AF386927

PANZER 35(t)

PANZER 35(t)

HISTORY, DESIGN AND OPERATIONAL USE OF THE LT vz. 35/PzKpfw 35(t)

JACEK ZABIELSKI

First published in Great Britain in 2026 by
Fonthill
An imprint of
Pen & Sword Books Ltd
Yorkshire – Philadelphia

ISBN 978-1-03619-281-5

A CIP catalogue record for this book
is available from the British Library.

Typeset in SabonLTStd 10/13 by
SJmagic DESIGN SERVICES, India.
Printed and bound in the UK by CPI Group (UK) Ltd, Croydon, CR0 4YY

The Publisher's authorised representative in the EU for product
safety is Authorised Rep Compliance Ltd., Ground Floor,
71 Lower Baggot Street, Dublin D02 P593, Ireland.
www.arccompliance.com

For a complete list of Pen & Sword titles please contact
PEN & SWORD BOOKS LIMITED
George House, Units 12 & 13, Beevor Street, Off Pontefract Road,
Barnsley, South Yorkshire, S71 1HN, England
E-mail: enquiries@pen-and-sword.co.uk
Website: www.pen-and-sword.co.uk

or

PEN AND SWORD BOOKS
1950 Lawrence Rd, Havertown, PA 19083, USA
E-mail: uspen-and-sword@casematepublishers.com
Website: www.penandswordbooks.com

Contents

List of Tables

Introduction

Designed by the Škoda company, the *Léhký Tank vzor 35* (Light Tank Model 1935, or LT vz. 35), later known by its German designation Panzerkampfwagen 35(t), stands as one of the most important tanks of the early stages of the Second World War, yet it is often overlooked. Developed during the mid-1930s, the LT vz. 35 was initially conceived as a light armoured fighting vehicle for the Czechoslovak army, reflecting the country's growing emphasis on indigenous modern mechanised forces. However, following the German occupation of Czechoslovakia in March 1939, over 200 of these tanks were absorbed into the Wehrmacht. There, the vehicle was redesignated as the PzKpfw 35(t)—with the '(t)' suffix signifying its Czechoslovak origin ('*tschechisch*')—and was pressed into front-line service by the German Panzerwaffe.

In its time, the LT vz. 35 was undoubtedly among the best tanks in its weight class. Despite its relatively light armour and compact design, the vehicle featured advanced systems such as pneumatic servo-assisted controls and a 37mm main gun effective against most early war armour. These characteristics made it highly effective during the rapid campaigns of 1939 and 1940 in Poland and France. The PzKpfw 35(t) continued to serve into Operation Barbarossa in 1941, where it was employed by Germany's 6.Pz.Div. in the early, mobile stages of the invasion. Though it quickly became outclassed by newer Soviet designs such as the KV and T-34, the 35(t)'s agility and low silhouette, and the quality of its crews, allowed it to remain relevant in a rapidly changing battlefield environment—at least for a time.

What is less well known, and forms a key focus of this monograph, is the widespread use of the LT vz. 35/PzKpfw 35(t) by Germany's Eastern European allies, particularly Slovakia, Romania and Bulgaria. These nations, aligned with the Axis powers, were recipients of surplus Czechoslovak and German stocks of the tank as Germany re-equipped its own divisions with newer models.

The Slovak army employed the vehicle from the very beginning of its involvement in the invasion of the Soviet Union in 1941, most notably as part of its Fast Division (*Rýchla divízia*). Later in the war, as Slovak morale declined and the German grip on its satellite states weakened, some of these tanks were used during the Slovak National Uprising against the Germans in 1944. Romania, too, incorporated the 35(t) into its armoured forces under the designation R-2. It served with Romanian armoured regiments on the Eastern Front, particularly during campaigns in Ukraine and around Stalingrad. The Romanian use of the tank extended into 1944, with several units continuing to fight even as Romanian forces were gradually pushed back and eventually switched sides following the coup of August 1944. Bulgaria also received a small number of LT vz. 35s, mostly for internal security and training purposes. However, by the time Bulgaria entered the war against the Axis in late 1944, most of these tanks were obsolete and of limited tactical value, though they still saw some localised action.

In tracing the LT vz. 35's journey from a product of Czechoslovak innovation to a battlefield tool in the hands of the Axis powers, this work offers in-depth insights into a tank that, although modest in appearance, left a lasting imprint on early Second World War armoured warfare. Through extensive archival research, rare photographs, detailed maps and original profiles, this book restores the LT vz. 35/PzKpfw 35(t) to its rightful place in the history of twentieth-century armoured combat.

A Note on Terminology and Structure

Given the multinational use of the vehicle and the wide range of source material consulted—including Czechoslovak, Bulgarian, Romanian and German-language documents—special attention has been paid to the accuracy and consistency of military terminology throughout this monograph.

German unit names are presented in full upon first mention, in their original form (for example, Panzer-Regiment 11), with abbreviations (Pz.Rgt.11) shown thereafter. The commonly understood term 'Panzer' is retained throughout due to its widespread recognition among English-language readers. Similarly, German military notation conventions are followed, such as using periods in ordinal numbers (for example, 6.Pz.Div. for the 6th Panzer Division) and distinguishing unit sizes with Roman numerals for battalions (I./Pz.Rgt.11—Abt.I) and Arabic numerals for companies (Kp.1, Kp.2, etc.). The term Abteilung (Abt.) is translated as 'battalion' when it refers to operational formations, and as 'detachment' when referring to non-combat or administrative elements.

A similar method has been applied to other national armies:

- in Czechoslovakia, *Pluk útočné vozby* (Armoured Regiment) is abbreviated as PÚV;
- in Slovakia, *Rýchla skupina* (Rapid Group) as RS, and *Rýchla brigáda* (Rapid Brigade) as RB;
- in Romania, *Divizia 1 Blindată* (1st Armoured Division) becomes D.1.Bl. and *Regimentul 1 Care de Luptă* (1st Armoured Regiment) as Rg.1.Cl.; and
- in Bulgaria, the *1-ви брониран батальон/полк* (1st Armoured Battalion/Regiment) is abbreviated as *1-ви ББ/БП/1-vi Broniran batalyon/polk*.

To aid clarity, all linear measurements in this book use the metric system (centimetres, metres, kilometres). Historical geographical names from the period 1938–1944 are used throughout (for example, Osterode, Deutsch Eylau, Lwów, Chişinău), with modern equivalents (Ostróda, Iława, Lviv, Kishinev) provided where appropriate to help orient the modern reader.

Sources and Visual Materials

This study is based on a broad range of primary and secondary sources, with a particular focus on original-language military records and rare wartime photographs. The book includes over 200 archival images, many of which are published here for the first time, as well as specially commissioned maps, organisational charts, and colour plates illustrating camouflage patterns and unit markings over time.

Photographs are sourced from the author's personal collection, public domain archives and various private and institutional collections, including (but not limited to) odkrywca.pl, wraki39.pobitwie.pl, worldwarphotos.info, pre-war Czechoslovak Army propaganda images, Škoda Works promotional materials and tank manuals, the photo collection of Lieutenant Sanders of the 6th Panzer Division, and public auction sites such as eBay. All graphics, including vehicle profiles and organisational charts, were created by the author.

Every reasonable effort has been made to obtain permission for copyrighted materials. Any inadvertent omissions are regretted, and readers are encouraged to contact the author with corrections for future editions.

1

Laying the Foundations

When the Austro-Hungarian Empire collapsed in 1918, the newly formed Czechoslovakia inherited a strong arms industry. Despite this, the country had no tank production capabilities, as the Austro-Hungarian military had not developed such weapons during the First World War. As a result, Czechoslovakia initially had to acquire armoured fighting vehicles from abroad, ordering a limited number of Renault FT tanks. However, the government was reluctant to purchase large quantities of foreign equipment and instead chose to focus its resources on domestic production. The Škoda Works in Plzeň (Pilsen) was expected to quickly initiate domestic production of armoured fighting vehicles, both for the domestic market and for export, as local demand was unlikely to support a large industrial base.

Although Škoda was formally controlled by the French Schneider-Creusot company, it was operated locally and independently of the French, which was advantageous for the Czechoslovak government and the military. Škoda's extensive experience in artillery production, as the sole supplier of artillery to the Czechoslovak army (including anti-tank and anti-aircraft guns), made it a logical choice for producing the new armoured vehicles. Moreover, the company already had experience in manufacturing armour, having constructed armoured turrets for the ships of the Austro-Hungarian navy.

Škoda initially produced armoured cars, starting with makeshift machines based on Fiat-Torino truck chassis. However, by 1923 it had designed its first original model, the PA-I, which in 1925 was further developed into the PA-II 'Turtle', widely regarded as one of the best armoured cars of its time. In the early 1930s, Škoda expanded its armoured vehicle development to include several types of tankette and a prototype light tank. However, progress was relatively slow compared to other European manufacturers and Škoda was further challenged by the emergence of a new domestic industrial rival.

On 1 January 1927 the Českomoravská Kolben-Daněk (ČKD) concern was founded, although its origins dated back to 1871. As a major producer of various types of machinery, including military electrical and mechanical equipment, aircraft engines and fully tracked artillery tractors, ČKD was well suited to tank production and the company was quick to seize the opportunity when the Czechoslovak army sought a manufacturer for its tankettes. ČKD's first major project was the licensed production of the British Carden-Loyd Mk VI tankette, which was modified for the

Above: ČKD tankettes (Tančík vz. 33) in the garage area of Milovice barracks, home of the 1st Czechoslovak Armoured Regiment (PÚV-1), preparing for field exercises in the mid-1930s. Note (*left*) the driver's fixed machine-gun mantlet and (*right*) the gunner's machine-gun mantlet. (*Czechoslovak Army propaganda materials [henceforth CzAPM]*)

Below: A platoon of Tančík vz. 33s in the spring of 1939, after the Milovice barracks were taken over by the Germans. The occupiers immediately dismounted the vehicles' armament and sent them to storage depots. (*Author's Collection [AC]*)

Czechoslovak LT vz. 35 tanks and tankettes were supported by the OA vz. 27 and later by OV vz. 30 armoured cars, designed and built by Tatra, which served in reconnaissance and support roles. Photo taken during a parade of the Czechoslovak army in May 1938. (*CzAPM*)

Czechoslovak army under the designation Tančík vz. 33. By the early 1930s ČKD had begun working on tank prototypes.

At the beginning of the 1930s, however, the development of tanks was slowing down, partly due to the effects of the Great Depression, which negatively impacted military budgets, and partly because of ongoing strategic debates over tank design and armoured warfare tactics.

The idea of using small groups of tanks for close infantry support was increasingly criticised as outdated, in contrast to the concept of large, massed tank formations. There was also no consensus on whether mechanised formations should be used to achieve breakthroughs during offensive operations or should be held back until the infantry had achieved a breakthrough, at which point the tanks would be deployed in the exploitation phase. This lack of tactical clarity led to the development of various types of tank designed for specific roles: slower tanks for infantry support and faster, more mobile tanks for cavalry and deep exploitation roles.

The Czechoslovak army, trained and led by the French Military Mission, finally adopted the French tactical perspective on tank usage and their integration into military formations. The army's official stance was published in a report on the role of tanks, written by the 3rd Department of the General Staff in 1932. While tanks were not yet regarded as a fully fledged offensive weapon, they were seen as an ideal tactical mobile defensive tool for Czechoslovakia, given the country's long borders. The army believed that its lack of manpower and artillery could be compensated for by fast, powerful and mobile tank formations.

Léhký Tank vzor 34 (Light Tank Model 1934, or LT vz. 34)

By the early 1930s both the army command and armour manufacturers had concluded that a completely new armoured fighting vehicle needed to be developed. In response, ČKD submitted to the Military Technical and Aeronautical Testing Institute a design for the P-II tracked combat vehicle. The P-II was a light tank weighing 7.5 tons, measuring 4.6 metres in length, and requiring a crew of three. It was designed to be armed with a 4.7cm Vickers 44/60 gun (for which ČKD had a licensing agreement) and two machine guns. The planned armour thickness ranged from 8 to 15mm, and its maximum speed was 30 km/h on the road, with an endurance of 8 hours.

The army accepted ČKD's proposal in 1931 and contracted the company to build a prototype. However, the P-II's development was slow, and it wasn't until November 1932 that the army accepted the prototype, which was assigned the serial number 13.363. The vehicle was placed under the supervision of the Military Technical and Aeronautical Institute, and testing was conducted by the armoured battalion in Milovice. By February 1933 the prototype had already covered 3,400 kilometres without any major issues.

On 17 February 1933 the Minister of National Defence met with the director of the Military Technical and Aeronautical Institute, who provided a favourable report on the new tank's performance. As a result, the minister decided to order fifty P-II tanks. The order, placed on 19 April 1933, called for the delivery of the first six tanks by 30 September 1933, another batch by 30 September 1934 and the final batch by 30 July 1935. The first six tanks were to be an evaluation series, and the production of the remaining tanks would only be approved after the acceptance of the first six. Some defects were found in the prototype after disassembly, requiring changes to the gearbox, reduction gear, radiator and exhaust system.

When the order was placed, the tank's armament had not been finalised, which meant ČKD could not complete the turret design. The army rejected the Vickers gun and the domestically designed ZB vz. 26 machine guns proposed by ČKD, instead requesting a Škoda-produced gun and heavy machine guns capable of sustained fire to arm the new tank. ČKD received the final turret design, featuring the Škoda 3.7cm A3 gun, in December 1933. By December 1934 the prototype was equipped with this gun along with two ZB vz. 53 air-cooled machine guns.

Production of the first six tanks began at ČKD's factory in Šlapanice in September 1933, with the understanding that they would be armed temporarily with two ZB vz. 26 machine guns. Simultaneously, the first batch of armour plates from the Poldi Steelworks in Kladno proved to be of poor quality, as they cracked when hit. This delayed production, with acceptable armour plates not arriving until December 1933. Consequently, the first six tanks were not handed over until 23 April 1934.

The new P-II tanks were assigned to the armoured battalion's 3rd Company, which had previously only operated the outdated Renault FT-17 tanks. After a brief training period, the new tanks (numbered 13.490 to 13.495) participated in trials in May 1934. The P-II tanks performed well in field conditions and were relatively easy to operate, though they were prone to frequent mechanical failures. As anticipated, coordination with tankettes proved ineffective; however, when deployed in platoon strength, the tanks offered effective support to cavalry units or infantry attacking unfortified positions. The new tanks were capable of reliably crossing barbed wire and shallow trenches, but concerns remained that their 15mm armour would be insufficient against enemy anti-tank weapons at close range.

Since the tanks lacked proper armament, the battalion command requested permission to install the 3.7cm guns from the Renault tanks on three of the new vehicles, for training purposes. This request was denied, and it was not until 18 months later that these tanks were fitted with the correct armament. The refitting took place between January and August 1936 at ČKD, and the tanks were then returned to Milovice barracks, where they remained in service with the 1st Armoured Regiment (*Pluk Útočné Vozby*, or PÚV-1) until September 1937, when the tank school moved to Vyškov.

On 13 July 1935 the Czechoslovak army officially accepted the P-II as the *Léhký Tank vzor* 34 (Light Tank Model 34, or LT vz. 34). The first forty-four production tanks were delivered to line units by the end of 1935, and the remaining tanks were delivered by mid-January 1936. Only after the production tanks were delivered were the six prototype tanks returned to the manufacturer for modifications and armament upgrades. These upgrades took place at ČKD Libeň between 15 January and 17 August 1936. The tanks were then handed over to the Assault Vehicle Training School (*Učiliště útočné vozby*) in Milovice, where they remained—after the training unit moved to Vyškov—in service with PÚV-1 beyond September 1937.

The rise of Nazi Germany prompted a re-evaluation of the Czechoslovak army's rearmament plans, as well as the combat usefulness of the LT vz. 34, which was

ČKD P-II-a prototype (serial no. 13.003) undergoing cross-country trials, painted in the standard three-tone camouflage scheme used by the Czechoslovak army. (*Author's Collection/ Public Domain [AC/PD]*)

Above: An LT vz. 34 (serial no. 13.496) in regular service, with its armament clearly visible—an A3 gun and two machine guns—the same configuration later used on the LT vz. 35. (*AC/PD*)

Below: Disarmed LT vz. 34 (serial no. 13.523) in 1939, captured as a war trophy by the German army. Due to its thin armour, it was deemed suitable only for reconnaissance roles. (*AC*)

classified as 'II category'. The 'Report on the Tank Situation', dated August 1934 and produced by the Ministry of Defence, identified the need for a new category of light tank, for both cavalry units and infantry support, which was classified as the 'II-a category'. The new type was expected to be better protected, with 25mm of frontal armour and 15mm on the sides and rear, and was intended to support cavalry and infantry during attacks on unprepared defences. The 'II-b category' was designed as an infantry-support tank with 25mm of armour on all sides. All three categories of light tank were to be armed with a 3.7cm gun and two heavy machine guns.

Medium tanks (III category) were expected to have 32mm armour and a 4.7cm gun, and were designed to support infantry in attacks on prepared defences and to fight enemy armoured vehicles.

Between 1934 and 1937 the army's budget allocated nearly 240 million koruna (approximately 10 million dollars) for the procurement of 279 light tanks (II-a/b) and forty-two medium (III) tanks.

While the LT vz. 34's light armour made it unsuitable for upgrading into a new II-a class, from 1937 they were reassigned to reconnaissance mixed units within infantry divisions. However, their low speed significantly hampered their effectiveness in this role.

Due to the differing roles of the assault vehicle regiments, the LT vz. 34s were redistributed among three armoured regiments: PÚV-1 received seventeen tanks, the 2nd Armoured Regiment (PÚV-2) retained its original eighteen and gained six additional vehicles from the 3rd Armoured Regiment (PÚV-3), leaving only nine LT vz. 34s stationed in Martin, Slovakia. During the September 1938 mobilisation, all planned LT vz. 34 units were successfully deployed; however, due to poor technical condition, some platoons were forced to return tanks for repairs. The overall combat

Czech armoured vehicles of PÚV-1 stored outdoors in 1939, including a Tančík vz. 33, LT vz. 34s on the right, and LT vz. 35s on the left in front of a truck. (*AC*)

Above: LT vz. 35 of PÚV-2 at Vyškov (serial no. 13.788) is marked on the rear of its turret with a red triangle, indicating 3rd Company, 2nd Platoon. Next to it is LT vz. 35 (serial no. 13.953), bearing a red square for 3rd Company, 3rd Platoon. On the far right is LT vz. 34 (serial no. 13.503). (*AC*)

Below: The OA vz. 27 Czech armoured car had a production run of fifteen vehicles, with the Germans taking control of nine of them during their occupation of Bohemia-Moravia in March 1939. There is no available information regarding the extent of their subsequent service. This photo was taken at the 1st Czech Armoured Regiment's barracks in Milovice. (*AC*)

readiness of these units was further hampered by the fact that they were manned by reservists with limited training and low morale. The most common technical issue continued to be thrown tracks.

Despite some disappointments with the LT vz. 34, the experience gained in its design and production played a crucial role in the development of its successor, the LT vz. 35, the II-a category tank.

2

Design and Development of the LT vz. 35

Škoda was frustrated by the success of its rival, ČKD, in supplying the Czechoslovak army with both tankettes and, later, LT vz. 34s. Determined to secure the next order for new light tanks, Škoda spared no effort—including allegedly resorting to bribes—to ensure that it would win the next tank contract. Indeed, the company was so determined to win the army deal that it entered into a cartel agreement with ČKD, under which both firms would share the production of whichever design won the army's approval. This strategic partnership soon paid off when, in 1934, the Czechoslovak army released its tank specifications in the 'Report on the Tank Situation' and invited the leading armament companies—Škoda, ČKD and Tatra—to submit prototypes for the new tank categories. The companies found particular success in the cavalry tank category (II-a).

ČKD leveraged its experience with the P-II type, which had already been adopted by the army as the LT vz. 34. Škoda, on the other hand, built upon its experience of developing several prototypes of tankettes in the early 1930s and a light tank, the *Střední Útočný Vůz* (Medium Attack Vehicle), all of which were rejected by the army.

Škoda ultimately emerged victorious from this competition, producing tank designs that were similar to the LT vz. 34 but featured improved armour and mobility. However, this success sparked considerable debate and criticism within Czechoslovakia, particularly in military and government circles. The controversy was largely driven by ČKD, which felt marginalised by the preference shown towards Škoda's design.

While the two companies' prototypes were not vastly different, the ČKD model P-II-a was simpler and closely followed the design of the earlier P-II (LT vz. 34), which made it seem incapable of further improvement. In contrast, the Škoda II-a (Š-II-a) was an entirely new design, with only the engine and steering borrowed from its predecessor. This suggested that the Škoda prototype would be more adaptable to future improvements, in line with the army's evolving demands. However, this expectation was not fully realised in practice, and ČKD's decision to exclude the Škoda prototype from its export offerings indicated that it did not view it as a viable product in the market.

The Škoda prototype (serial number 13.620) was transferred to the Armoured Corps School in Milovice, where it was frequently modified before becoming a fully operational combat vehicle. In September 1937 it was moved to Vyškov, and in

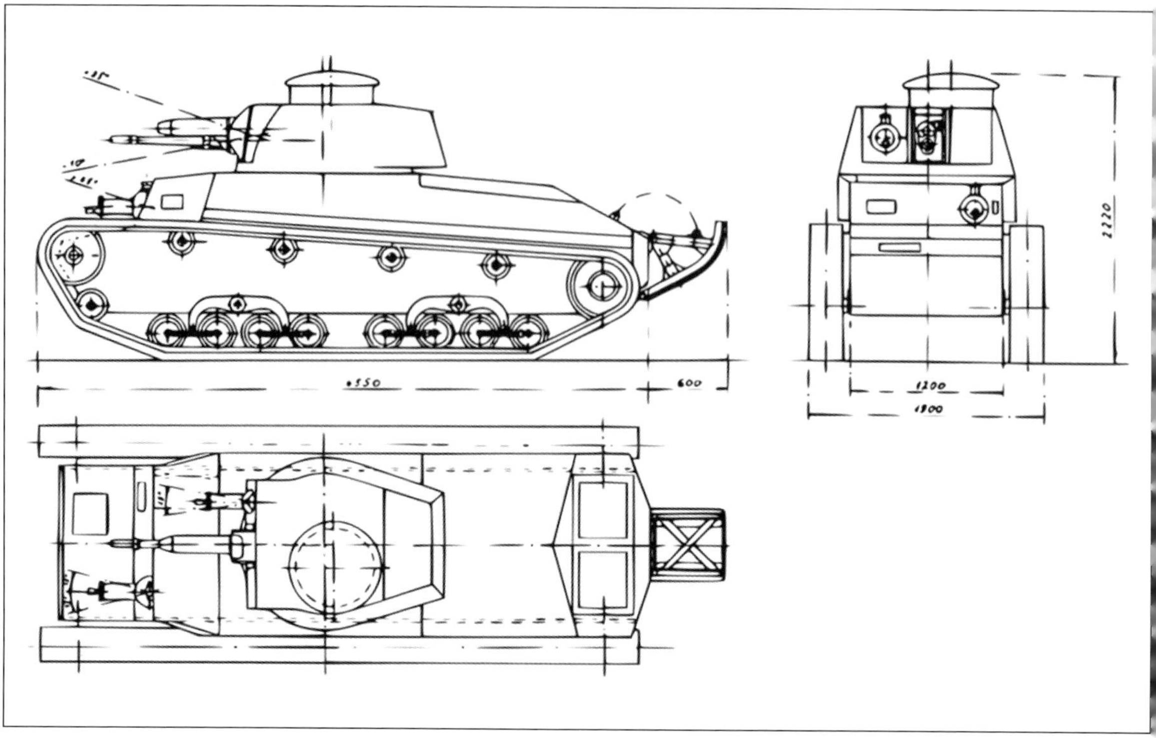

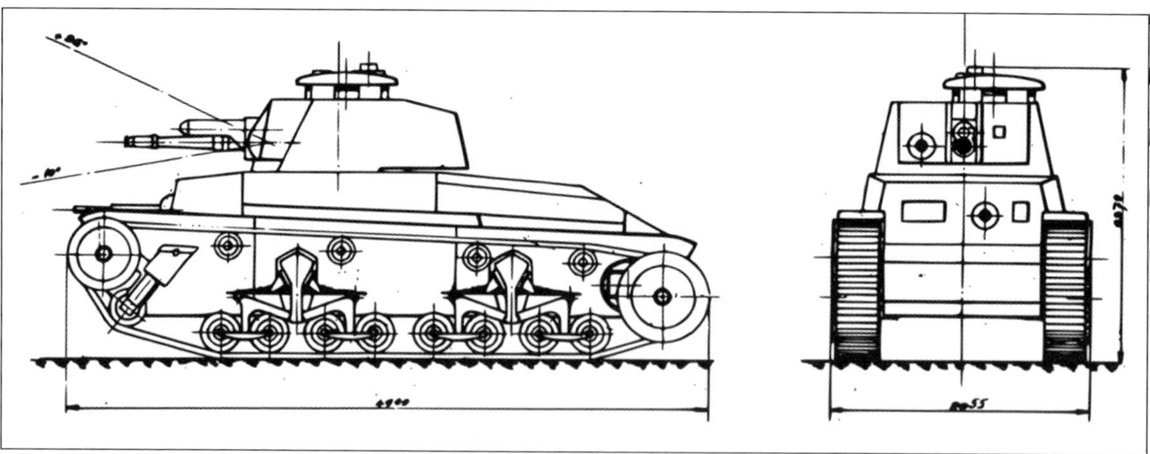

Above: Škoda's S-II-a: the initial design of February 1935. (*Škoda blueprint*)

Below: S-II-a/LT vz. 35: the final proposed designs. (*Škoda blueprint*)

August 1938 was shipped to Moscow along with one army-issued LT vz. 35 (serial number 13.903). Both vehicles were shown to a Red Army commission in Kubinka, and the Soviets expressed interest in purchasing one. However, Škoda suspected that the Soviets intended to engage in unlicensed production and declined the offer. On the return journey, Romania detained both vehicles, only releasing them on 14 March 1939—just one day before the German occupation of Czechoslovakia.

Manufacturing for the Czechoslovak Army

The Czechoslovak Ministry of Defence placed an order for a total of 160 LT vz. 35 tanks on 30 October 1935, to equip the tank battalions of four cavalry brigades. The order was split evenly between Škoda and ČKD, with each company responsible for producing eighty tanks. On 12 May 1936 an additional thirty-five tanks were ordered, followed by another 106 tanks a month later. In total, the army ordered 298 LT vz. 35 tanks (149 to be produced by Škoda and 149 by ČKD, in accordance with the cartel agreement, plus two prototypes), with deliveries scheduled between 30 September 1936 and 30 July 1937.

The guns for the tanks were to be supplied exclusively by Škoda, while the machine guns were provided by Zbrojovka Brno (ZB). The armour plates were manufactured by both the Poldi Steelworks in Kladno and the Vítkovické Hospodářské a Hutní Těšíctvo (Vítkovice Economic and Metallurgical Society) in Moravia, with each company supplying 149 sets of armour. When the initial contract for the LT vz. 35 was signed, the price was set at 524,640 koruna (21,000 dollars) for Poldi armour, and 527,840 koruna (21,100 dollars) for Vitkovice armour. This price did not include the armament, optical equipment, radio or nickel-iron (NiFe) batteries, which were billed separately. The total cost paid by the army for a complete vehicle amounted to 741,868 or 745,068 koruna (29,700 or 29,800 dollars).

At the end of the day, neither Škoda nor ČKD was able to meet the delivery deadlines, as the tank's design was not fully completed, and production was hindered by frequent changes and high rejection rates. ČKD participated in the process with little enthusiasm, taking every opportunity to accuse Škoda of technical incompetence or dishonest practices.

Concerns about the LT vz. 35's design led the army to order long-term tests using vehicles from the current production batch. The first test, conducted from January to March 1937, covered more than 4,000 kilometres and was moderately successful. However, the second test revealed several design shortcomings. Between 6 April and September 1937 three tanks (numbered 13.683, 13.696 and 13.721) each covered between 6,000 and 7,000 kilometres. After disassembly, excessive wear was found, caused by faulty design, poor assembly and substandard materials.

The disappointing results of these tests and the high defect rate of the tanks already in service led to a lack of confidence in the new vehicle. Faced with the deteriorating international situation, the Czechoslovak army needed to rearm quickly, but it had doubts about the quality of the delivered tanks. This, combined with the companies' intransigence in financial matters, created a strange situation with the third order for 106 LT vz. 35 tanks. Although the tanks had already been produced and partially shipped, the Ministry of Defence had not yet issued an official purchase order with the necessary budgeted funds. After tough negotiations between the army and the two companies, the Ministry of Defence agreed to issue the purchase order on 9 November 1937.

The army received its first LT vz. 35 tanks from Škoda on 21 December 1936. Škoda met its obligations, delivering the final three vehicles on 8 April 1938. ČKD delivered its 149 vehicles in 1937 but lost interest in the tanks as it had secured promising

Above and below: The bare hull of the LT vz. 35, as seen in a photo from the official Czechoslovak tank manual, reveals the vehicle's basic structural layout prior to the installation of its turret and armament. The armour protection on the LT vz. 35 was relatively light by late-war standards, but typical for mid-1930s designs. The frontal hull armour was 25mm thick, offering moderate protection against small arms fire and light anti-tank weapons. The side and rear armour measured 15mm, while the top and bottom plates were 8mm thick. The sloped armour design on certain surfaces offered slightly improved deflection capability, but the tank remained vulnerable to larger calibre anti-tank guns and heavy machine gun fire. (*Tank manual photo*)

A close-up view of the turret and its armament. The commander's hatch was dish-shaped and topped with a small cupola equipped with a periscope. Diagonal vision slits were present on both sides of the cupola to improve the commander's field of view. The photo is taken from documentation related to the tanks delivered to Romania—note the Romanian royal crest painted on the turret side. (*Tank manual photo*)

export orders for its own designs. Both companies still had to perform warranty repairs on all their vehicles, the extent of which was determined by feedback from the armoured units and long-term testing.

In December 1936 the first fifteen LT vz. 35 tanks arrived at PÚV-1 in Milovice, with the other regiments receiving their vehicles shortly thereafter. Of the 298 LT vz. 35 tanks, PÚV-1 received 197, PÚV-2 forty-nine and PÚV-3 fifty-two. All three regiments were tasked with supporting the four mobile divisions, each of which was to be equipped with ninety-eight light tanks, three OA vz. 27 armoured vehicles and nine OA vz. 30 armoured cars. Additionally, the regiments were required to supply thirty-four independent three-vehicle tank platoons for infantry divisions and border areas, as well as twenty-three tankette and six armoured car platoons for the border regions.

Following a meeting of the Military Technical and Aeronautical Institute on 30 May 1938, a complete list of necessary design changes was prepared, along with a plan for tank shipments from the units to the factories. Each factory was to modify twenty tanks per month in addition to performing normal repairs. At the same time, the ZB vz. 35 machine guns in the tanks were gradually replaced with the ZB vz. 37 model. As a result, by May 1938 the army had not yet received its full complement of tanks, and those it had were not fully armed with machine guns.

Exports and Espionage

The Czechoslovak tank industry, centred around Škoda and ČKD, had a production capacity that far exceeded the needs of the relatively small Czechoslovak army, and therefore it had to continuously seek foreign customers in order to remain viable. This meant that Czechoslovak arms manufacturers were deeply engaged in the global arms market throughout the 1930s. They aggressively marketed tanks and other armoured vehicles in Europe and South America, and even in parts of Asia. Countries such as Romania, Yugoslavia, Iran, Peru and China became important clients. Exporting was not simply a business strategy but a matter of industrial survival—keeping the factories running and workers employed, and retaining engineering talent.

Moreover, this export orientation influenced the design philosophy of Czechoslovak armoured vehicles. Tanks like the LT vz. 35 were built with reliability, ease of maintenance and adaptability in mind to appeal to a broad range of foreign militaries with varying logistical capabilities. However, prioritising exports also had drawbacks. At times, deliveries to the Czechoslovak army were delayed or reduced in favour of fulfilling export contracts, which inevitably weakened the nation's own military readiness—an especially critical factor during the mounting tensions of the late 1930s.

THE SOVIET UNION
Among the earliest foreign powers to express a serious interest in the Czechoslovak LT vz. 35 light tank was the Soviet Union. As part of its broader efforts to evaluate

The LT vz. 35 (S-II-a) undergoing testing at Kubinka near Moscow, shown driving on a slope. These three photographs were taken by members of the Czech delegation. (*PD*)

Above: Soviet officers observe the field trials of the Czech tanks with great interest, as the machines proved superior to the Soviet BT and T-26 models. (*PD*)

Below: The LT vz. 35 featured a relatively advanced suspension system and a well-balanced chassis, which gave it solid cross-country mobility for its time. (*PD*)

contemporary European armoured technologies, a Soviet military delegation visited Czechoslovakia in 1937. During this visit Soviet officers voiced admiration for Škoda's tank designs, particularly the LT vz. 35, which had already entered service with the Czechoslovak army. In response to this interest, the Czechoslovak Ministry of National Defence approved the dispatch of two tanks—serial numbers 13.903 and 13.620—along with a technical team to the Soviet Union for demonstration and evaluation. The delegation included two drivers, six mechanics and three officers. On 8 September 1938 the tanks arrived in Moscow by train, accompanied initially only by the drivers. The remainder of the team followed three days later.

Upon arrival, both tanks were delivered to specially prepared and sealed garages, underscoring the controlled nature of the trials. In accordance with Soviet stipulations, only tank 13.903 would undergo testing, while the second vehicle was to remain in reserve. The field trials began on 14 September and continued until 9 October. In the course of these exercises, tank 13.903 covered a distance of approximately 1,500 kilometres across a range of terrains. On paved roads it reached a maximum speed of 36km/h, while off-road performance topped out at 32.4km/h. Some mechanical wear was noted—particularly to the rubber pads on the road wheels—but overall, the tank demonstrated excellent mobility. It successfully climbed a 36-degree slope, broke through a 32cm-thick tree, crossed a 40cm-wide brick wall and bridged a 2.2m-wide trench. A single incident involving a thrown track on rocky ground was attributed to driver error rather than to a fault in the vehicle's design.

Weapons testing was conducted on 2 October but yielded mixed results. The technical crew, unfamiliar with the operation of the tank's weapon systems, struggled to optimise their performance. During the exercise fifty high-explosive shells, forty-nine armour-piercing rounds and some nine hundred rounds of machine-gun ammunition were expended. The Soviets were also permitted to test the tank's armour by firing small arms at the vehicle. While this resulted in minor damage to the front left bogie, the tank's armour effectively protected both the engine and crew compartments.

Tensions emerged during the trials when members of the Czechoslovak team observed Soviet personnel making detailed sketches of the tank's interior components. Concerned about potential violations of intellectual property and unauthorised replication, the team lodged a formal complaint. Following diplomatic intervention, the drawings were confiscated and destroyed in the presence of Czechoslovak officials. Ultimately, the Soviet Union expressed interest in acquiring a single example of the LT vz. 35 but categorically rejected the offer to purchase a production licence. This unwillingness to formalise a licensing agreement only deepened Czechoslovak suspicions. Fearing the Soviets intended to reverse-engineer the tank without compensation or oversight, the Czechoslovak government refused to proceed with the sale.

On 11 October the technical team returned to Prague. The tanks were scheduled to follow shortly thereafter, but the deteriorating political situation in Eastern Europe complicated their return. The vehicles were interned in Romania and remained there until 14 March 1939—just one day before the German occupation of Czechoslovakia. Upon their return, both tanks were rushed into service and participated in brief clashes with Hungarian forces in eastern Slovakia.

POLAND

Despite the strained diplomatic ties between Warsaw and Prague, Poland showed interest in the LT vz. 35 tank. A formal contract was out of the question owing to the ongoing political tensions, yet Polish intelligence officers managed to inspect the vehicles indirectly. In early 1939, as R-2 tanks were being shipped to Romania through

Above: The first series-produced LT vz. 35 (serial no. 13.666), officially accepted into army service on 21 December 1936, was initially assigned to PÚV-1 but was eventually transferred to the Romanian army. (*AC/PD*)

Below: While Poland showed some interest in the LT vz. 35, it ultimately chose to invest in its own domestically designed tank (7TP) based on the British Vickers model. The 7TP featured a specially developed turret housing a Bofors 37mm gun. Polish tanks saw their first 'combat' action in October 1938 during the annexation of Czech Trans-Olza, which was not resisted by the Czechoslovak army. (*Narodowe Archiwum Cyfrowe/PD*).

The LT vz. 35 variant produced for Romania, designated R-2c, was constructed with cemented (*cimentate*) armour and featured a modified rear turret shape (composed of two flat armour plates joined in a shallow 'V' shape). The R-2 seen here is participating in firing tests at Mihai Brăvia on 28 August 1941. Note the early registration number (010015). (*AC/PD*)

Polish territory, Polish operatives observed the convoy, gaining valuable insights into the tank's design and capabilities.

Later, on 9 March 1939, a Polish military delegation formally visited the Škoda Works in Pilsen. Their interest, however, had shifted towards a more advanced design—the heavier Š-II-c model. Negotiations never progressed beyond the preliminary stage, however, as the German occupation of Czechoslovakia that same month abruptly ended all independent export activity from the country.

Romania

The delivery of the LT vz. 35 to Romania—where it was redesignated the R-2— marked one of the most significant export successes of the Czechoslovak arms industry. For the Škoda Works, it was not only a commercial breakthrough, but a strategic validation of their armoured vehicle programme in a competitive interwar European market.

The initial deal was sparked by a Romanian purchasing commission's visit to Prague in November 1935. Following negotiations, a contract was signed on 14 August 1936, stipulating that Škoda would deliver a prototype of its Light Tank

Model 35 for testing within two months. Upon successful trials, full-scale production would commence, with the complete order expected to be fulfilled within ten months.

Škoda duly met the deadline for prototype delivery and trials began in January 1937. However, progress was quickly bogged down by persistent changes to the technical specifications demanded by the Romanians. These alterations disrupted production just as it was ramping up, leading to further delays. Compounding the issue was Škoda's difficulty in meeting concurrent delivery commitments to the Czechoslovak army. The ČKD company—responsible for manufacturing LT tanks for the Czechoslovakian army—was reluctant to prioritise the Romanian order, as its own production lines were focused on ČKD's proprietary tank designs.

Romania requested that Škoda deliver at least fifteen tanks by April 1937 in time for a major military parade in Bucharest. To meet this deadline, Škoda diverted eleven tanks from the batch intended for the Czechoslovak army and shipped them in April, with another four following in May. These vehicles remained in Romania until July 1938, and were primarily used for driver training. The combination of inexperienced Romanian crews and the rushed completion of the vehicles led to a host of technical problems. Škoda's resident mechanics in Romania found themselves constantly engaged in repairs, and the company incurred significant expense in shipping replacement parts at short notice. In the autumn of 1937 the R-2s participated in field

A view of the Škoda Plzeň Works production hall in February 1939, shortly before the delivery of the final R-2 tanks to Romania. The tanks were painted in overall green, with the dark grey royal crest insignia applied to the turret sides. (*Škoda Works promotional materials [SWPM]*)

manoeuvres, where their performance impressed on paper, but mechanical reliability issues led to one tank after another being sidelined.

Meanwhile, back in Czechoslovakia, Romanian evaluators remained dissatisfied with the prototype, particularly criticising its engine cooling system. Further deliveries were suspended until this issue could be resolved. The prototype was not formally accepted until 8 May 1938, and even then only conditionally, pending further trials on Romanian soil.

During this uncertain period the Romanian army seriously considered cancelling the entire order. It remains unclear whether this stemmed solely from dissatisfaction with the vehicles, or if ČKD, Škoda's rival manufacturer, had played a role in swaying Romanian preferences. While Romania had initially discussed increasing the order by another sixty-three tanks, by 1938 it was considering cutting the original contract in half or cancelling it altogether. The official justification pointed to the rapid pace of tank development in Europe, with which the Škoda design was allegedly no longer competitive. However, in a fortunate turn for Škoda, Romanian officials reconsidered and the order was salvaged, perhaps due to diplomatic pressure from the Czechoslovak military or to successful lobbying by Škoda representatives—possibly including the direct persuasion of General Negrei. According to Czechoslovak sources, Negrei was serving as Secretary General of the Romanian Ministry of National Defence in 1938 and was the key decision-maker in terms of armoured forces.

On 12 July 1938 three production R-2 tanks (serial numbers 17, 18 and 19) were sent to Romania for final evaluation. Škoda was informed in advance which vehicle would undergo testing (19) and ensured it was carefully prepared. The vehicle performed successfully during a 2,500-kilometre trial and returned to Škoda for

The LT vz. 35, known in Bulgarian service as the 'Škoda', was armed with the A3 cannon and a ZB machine gun. A total of twenty-six tanks in this configuration were delivered to the 1st Armoured Battalion of the Bulgarian army. (*AC*)

The T-11 model was nearly identical to the LT vz. 35, with the main difference being the installation of the more modern A8 gun. Originally developed for Afghanistan, ten of these tanks were eventually acquired by the Bulgarian army. *(AC)*

disassembly and inspection on 18 August. On 23 August the Romanian commission finally approved the tank for full production.

By then, the first fifteen R-2 tanks, which had remained in Romania for over a year (serial numbers 1–15) were being returned to Škoda for reworking to meet the newly approved standard. Simultaneously, production shipments resumed. In early September tanks 20–31 were delivered, followed by 32–41 a week later. Another batch (42–46) was sent on 15 September, but further deliveries were halted by the Czechoslovak army's general mobilisation in response to the escalating crisis in Europe. The military commandeered five completed tanks and rerouted six nearly finished ones to Slovakia. Škoda recovered these following the Munich Agreement and resumed deliveries on 15 October, shipping tanks 47–51, as well as 58 and 60.

Shipments were further disrupted by rising tensions with Hungary, as the rail route to Romania passed uncomfortably close to the Slovak–Hungarian border. At the end of 1938 Škoda secured Polish approval to use alternate transit routes across Polish territory. This allowed deliveries to resume at scale. On 22 December twenty tanks (52–57, 59 and 61–73) were shipped. The second batch (74–93) followed on 6 January 1939, and a third group (94–113) departed on 27 January. The final shipment of thirty vehicles, including those refurbished from the original batch, was dispatched on 22 February 1939.

Bulgaria

The Škoda T-11 light tank represented Škoda's final export version of the LT vz. 35 before the outbreak of the Second World War. The order for this model was placed by

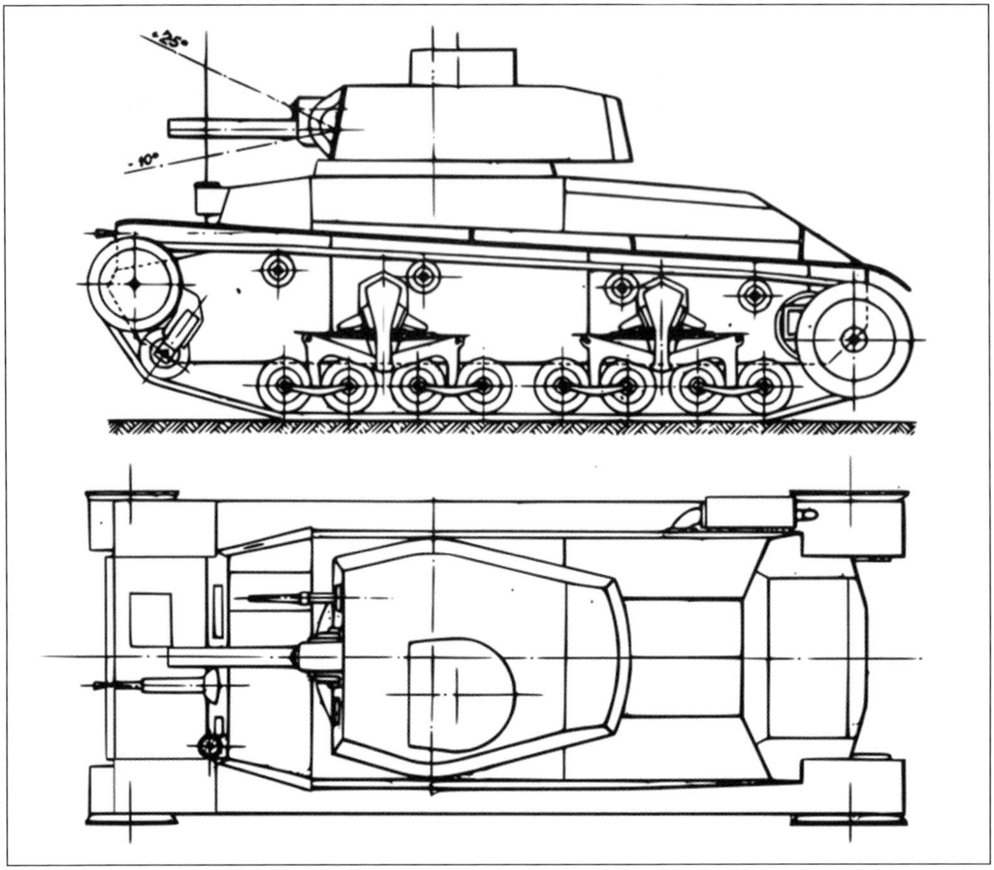

Above: S-IIa-j/T-12 prototype for Yugoslavia. (*Škoda blueprint*)

Below: The T-14 was the last Škoda design, but no prototype was built. (*Škoda blueprint*)

the royal government of Afghanistan. The T-11 designation was introduced following an internal Škoda directive issued on 26 May 1939, which aimed to simplify the previously complex nomenclature for special military vehicles (both wheeled and tracked). Under the new system, designations were based on function and weight class: 'T' stood for 'tank', the first digit '1' denoted a light tank, and the following number indicated its type within the series.

Under an agreement signed on 10 February 1939, Škoda was to deliver ten fully assembled II-a tanks (T-11s), valued at 11,229,120 koruna (equivalent to £83,550). However, production began only after the German occupation of Czechoslovakia, with approval from the German military arms office. Manufacturing was completed by February 1940, and an Afghan military commission formally accepted the tanks in March of that year. Due to wartime disruptions and logistical challenges, however, the vehicles could not be shipped to Afghanistan. Škoda was subsequently forced to seek an alternative buyer, though all negotiations were closely supervised by the German occupation authorities.

Bulgaria soon emerged as a serious customer. In early 1940 it had already received twenty-six LT vz. 35 tanks from German army stocks—vehicles originally belonging to the former Czechoslovak army and not supplied directly by Škoda. On 26 March 1940 Bulgarian representatives in Berlin inquired whether an additional forty new tanks of the same type could be acquired. Škoda responded on 31 May 1940, stating that it could supply only ten T-11 tanks, fully armed, equipped and cleared for export. A purchase contract was signed on 20 June 1940, with a delivery deadline set for 24 September. Deliveries began on 20 September and were completed by December 1940.

Compared to the original LT vz. 35, the T-11 featured several technical improvements. Notably, it was equipped with a gearshift controller to reduce mechanical failures and facilitate smoother gear changes. Communications were improved with the addition of a modern Telefunken radio system. A major enhancement was the installation of the Škoda A8 (model 1939) cannon, a 37.2mm weapon that maintained compatibility with the ammunition of the earlier A3 (3.7cm vz. 34) gun. The A8 featured a short-recoil system, an internal recoil mechanism, improved shell ejection and a semi-automatic breech. In terms of dimensions, armour thickness, weight and mobility, however, the T-11 remained largely consistent with the LT vz. 35.

Unlike the original LT vz. 35s, the T-11s delivered to Bulgaria were equipped with a Telefunken radio set.

The Forgotten Prototypes

The next development in Škoda's light tank programme was the T-12, a modified version of the original IIa prototype. Initially designated IIa-j ('j' for Jugoslávie, i.e. Yugoslavia), it represented an alternative structural configuration intended for future arms deliveries to the Royal Yugoslav Army. The T-12 was proposed as a replacement for the earlier II-j prototype (featuring a diesel engine), which had been ordered in 1937 but never completed due to persistent powerplant issues. In response to the failed diesel-powered project, Škoda engineers opted to develop a new prototype light tank using a gasoline engine and armed with a 47mm gun. The design phase began in late 1938, with construction starting in early 1939.

Structurally, the T-12 was derived from the LT vz. 35, retaining the same hull shape, mechanical systems and general powertrain layout. However, it featured a completely redesigned rotating turret to accommodate the more powerful Škoda A9 47mm tank gun. To counterbalance the increased weight of the main gun and coaxial machine gun at the front of the turret, the rear portion of the turret was extended. Additionally, the rotating commander's cupola was reworked to include a single observation episcope and a signal device mounted in the hatch, which also served as an emergency exit for the crew.

The engine, while based on the same type as that used in the LT vz. 35, was upgraded to produce 99.8kW (135hp) at 2,000rpm, enabling the tank to maintain competitive tactical and technical performance despite its increased total weight of 10,950kg.

The finished T-12 prototype underwent factory mobility and technical trials in Plzeň in early 1940. It was presented to a Yugoslav military commission, which ultimately postponed its purchasing decision. A second potential buyer, Hungary, evaluated the prototype during an official inspection between 7 and 9 May 1940, but likewise declined to place an order. As a result, the sole T-12 prototype remained at Škoda's facilities, serving primarily as a source of spare parts and components for other development projects. It did not survive the end of Second World War in complete form.

The T-13M (Mechanical) represented the final and most advanced development in the Škoda line of light tanks based on the LT vz. 35 platform. The project was initiated in the spring of 1940, without any official order; in effect it was an internal effort to continue development despite the German occupation. However, wartime demands and the production of other military equipment slowed progress.

A Škoda factory report dated 7 March 1941 confirmed the completion of design drawings, a finished prototype, and preliminary mobility and technical trials. This

A T-12 (S-IIa-j) designed for Yugoslavia, but still with its Czech registration number. (*SWPM*)

Above and below: The Škoda-owned T-13 prototype, equipped with the new 47mm A7 gun, undergoing testing in 1940. During the development of the T-13, Škoda also designed a dedicated flatbed trailer to be towed by the Škoda 6K lorry/tractor. This trailer was capable of transporting new tanks, allowing them to travel up to 20 per cent faster compared to moving under their own power. In contrast, tanks driven on their own often began to suffer mechanical failures after just 3,000 kilometres of heavy use. Although the T-13 never entered serial production, the Škoda 6K lorry was adopted by the Slovak army and assigned to the tank base at Turčiansky Svätý Martin. (*SWPM*)

prototype incorporated extensive structural and technical improvements, making it the most refined variant of the series. As with its predecessors, the T-13M was known for its stability, smooth off-road handling, robust track system and a spacious, unobstructed fighting compartment. Notably, molybdenum steel was used more extensively in place of chromium-nickel alloys, providing greater durability. The front armour of the hull and turret was thickened from 25mm to 30mm, while vertical armour plates increased from 16mm to 25mm, significantly enhancing protection.

The engine was upgraded from 120hp to 135hp (99.8kW) at 2,000rpm. This increase allowed the vehicle to maintain favourable performance despite its heavier armour. A major mechanical innovation was the elimination of compressed air in gear shifting and control systems, to be replaced by a fully mechanical set-up. The tank was also equipped with a dual-control system enabling smooth turning and pivoting on the spot, while a preselector gearbox simplified gear changes. Unlike the original LT vz. 35, the T-12 and T-13M versions were intended to carry German Fu2 or Fu5 radios operating in voice (phone) mode, in contrast to the radiotelegraph system used in the original Czechoslovak LT vz. 35 set.

To improve crew comfort and reliability in prolonged operations, a new direct-flow radiator and redesigned air intake/exhaust system were introduced. These improvements ensured cooling air did not pass through the crew compartment, reducing heat and dust exposure. Additional domestically produced equipment was integrated, with improved accessibility and functionality.

The T-13M prototype, measuring 4.9m in length, 2.1m in width, 2.3m in height, and with a ground clearance of 35cm, was capable of crossing a trench 2m wide with vertical walls, climbing over obstacles up to 80cm high, and fording water to a depth of 80–100cm. Its maximum gradient-climbing ability on solid ground was reported at 40 degrees. The overall dimensions and mobility characteristics of the other tanks in the series were virtually identical.

Despite all the technical improvements, no further development of the T-13M was recorded, and there is no known interest in the design from the German military or its allies. After the war, in a 1945 summary of Škoda's armament projects prepared for Allied reparations documentation, it was noted that one T-13M prototype remained at the factory as of 26 June 1945. Its ultimate fate is unknown.

Škoda also initiated a follow-up project, the T-14 light tank. This design was similar to the T-13M in structure but was planned to mount the more powerful Škoda A11 47mm cannon. Uniquely, it was intended for deployment in North Africa and featured 'tropicalisation' measures: improved engine cooling, better sealing against dust ingress, enhanced ventilation with air filters, and special internal and external coatings for harsh desert conditions. However, the T-14 never advanced beyond the design stage. Production limitations, combined with a lack of interest from the German military, which had already prioritised the T-15 reconnaissance tank in 1940, ended the project before a prototype was constructed.

The weight of the different prototypes (excluding the crew) varied depending on armour thickness, armament and installed equipment—reaching approximately 10,500kg for the T-11, 10,950kg for the T-12, around 12,600kg for the T-13M, and up to 12,950kg for the planned T-14. Each tank was operated by a four-man crew.

3

Technical Specification of the LT vz. 35/PzKpfw 35(t)

The LT vz. 35, which was redesigned in 1939 into the PzKpfw 35(t), was originally conceived as a light tank. Similar to British cruisers or Soviet BT fast tanks, it was primarily meant for use in cavalry roles, with infantry cooperation being an exception.

Crew

The LT vz. 35 had a crew of three: a mechanic/driver and a radio operator in the front of the hull, and the commander in the turret. The commander was responsible for loading and aiming the main armament, as well as operating the co-axial machine gun. Initially, the commander sat on a simple seat suspended by chains within the turret. However, this was later replaced by a more rigid seat fixed to the turret ring. An additional seat was added for the loader.

In Wehrmacht service, a fourth crew member was introduced, who was responsible for operating the main armament. This allowed the commander to focus on controlling the vehicle. The new crew member, known as the *Ladeschütze* (loader and turret machine-gun operator), increased the rate of fire, but did not resolve the core issue that the commander still had to serve as the *Richtschütze* (gunner). This became an even greater problem when the tank was assigned to higher command levels, such as a platoon leader or a company, battalion or regimental commander. If these commanders were tasked with aiming and firing the gun, they were neglecting their more critical responsibility of directing the tactical manoeuvring of their units.

Command and Control

The tank commander had at his disposal a monocular mirror periscope, 56.5cm in length, which could be extended through a hole in the cupola hatch. The periscope provided a 30-degree field of view with a 1.3x magnification.

The driver and radio operator/front machine-gunner sat in the front part of the fighting compartment, with the driver positioned on the right. The driver had a 390 x 90mm observation slot in the front plate, covered by an armoured shutter 28mm thick, and protected on the inside with 50mm-thick bulletproof glass. On the right side armour plate there was a smaller vision slit (120 x 3mm), similarly protected with 50mm-thick bulletproof glass. The driver was seated so that all control levers were within easy reach, preventing any unnecessary strain. On the right side of the front visor was a control panel with oil and air pressure gauges, a speedometer and an electric horn button. Additional switches for the electrical equipment and control lights were located on a panel on the right-hand side of the hull.

The radio operator had a smaller opening in the front plate, measuring 150 x 75mm. The machine gun was mounted centrally on the front hull plate in a ball mount, allowing a 30-degree field of fire with an elevation of 25 degrees and a depression of 10 degrees. The machine gun was equipped with a spotting telescope or could be fired using open sights built into the driver's visor. If necessary, the driver could lock the gun in the central position and fire it using a Bowden cable.

On the left hull wall was mounted the vz. 35 radio set and its accessories. The radio had a 2km range and operated in telegraphic mode. The operator used a Morse key to send messages and received communications via headphones in his helmet. Messages were transmitted via a rod antenna mounted on the left front fender.

When the Wehrmacht took over the LT vz. 35, the original radio system was removed and replaced with standard German tank radio and intercom equipment. Each tank was outfitted with components for the radio set, including two racks for receiver sets (Fu 2), one rack for a 10-watt transmitter (Fu 5), and a mount for three *Umformer* (rectifiers), allowing any tank to be used by the company or platoon

In Czechoslovak service the crew of an LT vz. 35 tank consisted of three members: the commander, the driver and the gunner. The driver was seated in the front right of the hull, while the gunner was positioned in the turret to operate the main 3.7cm gun and coaxial machine gun. While on duty, tank crews wore denim overalls and leather helmets quite similar in shape to the steel helmets vz. 32. (*CzAPM*)

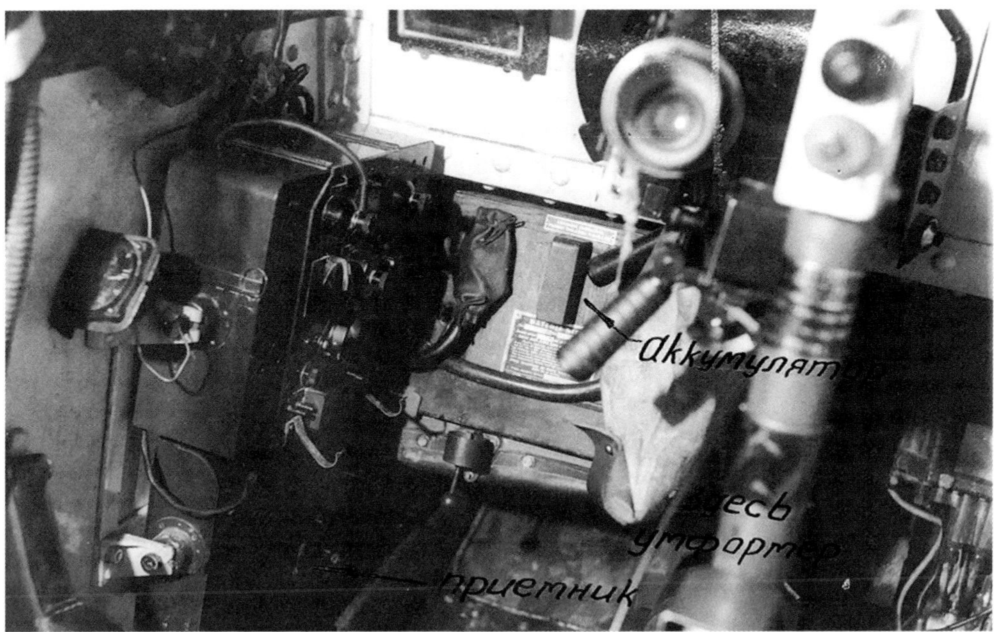

Above: The LT vz. 35 radio set was mounted on the left side of the hull. It operated in telegraph mode only and had a range of up to 2 kilometres. From top to bottom, the Russian annotations indicate the accumulator, the stick with three lights and the radio receiver. (*SWPM/Promotional materials for the Soviet Union*)

Below: The commander's cupola, showing the four episcopes, the armoured periscope and covers over the holes for signal flags and the signal lamp. (*AC/PD*)

commander, or even as a *Befehlswagen* (command tank) for the battalion commander. Additionally, a few tanks were equipped with radio gear in the signals ordnance depot as *Grosse Befehlswagen* (to replace the *Grosse Panzerbefehlswagen*, SdKfz 267) and were delivered to the *Regiments-Stab* (headquarters).

Internal communication within the LT vz. 35 between the driver and commander was limited to a very primitive system of coloured lights. On the left side of the driver's visor, at eye level, there were three signal lights: red, green and blue. The commander in the turret would convey his orders to the driver by lighting these bulbs in a prearranged code. The control buttons for these lights were located around the circumference of the turret. This rudimentary communication system did not perform well in combat, and as a result the Wehrmacht installed an intercom system in their PzKpfw 35(t)s. Crew members were connected via long cables to a central box mounted next to the radio set, communicating through throat microphones and headphones.

For external communication between tanks, signal flags (red and yellow) were used, with the commander displaying them through a hole in the cupola hatch. At night the commander could use a special signal light with colour filters.

Firepower

The LT vz. 35's primary armament was the Škoda 3.7cm semi-automatic anti-tank gun, introduced in 1934. It was coaxially paired with a heavy machine gun (7.92mm) produced by Zbrojovka Brno, both having a full 360-degree field of fire. The elevation of both weapons was 25 degrees, with a depression of 10 degrees. The 3.7cm gun was capable of penetrating 45mm-thick vertical cemented armour at 500 metres and could pierce 25mm armour at a 30-degree angle at 1,000 metres. The turret could be rotated in two ways: either by turning the wheel of the rotating mechanism (one full revolution equalled a 3-degree turn), or manually by applying force to the main gun after disconnecting the rotating mechanism. An arresting gear was used to stop the turret in any position.

Table 1. Škoda A3 tank gun specification

Type	A3 (3.7cm KPUV vz. 34, UV vz. 34)
Tank type	LT vz. 34, LT vz. 35, LTP
Calibre (mm)	37.2
Length of barrel (cal)	40.0
Muzzle velocity (m/sec)	675
Weight of shell (kg)	0.85
Muzzle energy (mt)	19.sie
Distance effective against 45mm armour @ m	500.0

The semi-automatic breech mechanism allowed for a high rate of fire—up to 15 rounds per minute according to Czechoslovak specifications. However, when the

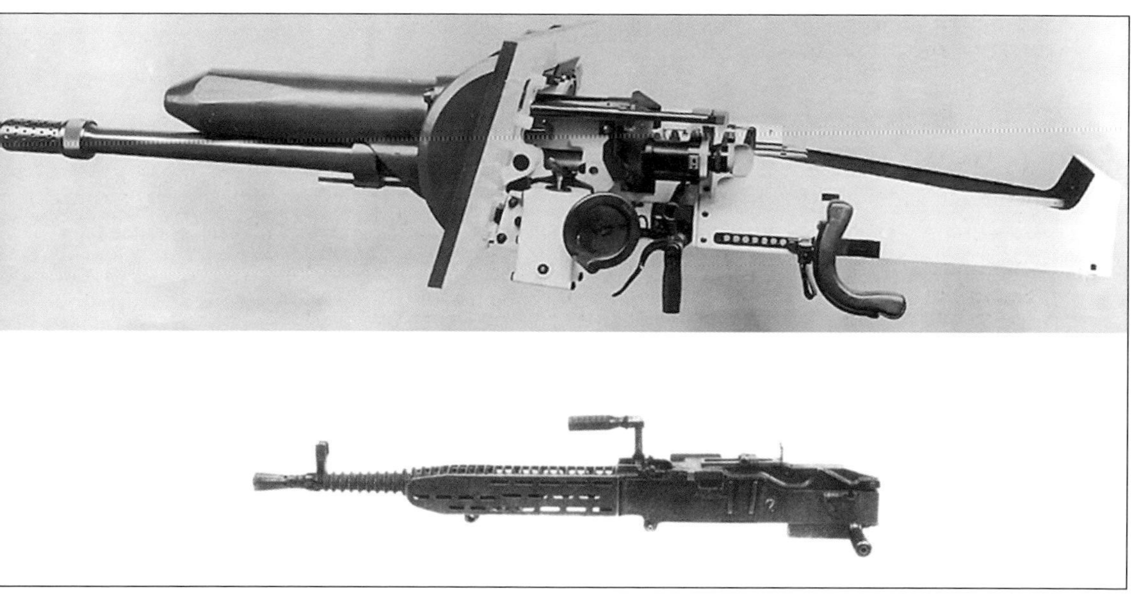

Above: The LT vz. 35's armament consisted of a 3.7cm gun and co-axial 7.92mm machine gun, with a further machine gun mounted on the front plate. The co-axial machine gun, mounted parallel to the main armament, allowed the crew to aim and fire both weapons in the same direction using the same targeting system. It was designed to engage infantry, soft targets or lightly armoured vehicles, thereby conserving the main gun's ammunition for heavier threats. (*AC*)

Below: A side view of the A3 gun and ZB machine gun. (*SWPM*)

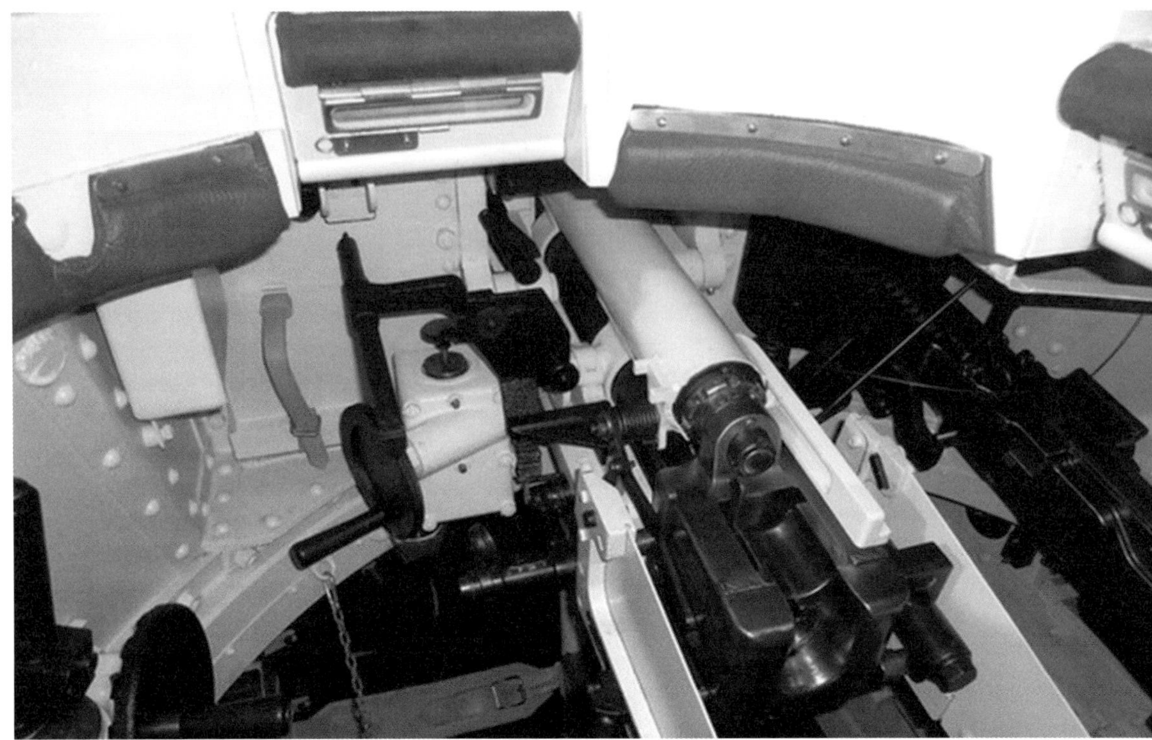

The gun breech block and front episcope. The A3 gun could penetrate up to 45mm of vertical cemented armour at 500m and 25mm of armour at a 30° angle at 1,000m. The weapon utilised a semi-automatic breech mechanism. (*Vojenském Technickém Muzeu Lešany*)

LT vz. 35 was tested by the Germans before employing it with line units, the actual sustained rate of fire was estimated at 8 to 10 rounds per minute, even with the additional crew member. The gun had a range of 4,000 metres with high-explosive rounds and 1,500 metres with armour-piercing rounds.

The gun was officially designated by the Czechoslovak army as the UV vz. 34 3.7cm gun, while Škoda referred to it internally as the A3. It was adapted from the towed KPUV vz. 34 anti-tank gun. However, modifications were needed, as the recoil from the infantry gun was too long, the recoil cylinder was positioned outside the turret and inadequately protected, the muzzle brake was not fully effective, and the spent cases were not ejected properly.

In 1935 the army found that the A3 gun could no longer penetrate the newly developed 30mm armour plates beyond a range of 550 metres, prompting the demand for a more powerful gun to be mounted on future tank models. Interestingly, the later vz. 37 gun outperformed the German 3.7cm PaK/Kwk 35/36 anti-tank gun and could penetrate the armour of all contemporary German tanks.

In Wehrmacht service A3 guns were used to fire either a 3.7cm PzgrPatr (HE-T) weighing 0.850kg at a muzzle velocity of 675m/s or a 3.7cm SprgrPatr.18 (HE-T) weighing 0.825kg at a muzzle velocity of 687m/s. A simple telescope with 1.25 x magnification and a 55-degree field of view was graduated to 1,500 metres for the gun.

Table 2. Weapons tests carried out by the German Waffen Pruf 1 on the Škoda A3 gun

Type	A3
German ammunition for PaK 35/36	3.7cm Pzgr(t) umg (High Explosive)
Projectile weight (kg)	0.815
Muzzle velocity (m/sec)	690
Range in metres vs. penetration @ 30°	
100	37.0mm
200	35.5mm
300	34.1mm
400	32.6mm
500	31.3mm
600	30.1mm
700	28.9mm
800	27.8mm
900	26.7mm
1,000	25.7mm
1,100	24.9mm
1,200	24.1mm
1,300	23.3mm
1,400	22.8mm
1,500	22.3mm

The export version of the LT vz. 35, developed for Afghanistan and designated the T-11, was armed with the new Škoda A8 3.7cm gun (UV vz. 39), which offered the same performance and used the same ammunition as the previously installed A3 cannon (UV vz. 34). The new cannon featured a modern design, with a brake recoil system housed inside the turret. It had a short recoil, improved shell ejection and a modified semi-automatic breech. Only ten such vehicles were produced, and they were ultimately sold not to Afghanistan but to Bulgaria.

In addition to the main gun, the tank was equipped with two ZB vz. 35 or ZB vz. 37 heavy machine guns, produced by Zbrojovka Brno (in the Wehrmacht these guns were designated MG 35/37(t)). These were mounted in special ball mounts, one in the turret and the other on the hull's front plate. The turret machine gun could be fired either coaxially with the main gun or independently.

The machine guns were gas-operated. The gases were bled from the middle of the barrel via a regulated opening and acted on a piston connected to the bolt. The barrel featured a finned cooling jacket and was easily removable without the need for tools. On the bolt side, it rested on springs that absorbed the vibrations caused by firing, which helped improve the gun's accuracy. Since the gun was also designed for anti-aircraft use, it had two rates of fire: 550 rounds per minute for use against infantry and 750 rounds

Above: The ZB vz. 35 machine gun was chambered for the standard 7.92 × 57mm Mauser cartridge and operated with a high degree of mechanical dependability—qualities that made it attractive beyond its original Czechoslovak users. (*CzAPM*)

Below: Large quantities of ZB vz. 35/37s were absorbed into German units under the designation MG 35/37(t). These weapons were typically issued to second-line units, training formations, rear-area troops and Waffen-SS units, especially early in the war when German small arms production was still ramping up. (*AC*)

The Luftwaffe repurposed MG 35/37(t) light machine guns for air defence and point-defence roles. The ZB's high rate of fire, reliability and portability made it well suited for engaging low-flying aircraft—especially when mounted on elevated tripods or anti-aircraft mounts, which provided the necessary elevation to effectively track and fire on aerial targets. (*AC*)

per minute in anti-aircraft mode. Unlike most guns, it lacked the usual cocking lever. The gunner simply pushed the two handles forwards until they engaged the bolt. By pulling them back, he cocked the gun, all without removing his hands from the firing handles or the firing buttons—an important advantage. The iron sights were initially set at 200 metres. After raising the distance frame, the sights could be adjusted from 200 to 2,500 metres. The sights featured two scales, one for light rounds and one for heavy rounds. On the right side of the bolt casing there were grooves for attaching a shoulder rest and an anti-aircraft sight. On the left side similar grooves were provided for attaching a spotting scope, which could be used in tanks and fixed fortifications.

The machine gun could be configured for single-shot or sustained fire. It was fed by metal link belts, available in 100- or 200-round configurations. Special ball mounts were developed for use in armoured vehicles, identical mounts being used in both the turret and the front wall of the hull. The protruding barrel was protected by a massive armoured trough. The gun also came with a cloth sack to catch the spent cartridges, and the muzzle was different from that of the infantry version. The tank version of the barrel was lighter than the infantry version and lacked the barrel handle. The gun measured 1,095mm in length, with a 733mm barrel. Its weight ranged from 18.88 to 22.05kg, depending on the barrel and other equipment. The muzzle velocity was 880m/s for light rounds and 780m/s per second for heavy rounds.

The first ZB guns were produced in 1935. Shortly thereafter, experience gained with the new gun led to several modifications. The updated version was designated the

Above: Already in German service, this LT vz. 35 (Serial no. 13.701) is seen during field manoeuvres in 1939, followed by PzKpfw IIs. It is not known why it has been disarmed. (*AC*)

Below: The heavy cast muzzle brake was perforated to minimise flash and to direct the recoil gases outwards, preventing them from entering the turret interior when the breech was opened. (*AC/PD*)

German soldiers inspecting the armament of a newly captured LT vz. 35 in March 1939. Its 3.7cm main gun was equivalent in calibre to that of the PzKpfw III—a significantly heavier and larger tank designed specifically for engaging enemy armour. (*AC*)

ZB vz. 37 and was officially accepted by the army on 19 January 1937. By September 1938 the army had acquired approximately 700 of these guns for its armoured vehicles, 1,464 guns for fixed fortifications and another 1,300 infantry versions, although the total order was for 9,334 guns. The ZB vz. 37 was also extensively exported from 1936 to 1948. In 1936 the manufacturing licence for the ZB vz. 37 was sold to England, where it was produced under the name BESA (Brno Enfield Small Arms). It was fitted to all British armoured vehicles during the war and remained in use into the 1950s.

All weapons were aimed using spotting scopes with a 2.6x magnification and a 25-degree field of view. The turret scope featured a distance scale for both the main gun and the machine gun, with machine-gun scopes scaled up to 1,600 metres. In the event of turret scope damage, the gun could be aimed up to 600 metres using open sights after opening an armoured cover on the turret's front plate. The machine guns could use iron sights after removing steel plugs from the ball mounts.

Most of the ammunition was stored in the turret overhang, in eight magazines, each holding six rounds. This set-up allowed for quick loading. A ready magazine with six rounds was mounted directly above the gun on the turret's ceiling, enabling the loader to fire the first six rounds almost immediately. The turret overhang also contained a toolbox for main gun repairs. Empty cartridge cases were collected in a bag, attached under the recoil frame, while the machine gun's spent cartridges were collected in cloth bags.

Ammunition for the main gun was primarily stored at the rear of the turret, with additional storage in the hull. A six-round stowage box was also mounted on the turret roof above the breech for immediate use. In Czechoslovak service the ammunition allocation consisted of twenty-four anti-tank rounds, fifty-four high-explosive rounds and 2,700 rounds of machine-gun ammunition (900 of which were vz. 31 armour-piercing rounds), stored in 100-round belts, with three belts per box. In Wehrmacht service this allocation was slightly reduced, owing to the addition of an extra crewman, to seventy-two rounds for the main gun and 1,800 rounds for the machine guns. Some references suggest the seventy-two rounds were exclusively high explosive, but it is more likely that the allocation was split between high explosive and anti-tank types. Command tanks carried even fewer rounds, as space was required for additional equipment, including a second radio and a gyrocompass.

Construction

The hull and turret of the tank were assembled using L-shaped steel profiles, to which flat armour plates were riveted. Both the rivets and screws were made from special steel. Up to a height of 100cm, all joints were sealed to be waterproof. The front plates of both hull and turret were 25mm thick, while the side and angled plates were 16mm thick; plates angled at more than 30 degrees were only 12mm thick. The bottom of the hull and the top plates were 8mm thick.

The 25mm front plates were impenetrable to armour-piercing rounds from a 20mm Oerlikon gun at ranges of 250 metres and beyond. The 25mm and 16mm plates could withstand vz. 31 armour-piercing machine-gun and rifle rounds at any distance. The safe distance for the 12mm plates against vz. 31 rounds was 100 metres, and for the 8mm plates, it was 125 metres. As a result, the armour protection of the LT vz. 35 was suitable only against small arms, but the relatively light armour allowed the tank to maintain a weight of 10.5 tons.

The hull was divided into the fighting and engine compartments by a 4mm-thick bulkhead. This firewall featured several openings, covered with wire mesh, allowing easy access to critical engine parts from inside the fighting compartment. This design was required by the cooling system, where air was drawn in through the commander's cupola and passed through the fighting compartment to the engine radiator. The disadvantages of this design included a constant draught in the fighting compartment, the risk of engine fires penetrating through the firewall and increased crew fatigue due to engine noise and heat. However, its main advantage was the excellent ventilation of the fighting compartment during weapon firing, which was a significant problem in other tanks. The fighting compartment beneath the turret provided enough space for the tank commander to service the tank's armament, and to accommodate the additional crew member introduced by the Germans.

The fully rotating turret sat in a ball-race ring, 1,267mm in diameter, located in the top plate of the fighting compartment. It was constructed in the same way as the hull. The front, straight, 25mm-thick armour plate housed the main gun, and on the right

Above: The front towing hooks on the LT vz. 35. After the German takeover, these hooks were often welded shut to accommodate the standard German towing shackles. The front guide roller was rigidly mounted and played a role in maintaining track tension at the front of the vehicle. Both the idler and drive sprockets were protected by large concave metal discs, which also helped to secure the track pins in place. (*CzAPM*)

Below: An LT vz. 35 on the move. The box located above the front guide roller was used to store track grousers, which were installed to improve traction in difficult terrain. This box was typically secured with a padlock. (*AC*)

Seen on the right is the forward section of the first suspension unit. The main suspension casting featured three ribs; the central rib supported the leaf springs. A raised, inverted 'V' on the outer rib functioned as a bump stop, working against an extension bolted to the main casting. The LT vz. 35 moved on nine pairs of rubber-tyred road wheels per side. (*AC*)

side was the ball mount for the turret machine gun. The turret sides were made from 16mm-thick armour plates, which were slightly curved, while the upper armour plate was 8mm thick. The upper plate featured an eccentrically positioned commander's cupola with an inner diameter of 570mm. The cupola's sides were 16mm thick, and the dished hatch was 8mm thick. The cupola was equipped with four episcopes, positioned at the front, rear and both sides.

The inner space of the fighting compartment and turret was fairly cramped owing to the small dimensions of the tank. Therefore, every effort was made to use the available space as efficiently as possible to accommodate all necessary equipment and armaments without hindering the crew's duties. In the fighting compartment of the hull the driver and radio operator sat next to each other on upholstered leather seats. The backs of their seats were formed by a wide leather strap, carrying a small cushion.

Escape from the fighting compartment was possible through the driver's hatch, the commander's cupola or through a floor escape hatch with a 50cm diameter.

Mobility

The LT vz. 35 was powered by an internal combustion, water-cooled, four-stroke, four-cylinder petrol engine, designed and built by Škoda. The engine had a rated output of 118–120hp (88.2–88.7kW) at 1,800rpm, which provided a top speed of 40km/h. With a bore and stroke of 140 x 140mm, the engine's displacement was 8,620cc. The cylinders were arranged in a single block, with a removable aluminium alloy head and a side-valve train. The crankcase was made of cast steel alloy, and the split crankshaft was mounted in main cylinder bearings. The engine was pressure-lubricated with a dry sump. Oil was circulated by a gear pump through a filter and oil cooler. The engine was capable of running on gasoline, alcohol-gasoline blends or Dynalcol.

Fuel was supplied by two fuel pumps: a mechanical diaphragm pump (AC pump) and an electrical pump (Autopulse). The main fuel tank had a capacity of 124 litres and was located on the left side of the engine (186 litres in total). An auxiliary tank with a capacity of 29 litres was positioned on the side of the fighting compartment, giving the tank an operational range of 190 kilometres on roads, and 120 kilometres cross-country.

The ignition system was a double magneto-electric set-up, with Scintilla 12V magnetos. Each cylinder had two spark plugs, firing from independent electrical circuits. The engine was started with a Scintilla starter that had an output of 2.94kW at 24V, but the tank also featured a provision for hand cranking from inside the fighting compartment.

Cooling water was circulated by a water pump through a tunnel radiator located on the right side of the engine compartment. The radiator was equipped with a fan powered by the engine. The total cooling capacity (including the equalising tank) was 50 litres. Exhaust gases were routed through an armoured elbow to a muffler situated on top of the right rear fender.

As the tank was pneumatically steered, it was equipped with two three-cylinder, two-stage compressors, driven by the main engine. The compressors had a working pressure of 810.6kPa, an output of 100 litres/min, and required 0.44kW of input.

The crankshaft was connected to the transmission using three triple planetary gears, which were constantly engaged with two cogs linked to shafts connected to the clutches of the individual gears. Additionally, a third cog wheel was attached to the reduction gear. The transmission featured three gears, with the first and second gears activated by pneumatically controlled belt brakes. The third gear (direct) was engaged through a dry multiple-plate clutch, also pneumatically controlled. The first gear could be engaged manually using a Bowden cable in case of emergency.

Behind the transmission, the reduction gear was made up of two stages, formed by gears engaged through a gear clutch, which was pneumatically actuated. In case of failure, the mechanical lever could be used. The gearbox provided six forward gears and one reverse gear.

The driving force from the transmission was transferred to the rear driveshafts via bevel gears, while the pinion engaged two dish-shaped bevel gears, which were freely mounted. Through the gear clutch, one of the bevel gears would engage the corresponding driveshaft to initiate either forward or reverse movement. The clutch was pneumatically actuated, with a manual back-up in case of emergencies.

For steering, each track was fitted with a planetary gear that allowed for independent movement of the tracks. The outer ring of the planetary gear engaged a pinion gear linked to the brake drum of the driving sprocket. When the brake was engaged using compressed air (or hydraulically in an emergency), the driving force was transferred from the planetary gear through a Cardan joint to the drive sprocket. Loosening the

The Škoda T-11/0 engine was a robust in-line, four-cylinder gasoline engine, designed to provide reliable performance for the LT vz. 35. It was water-cooled, which helped maintain optimal operating temperatures during extended periods of use and harsh battlefield conditions. With a displacement of 8,620cc, the engine was capable of producing 120hp (88.7kW) of power, enabling the vehicle to achieve high mobility on uneven challenging terrains. Weighing 900kg, the engine was not excessively heavy for its size, allowing for a balanced combination of power and durability. Its fuel consumption rate of 184g/kW/hr was typical for engines of that period, indicating a reasonable level of fuel efficiency for a military vehicle in the early 1930s. Despite the T-11/0's strengths, the engine did face limitations, including suffering wear and tear under continuous heavy use, which required maintenance and repairs to keep the vehicle in fighting condition during prolonged engagements. (AC)

brake allowed for gradual or sudden disengagement of the driving force from the track, enabling turns or pivoting in place.

The running gear consisted of two tracks, stretched over rear driving and front idler toothed sprockets, running wheels and return rollers. Each track had 111 links, each 320mm wide and 95mm long. The links were made from cast, hardened manganese steel, with a service life of 6,500 kilometres—well above the 1,600 kilometre life typically expected from tracks. There were 105 track links per side. The tank also carried grousers, which improved traction on ice and snow, and these were stored in boxes behind the front idler wheel on both sides. Thanks to its low ground pressure of only 0.51kg/cm², the LT vz. 35 could operate in terrain inaccessible to other tanks of its class. For example, the Renault R-35 had nearly twice the ground pressure.

The teeth of the driving and idler sprockets engaged the slots in the track links. Both sprockets had a diameter of 575mm and were equipped with two rings, each with nineteen teeth. Both sprockets were fitted with brakes. In the centre of each track link was a guide lug, which helped centre the track between the paired running wheels and in the grooves of the sprocket drum.

The track links were connected by link pins made of durable steel, which were loosely inserted into the links. This design allowed for the quick replacement of damaged track links or pins. To prevent the pins from loosening during operation, both the driving and idler sprockets were equipped with dish-like plates mounted on both sides, which pushed the loose pins back into the links. For particularly challenging terrain, grousers could be mounted on some pins, which were typically stored in metal boxes behind the front sprockets.

Detail view of the muffler. Note the track pins and the mud scraper in front of the rear drive wheel. (*AC*)

Above: Weighing approximately 10.5 tons, the LT vz. 35 was relatively light, which gave it a low ground pressure—a major advantage in soft terrain, where heavier tanks might become bogged down. Its compact size also allowed it to manoeuvre easily in tight spaces, making it well suited for reconnaissance, flanking actions and urban combat scenarios. (*AC*)

Below: Each track had 111 links, 320mm wide and 95mm long. The links were made from cast, hardened manganese steel, with a service life of 6,500km—well above the 1,600km life typically expected. (*AC*)

To reduce the accumulation of dirt and debris on the tracks, especially in wet and muddy conditions, large metal scrapers were bolted to the drive sprocket gear housings on both sides of the vehicle. These scrapers were positioned just ahead of the toothed driver sprockets, providing enough clearance to allow the wheel teeth to pass through.

The tracks were supported by two bogie carriages per side, suspended from cast steel brackets bolted to the hull. Each carriage had two independent swinging arms, each holding two pairs of road wheels connected by shallow, V-shaped swivel arms. Each wheel had a diameter of 350mm and a width of 94mm. The wheels were rubber-tyred and contacted the track on both sides of the guide lugs. Two pairs of wheels mounted on a common shackle formed a frame, and two such frames formed a wheel carrier, supported by 900 x 90mm leaf spring clusters.

At the front, under the idler sprocket, there was an unsprung double wheel of the same size and design as the running wheels. These wheels were fixed to lugs on the sides of the hull. Their primary function was to improve track centring, but they also enhanced the tank's ability to cross obstacles. The four pairs of return rollers on each side, measuring 200 x 60mm, were also rubber-tyred. Fixed blades mounted in front of the driving sprockets helped prevent them from becoming blocked by accumulated mud.

Though the suspension system on the tank was complex, it performed very well in cross-country conditions and demonstrated excellent durability. For example, a German commission that took over the tanks following the German occupation of Czechoslovakia in March 1939 deliberately attempted to shed a track while operating the tanks in rough terrain, but was unsuccessful. The only issue arose during high-speed driving on hard, stony surfaces, where the rubber tyres on the running wheels overheated and were prone to damage owing to their small size.

Despite the complexity of the suspension design, it was highly reliable and only failed after prolonged operation at high speeds over difficult terrain, such as during Operation Barbarossa in Russia. The main drawback of the system became apparent during harsh winter conditions when the running gear would frequently freeze solid. Breakages occurred when rapid defrosting was attempted; cold steel becomes brittle, and the application of heat causes it to expand suddenly, weakening the molecular structure and resulting in breaks when the vehicle was subjected to stress, such as moving.

The export version of 1939, the T-11, featured some improvements over the original LT vz. 35 model. One notable upgrade was the addition of a transmission controller that helped prevent malfunctions and facilitated the engagement of the reduction gear.

Steering

Škoda introduced pneumatic steering in all its tanks designed during the 1930s. The use of compressed air as the working medium eased the physical strain of operating a contemporary tank with mechanical steering. Compressed air was easy to supply to the various mechanisms, allowed fine control adjustments, acted quickly, and saved both weight and space in the fighting compartment. However, pneumatic steering was complex, which led to a higher incidence of breakdowns that were difficult to repair in the field.

Above: Interior view of the front section of the fighting compartment, showing the driving levers. (*Vojenském Technickém Muzeu Lešany*)

Below: The front road wheel was not sprung and was mounted in a fixed position. The storage box above it contained track grousers, which could be fitted onto the tracks to provide extra traction on ice or snow. The front mudguard was flanged and bolted to the top of the glacis plate. In service a leather apron was fitted to the front of the mudguard. (*CzAPM*)

The rear drive sprocket. Each of the two sprockets had nineteen teeth and each also had a mud scraper installed, as can be seen here. The large exhaust silencer was secured with metal straps to mounting brackets on the left side of the hull. (*AC*)

In the LT vz. 35 tank compressed air, provided by the compressors, was stored in an 18-litre pressure vessel mounted on the side wall of the fighting compartment. Gear shifting was controlled by an air controller located in front of the driver. By positioning the controller lever into the correct slot, air was directed through a system of valves to the pneumatic cylinders, activating the clutches or brakes.

To engage the reduction gear, the driver would depress the clutch pedal. A separate lever controlled the valve, feeding compressed air to the clutch, which engaged forward or reverse movement. In the event of a pneumatic system failure, first and fourth gears could be engaged mechanically using a hand wheel. A mechanical lever could also be used to engage the reduction gear and reverse.

Steering was managed by the driver using two steering levers connected to the distribution valves. By gradually pulling a steering lever towards himself, the driver disengaged the driving brake on the planetary gear, disconnecting the track from the driving force. Pulling the steering lever further fed compressed air into the main brake of the driving sprocket, which then braked the disconnected track, causing the tank to turn in a curve. If the lever was pulled all the way back, the track was fully braked, and the tank would turn on the spot. In this case the brake in the idler sprocket would stop the track. When moving in reverse, the driving sprocket brake would engage to stop the track.

By pulling both steering levers back simultaneously, the tank could be braked in a straight line. The sprocket brakes could also be controlled by a foot brake using pneumatic pressure. In an emergency the hand brake, which acted mechanically on the front sprocket brakes, could be used. This hand brake was also employed for parking.

If the pneumatic steering system failed, the tank could still be steered using two mechanical steering levers located on both sides of the driver's seat. These levers were mechanically linked to a hydraulic cylinder, whose piston connected to a lever that activated the planetary gear brakes. Naturally, steering this way required much more physical effort (65kg vs. 20kg for pneumatic steering).

This description of the steering system highlights its complexity: numerous pressure lines ran throughout the hull, with eleven actuating cylinders, two compressors, and many valves and stopcocks. All of these components were expensive to manufacture, required special materials and demanded meticulous assembly and maintenance. However, it is important to acknowledge that, despite its complexity, the system performed reliably in the field and had very few defects.

Additional Equipment

The fighting compartment of the LT vz. 35 was illuminated by a ceiling lamp mounted at the rear, while for external lighting two 5W contour lamps in metal casings were mounted on the front of the fenders. A similar lamp on the rear plate illuminated the vehicle's number plate. The tank was also equipped with a 50/35W headlight, 108mm in diameter, mounted between the visors on the front plate. With its long cable, this headlight could be used either as a spotlight or as a work light.

Starting in 1940, additional lighting was installed on the PzKpfw 35(t). A Notek light, mounted on the left front fender, provided diffused light for night driving.

Additional equipment mounted on the LT vz. 35 included a shovel and pickaxe on the left hull side above the fender, while a 6m-long towing cable with eyelets and a 10-ton capacity was carried across the upper engine-compartment hatches. (*AC*)

Above: By September 1939, after the LT vz. 35 was introduced into Wehrmacht service, some of the tanks were retrofitted with an NKAV smoke grenade rack mounted on the rear of the hull. (*AC*)

Below: In the spring of 1940, prior to the campaign in the West, 'Škodas' were upgraded with Notek-type night lamps, positioned on the left front fender. These lamps were shielded with a 'umbrella' cover, making it challenging for adversaries to detect vehicles using such lighting from the air during night operations. Additionally, two night searchlights were installed inside the hull. (*AC*)

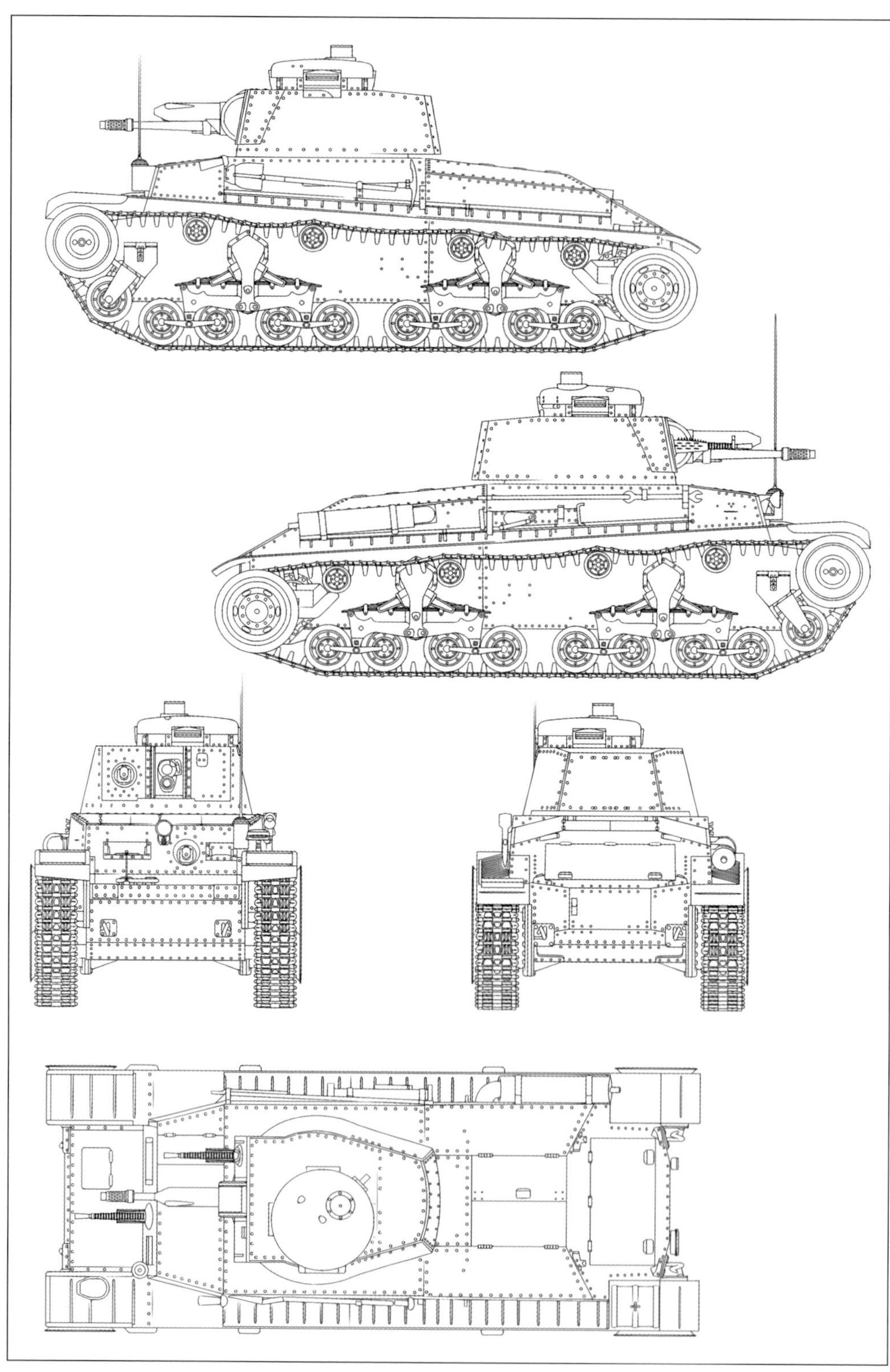

A 3D view of the LT vz. 35.

The rear plate illumination was removed and replaced with two new lights: on the left was a rear distance light (*Abstand Rücklicht*), and on the right an accessory rear light (*Zusatz Schlusslicht*). These lights, manufactured by Nove-Technik in Munich, were standard on all Wehrmacht vehicles. From October 1941 the accessory rear light was replaced by a rear brake light (*Bremseschlusslicht* DIN 72624FL).

The tank was powered by two 12V, 100Ah NIFE 9AL/10 alkaline batteries, stored in wooden compartments and charged by two dynamos connected to the engine.

In addition to tools and spare parts for both the vehicle and its armaments, which were mostly stored in wooden bins or leather bags within the fighting compartment, larger tools were carried externally. On the left hull side, above the fender, were mounted a shovel and a pick. On the right side an iron crowbar, an 8-ton jack and a wrench for track tensioning were attached. Two spare track links were stored on the rear of the left fender, while the right fender held a wooden block to support the jack. A 6m-long towing cable with eyelets and a towing capacity of 10 tons was carried on the upper hatches of the engine compartment. Additionally, the tank featured four towing hooks, two on each corner of the hull, each positioned 60 centimetres above the ground and capable of withstanding 5 tons of force.

Table 3. Technical specification of the LT vz. 35/PzKpfw 35(t)

Crew	3 (4 in Wehrmacht service)
DIMENSIONS AND WEIGHT	
Length x Width x Height (mm)	4900 x 2055 x 2370
Weight empty (tons)	9,76
Weight fully laden (armed, no crew) (tons)	10.5
ENGINE	Skoda T-11/0
Swept volume	8,620ccm
Output at 1800rpm	118–120hp/88.2–88.7kW
Engine weight (kg)	900
Fuel capacity (litres)	124 + 29
Oil capacity (engine/gearbox/oil cleaner) (litres)	12/13/6.5
Water capacity (litres)	50
Gearbox	6 forward and 1 reverse speeds
Speed at gear 1/2/3/4/5/6 (km/h)	3.5/5.6/8.8/13.7/21.8/34
Gearbox weight (kg)	500
Reduction	2 stages
Transmission	3 gears
MOBILITY	
Maximum speed (road) (km/h)	34
Maximum speed (off-road) (km/h)	12–16
Turning circle diameter (m)	3.5

Range road/off-road (km)	160/120
Ground clearance (cm)	35
Track width and length (mm)	320/19,545
Track ground contact length (mm)	3,240
Track contact area (cm²)	20,736
Ground pressure (fully laden) (kg/sqcm)	0.51
Stability (pitch and roll axes):	45°
Climb	87% (41%/0.716 rad)
Penetration of brick walls (mm)	450
Trench crossing (mm)	up to 2,000
Tree-felling capability (uprooting trees with a trunk diameter in mm)	up to 350
Ford depth (mm)	900
ARMAMENT	
Designation	Škoda A3
Originator and Producer	Škoda
Muzzle velocity (m/s)	675
Calibre (mm)	37
Length of tube (mm)	1,458
Standard recoil (mm)	460
Gun weight (kg)	235
Barrel endurance	3000 shots
Ammo carried	24 (armour-piercing) + 48
Round weight (kg)	1.44
SECONDARY ARMAMENT	
Machine guns ZB vz. 35/37	two
Calibre (mm)	7.92
Muzzle velocity (m/s)	750–830
Rounds carried	3,000
ARMOUR (mm)	25, 16, 12, 8, 5

4

In Czechoslovak Army Service

The foundation of Czechoslovakia's armoured forces began modestly in 1930 with the establishment of its first armoured battalion. This unit comprised two companies: one equipped with Škoda heavy armoured cars, and the other with light Tatra vehicles and ageing Renault FT-17 tanks. By September 1933 the battalion had been reorganised into a full armoured regiment—*Pluk Útočné Vozby*, or PÚV—which also included a company of armoured trains, a replacement unit and an armoured warfare training school. The tank battalion within the armoured regiment was composed of two companies equipped with tankettes, while a third operated LT vz. 34 light tanks. At the same time, armoured cars were assigned to a cavalry battalion comprising two reconnaissance squadrons.

The rise of Adolf Hitler to power in Germany in 1933 brought a significant shift in Czechoslovak defence planning. The General Staff undertook a major revision of its force structure, proposing the formation of four tank battalions and four armoured car battalions in direct support of the cavalry. Additional plans called for seven corps-level reconnaissance tank companies and fourteen more tank battalions to serve as strategic reserves. To support this ambitious structure, the army set high procurement targets: 373 cavalry (fast) tanks, 336 infantry tanks and 336 medium tanks—an extraordinary leap from the approximately two hundred armoured vehicles (including armoured cars) in service at the time.

In August 1935 the Ministry of National Defence ordered a sweeping reorganisation. A centralised armoured brigade was established in Milovice to oversee the creation of three armoured regiments and the Central Armoured Training Centre (*Učiliště Útočné Vozby*, or UÚV). The 1st Armoured Regiment (PÚV-1) remained in Milovice, while the 2nd Regiment (PÚV-2) was formed in Olomouc and relocated to Vyškov in 1937. The 3rd Regiment (PÚV-3) was based in Turčiansky Svätý Martin, Slovakia. Each regiment consisted of four battalions and an armoured train company. The 2nd and 3rd battalions within these regiments were built around three tank companies, two of which were reserve units equipped with the newly delivered LT vz. 35 light tanks.

The first fifteen LT vz. 35 tanks arrived in Milovice in December 1936, forming the nucleus of the modernised armoured forces. Of the 298 tanks produced before the Munich Crisis, PÚV-1 received 197 (a mix from Škoda and ČKD), PÚV-2 received 49 and PÚV-3 received 52. Production serial numbers were meticulously tracked, and tank distribution was carefully balanced between the two manufacturers.

Above and below: Czechoslovak military manoeuvres placed emphasis on coordination between tanks and infantry. Peacetime exercises sought to ensure that armoured units did not operate in isolation, which would leave them vulnerable to hidden enemy anti-tank guns or close-assault tactics—such as infantry using hand grenades or incendiary devices to disable them from behind or from blind spots. (*CzAPM*)

In the mountainous terrain of Czechoslovakia, tactical doctrine emphasised the importance of holding the high ground, which offered superior visibility, improved fields of fire and a natural defensive advantage. Czechoslovak tank crews were trained to operate effectively in these challenging environments, often practising manoeuvres and firing drills from elevated positions. (*CzAPM*)

Initially created in October 1935 to oversee training, logistics and personnel, the armoured brigade headquarters in Milovice was disbanded in March 1937 and its responsibilities transferred to the newly formed 7th Department for Armoured Troops within the Ministry of Defence. This shift ensured that the armoured forces had strategic representation at the highest levels of military planning.

Each of the Czechoslovak armoured regiments had developed distinct organisational structures by the mid-1930s:

- PÚV-1 (Milovice) fielded two battalions by 1936: the first battalion included a motorcyclist company along with two companies of tankettes and armoured cars; the second consisted of four tank companies. By 1937 it had expanded to four battalions, incorporating additional tank and anti-tank gun companies;
- PÚV-2 (Vyškov) followed a similar template. Its first battalion included motorcycles and armoured cars, while two battalions operated light tanks. Plans were in place to establish a fourth battalion equipped with medium tanks. By 1937 the first battalion had expanded to five companies, while anti-tank and medium tank elements were also reinforced; and
- PÚV-3 (Turčiansky Svätý Martin, Slovakia) initially fielded a first battalion with a mix of light vehicles and three tank companies, followed by two more tank battalions. By 1937 a fourth battalion was added, consisting of four anti-tank gun companies, with two additional anti-tank companies assigned directly to regimental command.

A fourth regiment, PÚV-4, was briefly established in Kolín in September 1938. It was intended to relieve PÚV-1 but its existence was short-lived due to the Munich Agreement and the resulting territorial losses.

By the eve of the crisis in 1938, Czechoslovak armoured forces had reached their most advanced organisational stage, boasting a planned personnel strength of 6,618 men. PÚV-1 accounted for 1,971 of them, PÚV-2 for 2,165, PÚV-3 for 930 and the nascent PÚV-4 for 1,405. The Armoured Training Centre maintained a cadre of 127 instructors and staff.

A major doctrinal milestone occurred on 1 October 1937 with the formal establishment of four mobile divisions (*Rychlá divize*, or RD), envisioned as the core of a modern mechanised force. Each division was to include ninety-eight light tanks, supported by armoured cars (three OA vz. 27s and nine OA vz. 30s per division). In parallel, the armoured regiments were tasked with fielding thirty-four three-tank platoons for infantry and border defence support, along with twenty-three tankette platoons and six armoured car platoons. Final organisation orders were issued in the winter of 1937, and the divisional headquarters were officially established on 1 January 1938. The 1st Mobile Division (RD-1) was stationed in Prague, RD-2 in Brno, RD-3 in Bratislava and RD-4 in Pardubice.

The mobile division structure embodied a hybrid concept, combining a cavalry brigade (comprising dragoon regiments, cyclists and horse-drawn artillery) with a mechanised brigade (including two tank battalions, two motorised infantry battalions and motorised artillery). Each division also featured a reconnaissance battalion, equipped with its own light tank company.

All these developments enabled Czechoslovakia to build one of the most advanced armoured forces in Central Europe—well organised, partially mechanised and strategically ambitious. This solid foundation held great potential for further growth, had it not been abruptly disrupted by the geopolitical upheavals of 1938.

The Challenges of Mobilising the Mobile Divisions

At full strength, each Czechoslovak mobile division was intended to field an impressive array of resources: 11,000 personnel, 2,832 horses, 298 motorcycles, 1,009 motor vehicles, ninety-eight tanks, twelve armoured cars and sixty-eight artillery pieces—including anti-tank, anti-aircraft and field guns. However, translating this ambitious blueprint into a fully functional combat formation by 1938 proved significantly more difficult than anticipated.

The most immediate and critical issue was a chronic shortage of tanks. Although each of the four mobile divisions was slated to receive ninety-eight tanks (a total requirement of 392), the Czechoslovak army possessed only about 88 per cent of that number. This included approximately fifty LT vz. 34s—mechanically worn and increasingly obsolete—and 298 LT vz. 35s, still plagued by technical teething issues. Many LT vz. 35s had to be returned to the manufacturers for urgent modifications shortly after field delivery. Further straining resources, the first fifteen tanks of this type were loaned to Romania, as export commitments were often prioritised over domestic military requirements.

Above: LT vz. 35 (Serial no. 13.666) of PÚV-1 pictured during field manoeuvres in September 1938, skilfully concealed within a wooded area. Utilising the natural cover provided by the trees, the crew practised ambush tactics. (*CzAPM*)

Below: Following an LT vz. 35 driving across open fields at half speed—around 20 km/h—was a challenging task for the infantry. (*CzAPM*)

A platoon of LT vz. 35 tanks of PÚV-1 during a break in manoeuvres, with their crews taking a moment to rest and discuss tactics. (*CzAPM*)

More serious, however, were the organisational shortcomings. Mechanised brigade headquarters—central to each mobile division's structure—existed only on paper during peacetime and were intended to be formed ad hoc during mobilisation. This presented serious coordination challenges. Compounding the issue was the lack of dedicated motorised infantry units. Under mounting political pressure in the summer of 1938, these formations had to be hastily improvised, often by reassigning training battalions or border security units. RD-1, for example, was reinforced with two training battalions, while the other divisions each received a single border battalion as a temporary measure.

Additional complications arose from the cavalry arm, which traditionally formed the backbone of the mobile divisions. Rather than being an elite force, the cavalry often suffered from underqualified leadership and a high proportion of conscripts from ethnic minorities—factors that undermined morale and cohesion. Cavalry training emphasised dismounted combat, with troops acting primarily as dragoons supported by mortars and machine guns; horses served merely as a means of cross-country mobility.

The First Test (May 1938)

Rising tensions in the Sudetenland, the Czechoslovakian border area populated by a German minority, prompted the first real test of Czechoslovakia's mobile divisions. On the night of 20 May 1938 the government ordered a partial mobilisation in response to escalating German provocations. The mobile divisions deployed to their designated wartime positions and remained on high alert until 8 June. During these three weeks in the field numerous and often critical deficiencies were exposed.

Above: LT vz. 35 (Serial no. 13.846), manufactured by Škoda, was officially accepted into service with PÚV-3 based at Turčiansky Svätý Martin in Slovakia. (*CzAPM*)

Below: A platoon of LT vz. 35 tanks belonging to PÚV-1 pictured during training at Milovice. These tanks (Serial nos 13.676 and 13.685) had been delivered by Škoda between December 1936 and January 1937, as part of the first operational batch of LT vz. 35s. In this photograph the military censor eliminated the hull machine guns. (*CzAPM*)

A full company of PÚV-1 LT vz. 35 tanks during manoeuvres in the autumn of 1938. The photo likely depicts one of the large-scale training operations conducted in response to the mounting threat posed by Nazi Germany, showcasing the regiment's combat readiness and coordination before the eventual disintegration of Czechoslovakia. (*CzAPM*)

Most crews and commanders lacked adequate training, particularly in the operation of armoured vehicles under field conditions. Many officers had only recently transferred from the infantry or cavalry, having completed a mere four-month course at the armoured warfare school. Enlisted personnel, meanwhile, were drilled only at platoon level and frequently lacked the technical skills needed to maintain or operate their vehicles effectively.

Weapons readiness was another major concern. The transition from the older ZB vz. 35 to the newer ZB vz. 37 machine guns had left nearly half of the tanks unarmed at the time of mobilisation. The new guns were incompatible with existing mounts, forcing many tanks to deploy with their machine gun ports sealed by makeshift metal covers. Factory teams were dispatched to retrofit the tanks in the field, but the delays and disruption were considerable.

Additional problems included a shortage of armour-piercing ammunition—a situation that was only partially resolved by September 1938—and critical gaps in equipment such as optical sights, bulletproof visors, radios, towing cables and ammunition belt loaders. Most seriously, the army lacked a mobile repair and recovery system. In the absence of field workshops or dedicated recovery units, even minor mechanical issues required the return of vehicles to the factory. Although some of these logistical shortcomings were addressed in the following months, technical support remained the armoured force's most significant vulnerability.

ESCALATION AND READINESS (SUMMER 1938)

By early 1938 the Ministry of National Defence was increasingly concerned about mounting unrest among the ethnic German population in the Sudeten border regions. As political agitation escalated into violent incidents and sabotage, it became clear that regular army units would be needed to support border security and internal defence.

On 25 July 1938, amid the deepening crisis, the ministry ordered the rapid formation of 'ready units'—specialised mobile formations capable of immediate deployment along the frontier. A total of forty-one such units were created, each comprising three platoons of tankettes, six of light tanks and eight of armoured cars, as well as four motorcycle platoons. These forces were strategically positioned in vulnerable areas, providing a visible and rapid-response deterrent to unrest.

Despite frequent redeployments and long-distance marches, the armoured vehicles assigned to these formations performed reliably, covering thousands of kilometres without a notable increase in mechanical breakdowns. This performance reflected both improvements made by the manufacturers and the growing familiarity of the crews with their equipment. Interestingly, the most common malfunctions were electrical in nature, rather than issues with the more complex pneumatic systems used in the LT vz. 35.

By late August 1938 twenty-nine additional 'ready groups' were added to the original force structure, each reinforced with an armoured car. These mobile units played a key role in quelling pro-Nazi uprisings in the Sudetenland. However, their creation came at a significant cost: most of the vehicles assigned to these new groups were drawn from the mobile divisions' front-line strength, weakening the larger formations precisely when they were most needed.

The Sudeten Crisis (September 1938)

Despite nearly a decade of planning, by September 1938 Czechoslovakia's mobile divisions were still far from achieving their intended wartime strength. Of the thirty-six tank companies originally envisioned across the four divisions, only thirteen had been fully formed. The shortfall in armoured vehicles was particularly stark: RD-1 could field just thirty-eight tanks, RD-2 forty and RD-3 only sixteen; RD-4— somewhat better equipped—had seventy-six. An additional thirty-seven tanks were assigned to an independent battalion supporting fortress troops. In total, only 207 light tanks were operational—less than half of the 440 tanks planned for the mobile divisions, and significantly below the total combined inventory of 348 LT vz. 34 and LT vz. 35 tanks available at the time.

The political crisis reached breaking point on the night of 12 September 1938, when the Sudeten German Party, with support from Berlin, orchestrated widespread demonstrations and riots throughout the borderlands, demanding annexation to Nazi Germany. The following day martial law was declared in eleven frontier districts, but overstretched police and army units struggled to restore order. In response, the army deployed the motorised brigades of the mobile divisions to the most threatened regions. Supported by artillery and armoured vehicles, these units proved highly effective in suppressing the unrest and re-establishing state control.

Above: Milovice Barracks, mid-1920s. Originally constructed as an infantry facility with several single-storey buildings, the barracks were not designed to accommodate armoured vehicles. When the tanks arrived in the mid-1930s, they were parked together under a single roof, as dedicated mortar garages were not available. (*AC*)

Below: Two LT vz. 35 tanks, manufactured by Škoda in 1937 and assigned to PÚV-1, pictured in a temporary parking area. (*AC*)

A rare and revealing photograph shows a Luftwaffe soldier posing proudly next to a captured LT vz. 35 tank. The image reflects a common practice among German troops during the occupation of Czechoslovakia in March 1939—posing with seized military equipment as symbols of triumph. Note the red rhombus identifying the Czechoslovak 4th Company/4th Platoon. (*AC*)

With tensions mounting and war appearing imminent, Czechoslovakia ordered full mobilisation on 23 September. In the three weeks between 12 September and 4 October Czechoslovak forces engaged in at least sixty-nine armed clashes with the Sudetendeutsches Freikorps—a German-backed paramilitary force composed of Sudeten German militants. Supplied and directed by the Third Reich, Freikorps units frequently crossed the border to attack military and police outposts. In response, Czechoslovak armoured formations—typically organised into three-vehicle platoons of light tanks, tankettes or armoured cars—were routinely deployed to counter these incursions.

The first combat use of Czechoslovak armoured units during the crisis occurred on the night of 12 September, in towns such as Stříbro, Planá u Mariánských Lázní and Jáchymov. One of the most intense engagements took place on 22 September near Cheb, where a motorised brigade launched a counterattack against Freikorps forces that had crossed into Czechoslovakia from German territory. Working in concert with infantry, the tanks quickly overwhelmed the insurgents.

Clashes also erupted in Kraslice and soon spread to Varnsdorf and nearby towns. In these engagements the tanks proved decisive. Their firepower was used to break barricades and neutralise machine-gun nests, while their mere presence often dispersed crowds and demoralised attackers. The insurgents, lacking effective anti-tank weapons and relying mostly on grenades, were unable to halt the armoured advances. In many instances the appearance of a single tank or armoured car was enough to scatter the enemy.

On 17 September 1938 the situation escalated further as Germany effectively initiated a low-intensity, undeclared war against Czechoslovakia through cross-border provocations and insurgent support. In response, Britain and France began exerting diplomatic pressure on Prague. On 20 September both powers formally urged the Czechoslovak government to cede the Sudetenland to Germany in an effort to preserve peace.

The final days of September saw the most intense fighting. Between 26 and 29 September, in the vicinity of the villages of Budislav and Přesdíbor, forty Czechoslovak tanks were engaged in sustained clashes—the heaviest of the crisis. By the end of the month no fewer than 150 LT vz. 35 tanks had been committed to border operations, drawn from the 2nd, 3rd, 7th and 8th light tank battalions. Additionally, 102 more LT vz. 34 and LT vz. 35 tanks were fielded by thirty-four independent armoured platoons assigned to the Border Guard.

With full mobilisation under way and an invasion appearing likely, the Ministry of National Defence placed an emergency order with Škoda for 105 additional LT vz. 35 tanks. This was a stopgap measure intended to compensate for delays in the delivery of the newer LT vz. 38, then in production by ČKD. However, this order was swiftly cancelled following the signing of the Munich Agreement on 30 September. Nonetheless, the army hoped to retain some of the tanks then being built for Romania under existing export contracts as R-2s.

The Munich Conference, held on 29–30 September 1938, brought the crisis to a bitter end. In a meeting from which Czechoslovakia was deliberately excluded, the leaders of Germany, Britain, France and Italy acceded to Hitler's demands. The Sudetenland would be ceded to Germany without resistance. Between 1 and 10 October 1938 German forces occupied the region, seizing not only territory but also much of the nation's fortified defensive line. With a single diplomatic stroke, Czechoslovakia lost its most defensible frontier—and the strategic balance of Central Europe was irrevocably altered.

The Clash with Hungary

Following the Munich Agreement and the cession of the Sudetenland to Germany, most Czechoslovak army units returned to their peacetime garrisons. However, this period of relative calm was brief. By mid-October 1938 it became clear that Hungary—emboldened by the weakening of Czechoslovakia's defensive posture—was preparing to press its territorial claims, particularly in Slovakia and Transcarpathian Ruthenia.

In response, Czechoslovakia began assembling armoured detachments specifically to counter the potential Hungarian threat. Starting in mid-October, tanks from the 2nd and 3rd light tank battalions were deployed to Nitra, where a combined force of forty tanks, ninety-six motor vehicles and some four hundred and fifty personnel was stationed. However, by the end of the month most of the 2nd Battalion's tanks had returned to their home garrisons. Vehicles from the 3rd Battalion, along with companies from the 7th Battalion, were redirected to reinforce positions throughout Slovakia. The 3rd Battalion remained in the region until mid-December before it, too, withdrew. Nevertheless, the 2nd Company—with thirteen tanks—remained in Bratislava to support the 12th Infantry Division, and a mixed company from the 7th Battalion continued operating in Slovakia until March 1939.

The harsh winter of 1938/1939 revealed critical mechanical vulnerabilities in the LT vz. 35 tanks. Cold temperatures caused the oil to thicken, making engines difficult to start. The tanks' pneumatic systems also malfunctioned in sub-zero conditions. Lacking antifreeze, crews were forced to drain the radiators each night to prevent freezing and refill them the next day—an arduous task that often delayed the tanks' readiness by several hours every morning.

On 15 February 1939 the Czechoslovak army formally ended its defensive operations along the Hungarian border. Although the 12th Infantry Division in Transcarpathian Ruthenia had initially been ordered to return all its armoured assets, it retained a company of LT vz. 35 tanks in Michalovce and a combined unit of tanks and armoured cars in Chust and Sevluš (present-day Vynohradiv).

The German Invasion (March 1939)

The Munich Agreement effectively marked the end of Czechoslovakia as a sovereign, unified state. On 5 October 1938 President Edvard Beneš resigned; he left the country three weeks later. He was succeeded by Emil Hácha, a respected legal scholar, who

The Czechs were generally neither allowed nor inclined to assist the invaders while they inspected captured tanks. Due to this reason Germans initially encountered challenges in integrating ex-Czech vehicles into their armoured forces as all technical documentation, manuals and instructions were in Czech. (*AC*)

was elected president on 30 November. In the aftermath of the president's resignation, Slovakia declared autonomy on 6 October 1938—a move officially recognised by the central government in Prague. On 19 November the state was formally reconstituted as the 'Czecho-Slovak Republic', adopting a federal structure. This marked the transition from the First Republic to the so-called Second Republic.

Rudolf Beran was appointed prime minister of the new republic and embarked on a programme of authoritarian reform in the name of national unity. His government imposed strict censorship, outlawed most Czechoslovak political parties and established internment camps in Lety and Hodonín. Simultaneously, efforts to curtail regional autonomy further alienated Slovakia and other provinces, deepening the political instability.

These centralising measures provoked widespread resentment among Slovaks. In early March 1939 the Prague government attempted to reassert direct control over Slovakia. On the night of 9/10 March a presidential decree revoked Slovak autonomy, declared a state of emergency and triggered mass arrests of Slovak political activists. The crackdown provoked an immediate backlash, with protests erupting across the region. Casualties occurred as Czechoslovak troops attempted to suppress the unrest. The operation, widely viewed as a failed coup, ultimately backfired.

The Czechoslovak government's violation of the federal agreement—and its inability to effectively address renewed Hungarian territorial ambitions—prompted

Two PÚV-1 LT vz. 35s transported from Milovice barracks near Prague to Pz.Rgt.11 at Paderborn barracks. The transfer was conducted by rail, facilitated by the railway stations in both towns being equipped to handle flatbed cars for armoured vehicle transport. (*AC*)

The LT vz. 35, tested by crews of Pz.Rgt.11, demonstrated excellent cross-country mobility thanks to its light weight of approximately 10 tons—only slightly heavier than the PzKpfw II, but armed with a significantly more powerful 3.7cm gun compared to the PzKpfw II's 2cm cannon. (*AC*)

Slovakia to declare independence on 14 March 1939. The very next day, on 15 March, President Emil Hácha was summoned to Berlin, where Adolf Hitler coerced him into accepting the German occupation of the remaining Czechoslovak lands. That same morning German forces—led by Panzer and *Schnelle Truppen* (armoured and fast troops) formations—entered Bohemia and Moravia. Facing no meaningful resistance, they completed the dismemberment of the Czechoslovak state within the next few days.

5

In German Army Service

The German occupation of Czechoslovakia in March 1939 had immediate and far-reaching consequences for the expansion of Germany's armoured and motorised forces. Among the most valuable assets seized was a stockpile of 469 armoured fighting vehicles, including 244 LT vz. 35 light tanks. Of these, fifty-two remained in service with the newly established Slovak army, while the remainder were absorbed into the Wehrmacht, significantly strengthening Germany's Panzer forces ahead of the impending invasion of Poland.

Following a thorough technical evaluation, the German Army High Command (*Oberkommando des Heeres*, or OKH) determined that more than fifty of the LT vz. 35 tanks required refurbishment before they could be deployed. These vehicles were sent to the Škoda Works in Pilsen for overhaul. Meanwhile, combat-ready tanks were prepared for transport to Germany as early as April 1939, with the refurbishment programme continuing into the summer months.

By 1 September 1939 a total of 202 LT vz. 35 tanks had been fully integrated into the German military inventory. Although the Wehrmacht readily incorporated the captured Škoda tanks into its front-line units, it made no effort to resume production of the type. This decision was largely due to the German military's mistrust of the LT vz. 35's complex pneumatic control system, which was considered unreliable and overly complicated for mass deployment.

Integration of the LT vz. 35 into the Wehrmacht

The operational LT vz. 35 tanks captured during the German occupation of Czechoslovakia were primarily distributed among several key units: the 11th Armoured Regiment (*Panzer-Regiment 11*, or Pz.Rgt.11), stationed in Paderborn, the 65th Armoured Battalion (*Panzer-Abteilung 65*, or Pz.Abt.65), based in Sennelager, and the 82nd Armoured Signal Battalion (*Panzer-Nachrichten-Abteilung 82*, or Pz.Nacht.Abt.82) of the newly formed 1st Light Division (1. *leichte Division*, or 1.le. Div.). This division had been established on 10 November 1938, evolving from the 1st Light Brigade.

Although modelled on the French *Division Légère Mécanique*, 1.le.Div. would be more accurately described as a fast motorised division (*Schnelle Division*) or a form of armoured cavalry (*Panzerkavallerie*) formation. Compared to standard German armoured divisions, these new motorised cavalry formations were less resource-intensive and easier to manoeuvre and conceal, offering a cost-effective solution during a period of rapid expansion and limited industrial output.

Although it was armed with a 3.7cm main gun, nominally similar in calibre to that of the German PzKpfw III, the LT vz. 35 was not considered the PzKpfw III's tactical or technical equal. The tank's three-man crew (with the commander also serving as gunner and loader) was seen by German tank doctrine as a significant operational flaw. To address this, a directive issued in July 1939 ordered the addition of a fourth crew member—a dedicated loader—to improve firing efficiency and reduce crew fatigue.

Another key deficiency was the LT vz. 35's original radio system, which lacked the range and reliability of German communication equipment. By July 1939 all the tanks had been retrofitted with Fu 2 receivers, while company commanders' tanks were equipped with Fu 5 transceivers. Soon afterward, Fu 5 sets became the standard across all vehicles, with command tanks featuring both Fu 2 and Fu 5 systems.

A dedicated command variant was also developed: the *Panzerbefehlswagen* (PzBefWg 35(t)), classified as SdKfz 267 or 268. These tanks featured enhanced communications suites, including Fu 5 and Fu 8 transceivers, along with a prominent 2m-long rod antenna (*Stabantenne*) and the distinctive frame antenna (*Rahmenantenne*) mounted on the rear deck. In these variants, the turret-mounted machine gun was retained, while the hull machine gun was removed to make space for the added radio equipment.

All vehicles were repainted in the standard Wehrmacht camouflage pattern of dark grey (*Dunkelgrau* RAL 7021) with dark brown (*Dunkelbraun* RAL 7017) patches, in accordance with contemporary German regulations.

The first testing of LT vz. 35 tanks taken over from PÚV-1 by Pz.Abt.65 took place at the Senne/Haustenbeck Proving Ground in April 1939. As seen here, the vehicles were still painted in Czechoslovak camouflage and bore their original Czech registration numbers (13.683 and 13.676). (AC)

Above: Delivery of LT vz. 35 tanks converted into the command and communications variant, known as the PzBefWg 35(t). These vehicles were equipped with long-range radios and distinctive frame antennas. Since tanks were not permitted to travel on public roads during peacetime, they were transported to Paderborn barracks on flatbed trailers towed by SdKfz 9 half-tracks. (*AC*)

Below: Tanks of Kp.5/Pz.Rgt.11 during spring field manoeuvres in 1939. A heavier and more powerful 'Škoda' is seen pulling a PzKpfw II out of a sand pit at the Senne Proving Ground. (*AC*)

Initially recorded in official documents as *Panzerkampfwagen* (3.7cm) 'L.T.Sk.35s', the tanks were officially redesignated *Panzerkampfwagen* 35(t)s (PzKpfw 35(t)s) in January 1940, with the suffix '(t)' denoting their Czechoslovak origin. Among Wehrmacht crews, the PzKpfw 35(t) earned mixed reputations. Some ironically referred to it as the 'Škoda Super Sport', a nod to its relatively smooth ride and mechanical reliability—though the nickname carried a sarcastic edge due to the tank's outdated design. Others simply called it the '*alte Kiste*' ('old bucket'), reflecting its perceived obsolescence.

Nevertheless, the integration of the LT vz. 35 significantly bolstered the strength of the *Panzerwaffe* at a critical moment. As of September 1939, only ninety-eight PzKpfw III tanks were available. The seventy-five PzKpfw 35(t)s assigned to Pz.Regt.11, Pz.Regt.37 and Pz.Abt.65 more than doubled the Wehrmacht's inventory of medium tanks, not to mention the additional ex-Czechoslovak PzKpfw 38(t) tanks also entering service.

As of 31 August 1939, the total inventory of these Czech-built tanks in German hands stood at: 164 operational tanks, four in *Heereszeugämter* (Army Ordnance Depots) and thirty-four in the *Ersatzheer* (Replacement Army), for a total of 202 LT vz. 35 tanks available to the Wehrmacht.

Table 4. 1.leichte Division—Order of Battle and Equipment, 1 September 1939

Pz.Regt.11	HQ Kp	I.Abt (1st Bn)			II.Abt (2nd Bn)		
		Kp.1	Kp.2	Kp.3	Kp.5	Kp.6	Kp.7
Tank types	PzBefwg—6; Pz.II—45; Pz.35(t)—75; Pz.IV—27						
Pz.Abt.65	HQ Kp	Kp.1	Kp.2	Kp.3			
Tank types	PzBefwg—2; Pz.II—20; Pz.35(t)—37; Pz.IV—14						

A PzKpfw 35(t) passes by typical Fachwerk buildings in the Paderborn garrison area of Nordrhein-Westfalen, built using the traditional construction technique in which a wooden beam framework is filled with clay, brick or stone. (*AC*)

Above: The Paderborn garrison, home to Pz.Rgt.11, traced its origins to the Infanterie-Kaserne (Reichswehr infantry barracks) built in the early twentieth century. In the 1930s a new Panzer-Kaserne was constructed on Driburger Strasse, featuring modern facilities, including large garages and workshops. (*AC*)

Below: A PzKpfw 35(t) during manoeuvres in the spring of 1939. As field exercises were used mainly to master mobility, the machine guns were often dismounted, as here. (*AC*)

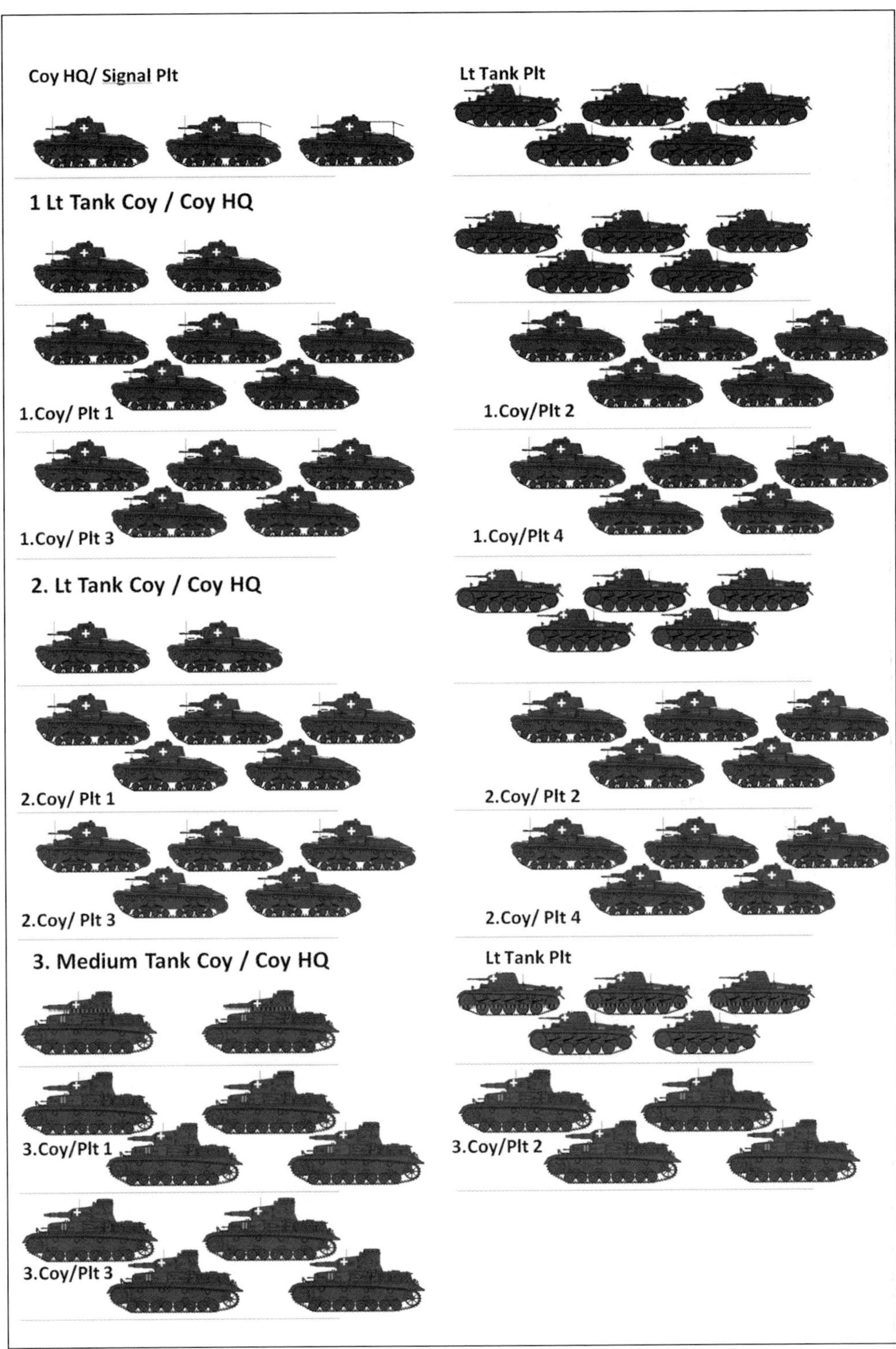

Table of Organisation and Equipment: Pz.Abt.65, August 1939. Only Kp.1. and Kp.3 of Pz.Abt.65 participated in the Polish Campaign, while Kp.2 was kept in reserve.

The Polish Campaign (September 1939)

Following the annexation of the remaining parts of Czechoslovakia in March 1939, Hitler swiftly turned his attention to his next target: Poland. As early as 3 April 1939, the German High Command of the Armed Forces (*Oberkommando der Wehrmacht*, or OKW) issued a directive to all three branches of the military to begin preparing operational plans for the invasion of Poland under the codename 'Fall Weiss' (Case White).

The attack was originally scheduled for 26 August 1939, but international developments forced a last-minute change. On 24 August Britain issued formal guarantees to Poland, pledging that both the United Kingdom and France would support Poland if it were attacked. In response, late on 25 August Hitler postponed the offensive, despite the fact that many German units—including elements of the *leichte Divisionen* (light divisions)—were already en route to their designated staging areas. In many instances senior officers and even divisional commanders had to physically intercept the advancing columns to deliver the order halting the attack.

Among the formations assigned to Tenth Army was 1.le.Div., which began its movement towards the Polish border around 20 August. The wheeled elements of the division advanced via main highways towards the Liegnitz (modern-day Legnica) region, then switched to country roads to reach forward positions near the frontier. The final assembly zone stretched between Kluczbork (Kreuzburg) and Tarnowskie Góry (Tarnowitz), with motorised cavalry units billeted in the surrounding villages. To conserve mechanical reliability, the Panzer battalions were transported as far as possible by rail or heavy trucks, only driving the last kilometres under their own power.

On 31 August 1939 Hitler issued Directive No. 1 for the Conduct of the War, officially setting the start of the invasion at 4.45 am on 1 September. That same day the OKH relocated to its forward operational headquarters in Zossen, south of Berlin, to oversee the campaign.

THE ADVANCE TO THE WARTA RIVER

At dawn on 1 September 1939 General Reichenau's Tenth Army—which included the 1st, 2nd and 3rd *leichte Divisionen*—advanced towards Warsaw as the central spearhead of Army Group South. This army fielded the highest concentration of armoured units among the German forces and was deployed on a narrow front with significant operational depth, underscoring its role as the main striking force.

Opposing the Tenth Army were four Polish infantry divisions and a cavalry brigade from the Łódź army. These units were deployed partly behind an incomplete defensive line of bunkers along the Warta (Warthe) river and partly west of Częstochowa. Additional Polish divisions and another cavalry brigade were held in reserve further east, but too far away to offer immediate reinforcement. Although the Polish army lacked armoured formations in the sector attacked by 1.le.Div., each infantry division was equipped with thirty-nine 37mm Bofors anti-tank guns, which were capable of penetrating the frontal armour of all the German tanks used in the campaign at effective combat ranges of 200–300 metres.

Above: By demolishing the bridge over the Prosna river the Poles managed to delay the advancing German tanks by approximately 10 hours during the first day of the war. However, despite this initial success, the delay was not enough to stop the advancing forces. This PzKpfw 35(t) from Kp.2/Pz.Rgt.11 eventually found a way to bypass the border town of Praszka, seen in the distance with its church with two tall towers. (*AC*)

Below: A PzKpfw 35(t) rolls into the city of Wieluń, which had been brutally bombed by Ju-87s and left in ruins. It was captured on 2 September 1939, with little opposition from Polish forces. The tank bearing tactical no. 511 belonged to Kp.5/Pz.Rgt.11. (*AC*)

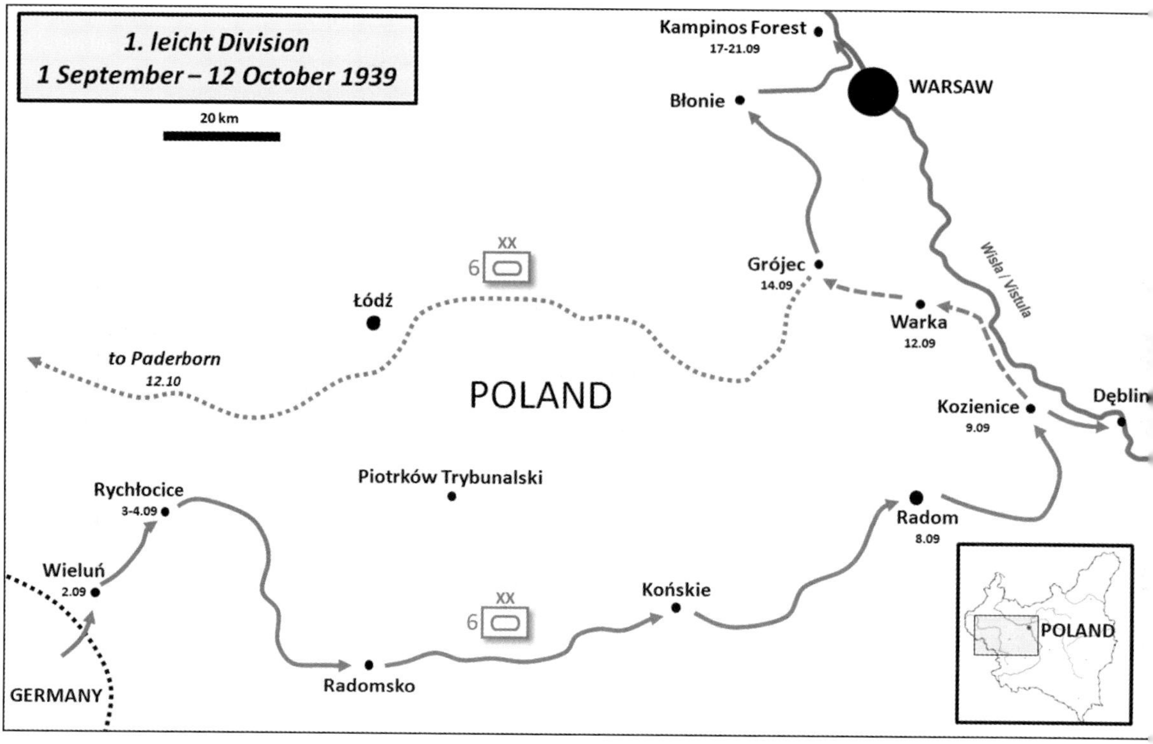

Battle trail map, 1939.

The Polish forces had no tanks in the path of the 1.le.Div.'s advance, allowing German 'Škodas' to move forwards largely unopposed, encountering resistance only from occasional ambushes by Bofors anti-tank guns. (*AC*)

Above: On 3 September Pz.Rgt.11 entered the small town of Radomsko, where it stayed for a few hours before resuming its advance. (*AC*)

Below: After piercing the Polish border zone, tanks of 1.le.Div. were placed onto trucks and tank trailers and driven deep into Polish territory against weakly fortified targets. This photo, taken in Włoszczowa market, showns PzKpfw 35(t) tanks of Pz.Rgt.11 ready to be transported. (*AC*)

At 4.45 am the Luftwaffe launched an air raid on the small Polish town of Wieluń, destroying approximately 70 per cent of the town's infrastructure, including the hospital and much of the city centre. Although 1.le.Div. was advancing towards Wieluń, it did not reach the town on the first day. While Wieluń burned, elements of the German 18th Infantry Division and reconnaissance units from 1. le.Div. crossed the border and engaged the forward positions of the Polish Łódź army. By the evening German troops had captured Wierzbie, Ożarów and the high ground north of Ożarów. They encountered stiff resistance from the Polish 36th Infantry Regiment, sustaining several casualties in the process.

Meanwhile, Pz.Regt.11, equipped with PzKpfw 35(t) tanks, had assembled near Landsberg (present-day Gorzów Śląski), on the Prosna river opposite the Polish town of Praszka. To the north, Pz.Abt.65 was positioned at Gołkowice, near another border crossing.

As Polish forces began a hasty retreat towards the Warta river line, the German motorised cavalry encountered increasingly difficult terrain that slowed its progress. By nightfall on 1 September the majority of the German forces had reached the vicinity of the Warta. They were anticipating stronger resistance along its banks as Army Group South commanders assumed the Poles were attempting to establish a firm defensive line behind the river.

At 3.30 am on 2 September Pz.Regt.11 began its advance towards the border. The regiment passed through Josefsberg and had crossed the Prosna river by 5 am. By 7 am German tanks had arrived at a designated assembly point in the forest approximately a kilometre southwest of Sołtysy, near the Praszka-Wieluń road. At 7.30 am I./Pz.Regt.11 was temporarily attached to the German 6th Motorised Cavalry Rifle Brigade, which had orders to dislodge the Polish forces defending Gaszyn, located 2 kilometres south of Wieluń.

By 9 am I./Pz.Regt.11 had secured the area east of Gaszyn and pushed northwestwards, reaching the southern outskirts of Wieluń. The town was taken at 10.30 am with minimal resistance and no German casualties. The operation was supported by II. and III. battalions of the 4th Motorised Cavalry Rifle Brigade.

Simultaneously, Pz.Abt.65, following Pz.Regt.11, crossed the border near Praszka around 6 am. Its 4th Tank Company passed through around noon, preceded by armoured cars from the 6th Reconnaissance Battalion, which reported that retreating Polish troops had already sabotaged key bridges.

By the morning of 3 September the Tenth Army had successfully crossed the Warta river in two locations, disrupting Polish plans for a prolonged defensive action. General Reichenau now committed his reserves for the next phase and transferred 1.le.Div. to the command of XIV Motorised Army Corps.

The Polish 28th Infantry Division, recently brought forwards to try to halt the German advance from Wieluń, engaged in a sharp encounter west of the Warta. One of its regiments was heavily mauled, forcing a withdrawal across the river. The division attempted to regroup and establish a defensive strongpoint at Konopnica village, but German forces—led by PzKpfw 35(t)s of I./Pz.Regt.11—crossed the river before the Polish defences could fully solidify.

Above: The HQ platoon of Pz.Rgt.11 is identifiable owing to its command-radio tanks. The two white stripes on the front armour may identify machines of Abt.II. (*AC*)

Below: 'Škodas' damaged during the Polish campaign were gathered in the courtyard of the Radom Arms Factory. The motorcycle posing in front of the panzers belongs to an unidentified Luftwaffe formation, likely from a forward observation unit attached to a motorised division. (*AC*)

A PzKpfw 35(t) is seen parked at the edge of an unpaved road somewhere in the Polish countryside, likely at Wola Gulkowska. The autumn of 1939 was unusually hot and dry, which made travelling along sandy roads particularly difficult. Clouds of dust trailed behind advancing columns, reducing visibility, clogging engines and filters, and adding to the already challenging conditions faced by German motorised units during the campaign. (*AC*)

By 2.10 pm II./Pz.Regt.11 had reached Małyszyn, 3 kilometres northeast of Wieluń, finding the town ablaze. Engineers were tasked with repairing the destroyed bridge at Borowiec.

At 4.45 pm the PzKpfw 35(t)s of the 7th Company of Pz.Regt.11, reinforced by a platoon of PzKpfw IVs from the 6th Company, moved to a crossroads 2 kilometres northeast of Wielgie with orders to support an infantry assault. At 6.40 pm the tank company, under Hauptmann Streger, began its advance, followed by three PzKpfw IVs and two platoons of PzKpfw 35(t)s. Approaching Rychłocice, the German tanks positioned themselves on either side of the road and opened fire to suppress enemy positions. Under this covering fire, infantrymen crossed open ground dragging small dinghies and began to ferry troops across the Warta river. The operation was successful, and a bridgehead roughly 2 kilometres deep was established on the far bank.

Following the successful crossing, 1.le.Div. continued its advance—led by Pz.Abt.65 and Pz.Regt.11—towards Widawa via Rogoźno. However, its progress was impeded by marshy terrain, anti-tank obstacles and artillery fire. During this phase a tank commanded by Lieutenant Wendland took a direct hit, killing both Wendland and an *Unteroffizier*—marking the first losses for Pz.Abt.65.

By the end of 3 September 1.le.Div., operating under XVI Motorised Army Corps, had captured Osjaków after a sharp engagement and succeeded in securing a second bridgehead across the Warta river, enabling the continued German advance deeper into central Poland.

Polish Forces Fall Back

At dawn on 5 September 1939 Hoepner's XVI Motorised Army Corps launched an assault on Piotrków Trybunalski. After intense fighting, the Polish defensive line was breached, allowing German armoured units to surge forwards. Simultaneously,

Right and below: On 8 September 1.le.Div. captured Radom after advancing through difficult terrain, including dense forests along the northwestern slopes of Łysa Góra, and encountering heavy resistance. By the following day elements of the corps had reached the Vistula river bridges at Dęblin and Kozienice. (*AC*)

Newly incorporated into the German army, the 'Škodas' were not yet widely familiar to many German soldiers. As a result, they often attracted considerable attention and curiosity, especially among infantry units encountering them for the first time. (*AC*)

German forces penetrated Polish positions near Tomaszów Mazowiecki, forcing the northern elements of the Prusy army into a retreat eastwards towards Dęblin. Encircled north of Radom after engagements at Odrzywoły, Jedlnia and Maciejowice, these Polish units were crushed by the German 13th Motorised Infantry Division, followed closely by 1.le.Div., led by 'Skodas'.

Despite difficult terrain and heavy resistance, the XIV Motorised Army Corps, with 1.le.Div. in the lead, fought its way through dense forested areas along the northwestern slopes of Łysa Góra, capturing Radom on 8 September. By the following day elements of the corps had reached the Vistula river bridges at Dęblin and Kozienice.

On 6 September the Polish 29th Infantry Division was ordered to retreat across the Pilica river using a temporary pontoon bridge. Meanwhile, 1.le.Div. crossed the Pilica at Przedbórz and, operating from the Czermno area, reached the 1st Battalion of the 163rd Infantry Regiment at Ruda Maleniecka around 8 pm. Attempting to seize the crossing on the move, they were repelled by the Polish 3rd Company and a cavalry platoon. The defenders pushed the Germans out of the town and then destroyed the bridge and nearby dams before withdrawing to the river's eastern bank.

As Polish resistance in the area collapsed, 1.le.Div. dispatched Battlegroup von Ravenstein northeastwards to pursue the retreating enemy forces towards Łask. At 11 am orders were issued for I./Pz.Regt.11, Pz.Abt.65 and II Battalion of the 4th

Motorised Cavalry Rifle Regiment to advance in that direction and cut off the Polish retreat.

By 9 September German tanks from 1.le.Div. had reached the railway bridge at Dęblin. Despite coming under fire from nearby fortifications, and sustained artillery and anti-tank fire from across the Vistula, the German Panzers fired on retreating Polish infantry using the bridge, eventually gaining control of the area. That same day Kozienice was also captured, effectively trapping the remnants of the Polish forces withdrawing from Kielce towards Warsaw in what became known as the Kielce-Radom Pocket—the first major encirclement of the Second World War, resulting in the capture of approximately sixty thousand Polish troops.

As the Germans closed the pocket from the north, 1.le.Div. intercepted the retreating Polish 13th Infantry Division, which had earlier engaged German forces near Tomaszów Mazowiecki. Still organised, and supported by artillery and tanks, the 13th Division was attempting to reach the Vistula to establish a new defensive line. Before dawn on 10 September, unaware that Głowaczów had already been taken by German motorised cavalry, Polish forces entered the town. Their vanguard, consisting of engineers, was ambushed and most were captured. A fierce battle ensued as the full strength of the Polish 13th Infantry Division arrived. Initially pinned down by heavy fire, the Polish signal and heavy machine-gun company commanders were killed. However, the 44th Infantry Regiment counterattacked, supported by artillery and a company from the 1st Light Tank Battalion. Seven Polish 7TP tanks were brought into the fight, although four became stuck in the marshes near Lipa and were later destroyed by their crews. The remaining three entered the burning town and, according to Polish sources, destroyed two German PzKpfw 35(t) tanks from Pz.Regt.11. The remaining German tanks were reportedly forced to retreat. During the same engagement a PzKpfw IV was destroyed by Polish infantry in the town square—allegedly set ablaze with gasoline and a grenade.

After 2 hours of brutal combat, the Poles recaptured Głowaczów and forced the Germans back across the Radomka river. At least eighty-six Polish soldiers were killed in the engagement, with many more wounded. Due to severe fuel shortages, only one Polish tank was able to withdraw from the town. It reached Lipinki, where it was destroyed by its crew after running out of fuel.

Eventually, Polish forces reached the Vistula near Magnuszew and managed to cross using improvised means. After their departure, Głowaczów was reoccupied by elements of 1.le.Div. German troops found several abandoned Polish tanks in the bogs surrounding the town. One of them, still fully operational, was recovered, repainted with German markings and reportedly integrated into Pz.Regt.11 under the name 'Friedel' with the tactical number B5 (B for '*Beute*' or captured tank).

THE BATTLE OF THE BZURA

By 8 September 1939 advanced German units had reached the outskirts of Warsaw, marking the beginning of the siege of the Polish capital. Meanwhile, the Wehrmacht had lost contact with the Polish Poznań army, which had been retreating eastwards towards the Vistula river during the first week of the campaign. On the night of

9 September the Poznań army launched a surprise counteroffensive south of the Bzura river. The attack targeted German forces of the Eighth Army advancing between Łęczyca and Łowicz towards Stryków. The Polish assault achieved early success, inflicting significant losses on the German defenders—around one thousand, five hundred men were killed or wounded, and another three thousand taken prisoner during the initial thrust.

Underestimating the scale and coordination of the Polish counterattack, the German command initially delayed its response. On 11 September, however, major elements of the Tenth and Fourth armies, as well as strategic reserves from Army Group South, were redirected towards the Bzura front.

By 15–16 September the Polish forces had withdrawn to defensive positions on the north bank of the Bzura. In response, the Germans sought to encircle and annihilate them, committing to the action much of the Tenth Army—including two armoured divisions, one motorised division and three light divisions—supported by approximately eight hundred tanks. The German assault began on 16 September, bolstered by concentrated Luftwaffe air support. After two days of intense combat, and with no remaining ammunition or food supplies, the Polish defenders were unable to mount further breakout attempts. Only scattered units managed to escape the encirclement.

Tanks of Pz.Rgt.11 during a combat break. Clearly visible are the tactical markings used in September 1939: white crosses on the turret and a white rectangle across the upper engine hatch. (*AC*)

Above: German tanks in Kozienice, a town located just a few kilometres from the Vistula river—one of Poland's most significant natural barriers. The river, which cuts the country roughly in half, represented the last major potential line of defence for the Polish army during the 1939 campaign. (*AC*)

Below: Wrecked tanks from 1.le.Div., damaged during the fighting near Kozienice, gathered by the wall of the Jewish cemetery. A few weeks later the nearby synagogue was set on fire by the Germans, who prevented the local fire brigade from extinguishing the flames. The synagogue was never rebuilt after the war. (*AC*)

Above and below: The crew of the PzKpfw 35(t) commanded by Prince von Ratibor (first on the left in black uniform), photographed at the beginning of September 1939, and the same vehicle destroyed by Officer Cadet Orlik near Pociecha (Kampinos forest) on 18 September. (*AC*)

German soldiers pose next to a TKS tankette from the Polish 71st Armoured Squadron, captured after the fall of Warsaw. Its 20mm gun suggests the vehicle most likely belonged to Officer Cadet Orlik—one of the first tank aces of the Second World War. (*AC*)

Despite the defeat, thousands of Polish soldiers who had fought at the Bzura managed to reach Warsaw from the northwest through the dense Kampinos forest. On 18 September General Reichenau ordered 1.le.Div. into the woodland to block this route, expecting to encounter only disorganised stragglers. Instead, the division ran into the well organised Wielkopolska Cavalry Brigade, which retained artillery, anti-tank guns and several TKS tankettes.

The Polish cavalry brigade fought a series of fierce close-quarters engagements, demonstrating tactical proficiency and boldness. On the morning of 18 September a platoon of three TKS tankettes under Officer Cadet Roman Edmund Orlik was sent to scout a clear path towards Warsaw. At the village of Pociecha, Orlik set up an ambush position. His tankette was among the few fitted with a new 20mm autocannon, giving it a rare anti-tank capability. Soon a German tank platoon—two PzKpfw 35(t)s and one PzKpfw IV—from 1.le.Div. approached. At less than 100 metres Orlik opened fire, destroying all three tanks in rapid succession. The German platoon commander, Prince Viktor Albrecht von Ratibor IV, died after being pulled from his burning tank.

That night (18/19 September) dismounted troops of the Wielkopolska Cavalry Brigade seized the village of Sieraków, 15 kilometres northwest of Warsaw. In a remarkable success, the Polish cavalry captured thirty-four German supply trucks from 1.le.Div., filled with fuel and equipment. Polish accounts report that approximately seventy Germans from II.Battalion of the 4th Motorised Cavalry Rifle Regiment were taken prisoner.

At around 10 am on 19 September 1.le.Div. launched a counterattack on Sieraków. Two German armoured groups from Pz.Regt.11 and Pz.Abt.65 attacked from different directions, but were repelled by coordinated Polish artillery and anti-tank fire. The first German group lost twenty-seven tanks, most of them being damaged. Orlik, still operating his 20mm-armed TKS, is credited with destroying seven of them, making him one of the earliest tank aces of the Second World War. Additional German tanks were knocked out by the Polish 7th Light Artillery Regiment (firing in direct mode) and the 7th Cavalry Rifle Regiment, equipped with 37mm Bofors anti-tank guns. Polish losses in this engagement were fourteen killed and forty-two wounded.

The second German group lost eleven tanks. Two were destroyed by direct fire from an artillery platoon of the 14th Light Artillery Regiment, led by Lieutenant Orzeszko. Another three were taken out by a platoon of Bofors guns under the command of Lieutenant Ziemiński of the 14th Uhlan Regiment, who personally accounted for two of them. The remaining six tanks were eliminated by elements of the 17th and 14th Uhlan Regiments and the 9th Cavalry Rifle Regiment.

According to German sources, Pz.Abt.65 alone suffered twenty-six killed or wounded during the Sieraków action, including four officers, five non-commissioned officers and seventeen enlisted men. The surviving German tanks withdrew towards Hornówek and Lipków. Total German tank losses at Sieraków are estimated to have been as high as thirty-one either destroyed or severely damaged.

Later on 19 September an improvised Polish battle group—composed of the 14th Uhlan Regiment and elements of the 9th Uhlan Regiment—emerged from the Kampinos forest and attacked 1.le.Div. near Wólka Węglowa. The Polish commander ordered a cavalry charge—the largest of the 1939 campaign. The initial assault caught the German motorised units by surprise, but hidden machine guns and tanks opened fire as the charge progressed. Despite heavy losses, the Poles broke through towards Warsaw as planned. But the cost was steep. Of the thousand Polish cavalrymen who began the charge, 105 were killed and another 100 wounded—roughly 20 per cent of the attacking force. However, their sacrifice opened the way for other Polish units following behind to reach the capital.

German losses after the charge were estimated at fifty-two killed and seventy wounded. On the night of 19/20 September most of the Polish cavalry, including Orlik's TKS tankettes, successfully entered Warsaw. These would be the only armoured vehicles from the Battle of the Bzura to reach the city. The arrival of other Poznań army elements allowed General Juliusz Rómmel to form a tactical reserve of three infantry battalions within the capital.

THE LAST BATTLES

On 17 September 1939 Soviet forces invaded Poland from the east, in accordance with the secret protocols of the Molotov-Ribbentrop Pact. At that time several Polish units were still actively resisting German forces. Major concentrations of Polish troops remained in the garrisons of Warsaw and Modlin. A small mixed force continued to defend Lwów, while a significant number of reserve formations were positioned around Dęblin and Lublin. Despite this, Warsaw surrendered unconditionally on 27 September, after enduring a week of relentless artillery and aerial bombardment. The city's garrison—more than a hundred thousand men—capitulated, although German forces did not formally occupy the city until 5 October. Modlin, which had served as a fortress since 13 September, surrendered the following day, on 28 September, with twenty-four thousand troops taken prisoner. Organised Polish resistance ended on 5 October near the town of Kock, where approximately eight thousand men laid down their arms. With this, the last regular Polish military formations ceased combat operations.

Following the campaign, Germany's 1.le.Div. returned home in October 1939 for reorganisation and re-equipment, and would soon be converted into a full Panzer division.

Lessons Learned

After-action reports compiled in October 1939 highlighted several important operational insights. Strategically, the light divisions proved effective in their role as motorised cavalry, particularly when equipped with Czechoslovak tanks. However,

Crews of Pz.Rgt.11 resting during a brief halt in the advance towards the Modlin fortress, which served as a defensive stronghold for nearly twenty-five thousand Polish troops from 13 to 29 September 1939. Notably, the last tank in the column (tactical no. 246) bears a white cross with a diagonal stripe across the centre—a tactical marking used by some vehicles of Abt. I (AC)

Above: A PzKpfw 35(t) of Kp.2/Pz.Rgt.11 photographed after the end of hostilities in Poland. The tank has been stripped of both its machine guns, likely due to maintenance or servicing. (*AC*)

Below: The tragic consequences of a direct hit to the ammunition storage bin by a Polish Bofors anti-tank gun are clearly visible. The resulting internal explosion, triggered by the detonation of stored shells, violently vented through the upper section of the turret, where the armour was thinner and less reinforced. (*AC*)

opportunities for tank-on-tank combat were limited, as the Polish Army fielded few armoured units capable of directly challenging German armour. One surprising revelation from the initial days of the campaign was that anti-tank hits did not necessarily result in the deaths of all crew members. Of five recorded hits, only one successfully penetrated the armour. In many cases only one crew member was killed—typically the driver or the radio operator, who were most exposed in the vehicle layout.

The PzKpfw 35(t) tanks were found to be effective against infantry targets, while the PzKpfw IV performed especially well when engaging fortified or heavily protected positions. However, mechanical reliability proved to be a significant issue. In 1.le.Div. 131 out of 259 tanks suffered mechanical breakdowns, primarily due to unspecified technical failures. A major problem was the rapid wear of tank tracks, which began to fail after reaching 3,000 kilometres in service. A technical readiness report from 1.le.Div. noted:

> More than four weeks are needed to repair the Panzers if the necessary spare parts are delivered. All *Panzerkampfwagen* and 50 per cent of the artillery *Zugmaschinen* [prime movers] require new tracks. Due to these worn-out tracks, *Panzer-Regiment 11* will be immobilised once transported by rail back to its home garrison.

These mechanical shortcomings underscored the logistical and maintenance challenges facing fast-moving armoured units in extended operations—an issue the Wehrmacht would need to address as it prepared for future campaigns.

Glory Days in France (May–June 1940)

In mid-October 1939, less than two weeks after the end of 'Fall Weiss', the 1st, 2nd and 3rd light divisions began converting into the 6th, 7th and 8th armoured divisions. Thus, 1.le.Div. became the 6th Armoured Division (6.Pz.Div.), under the command of *Generalmajor* Werner Kempf; it consisted of the 6th Motorised Rifle Brigade (including the 4th Motorised Cavalry Regiment (*Schützen Regiment 4*, or Schüt.Rgt.4), the 14th Rifle Regiment (Schüt.Rgt.14) and the 6th Motorcycle Battalion); the 11th Panzer Regiment (Pz.Rgt.11), under *Oberst* Wilhelm Phillips, which was still organised in two battalions, I./Pz.Regt.11 commanded by Major Stephan and II./Pz.Regt.11 by Major Koll, who in January 1940 replaced *Oberst* Wilhelm Phillips as regimental commander; Pz.Abt.65 commanded by Major Thomas; the 76th Panzer Artillery Regiment (Art.Rgt.76); and associated divisional troops. The new tank division was smaller than the panzer divisions created earlier and was still mainly equipped with PzKpfw 35(t) tanks.

A status report dated 5 February 1940 revealed that 6.Pz.Div. was slightly overstrength, with additional PzKpfw 35(t) tanks in the 1st and 2nd companies of Pz.Regt.11 and the 1st and 3rd companies of Pz.Abt.65. These extra tanks, which exceeded the unit's standard Table of Organisation and Equipment limits, were to be deployed when the division was sent into action.

Table 5. Table of Organisation and Equipment, 6.Pz.Div., February 1940

	PzKpfw 35(t) (combat tanks)		PzBefWg 35(t) (command tanks)	
	Authorised	Available	Authorised	Available
11th Panzer Regiment	1	1	2	2
I.Bn HQ	1	1	2	2
1st Company	17	18		
2nd Company	17	19		
II.Bn HQ	1	1	2	2
5th Company	17	17		
6th Company	17	17		
65th Panzer Bn HQ	1	1	2	2
1st Company	17	19		
3rd Company	17	19		
Total	106	113	8	8

While the PzKpfw 35(t) proved to be fully capable of performing its assigned tasks during the Polish Campaign, the PzBefWg 35(t) command tanks were inadequate for the role assigned. Their optical devices had too small a field of view, making observation difficult and hindering command effectiveness. As a result, XV Corps Command (Korps-Kdo.XV) requested that the 4th Army High Command (AOK4) replace the PzBefWg 35(t)s with PzKpfw IIID command tanks. However, this request was denied on 29 February 1940.

While 6.Pz.Div. was allocated slightly over a hundred PzKpfw 35(t) tanks, the Army Weapons Office (*Heereswaffenamt*) still held 195 of this type in strategic reserve. However, by 1 May 1940 this number had been reduced to 143, as twenty-six tanks were sold to Bulgaria in February and another twenty-six were withdrawn for major repairs in March.

On 30 January 1940 6.Pz.Div. left its home garrison at Wuppertal and assembled in the Euskirchen area on 2 February, with the divisional command post located in Münstereifel. The period of relative quiet on the Western Front allowed the newly formed division to conduct regimental exercises.

On 1 March 1940 6.Pz.Div. moved into the Westerwald, where, one week later, it was incorporated into XXXXI Army Corps (also known as XLI Panzer Corps) under *General der Panzertruppe* Hans-Georg Reinhardt. Also included in XXXXI Corps were the 8th Armoured Division (8.Pz.Div.) and the 29th Motorised Infantry Division. The corps was one of three assigned to Operation Sichelschnitt (Sickle Cut), the German armoured thrust through the Ardennes. By the end of April 1940 all the tracked vehicles were concentrated across the Rhine in the Mayen area, while the bulk of the division remained in the Westerwald. At the beginning of May 6.Pz.Div. was tasked with invading France by crossing the Meuse at Monthermé, approximately 32 kilometres north of Sedan, while 8.Pz.Div. advanced towards Nouzonville to the south.

Above: On 30 January 1940 6.Pz.Div. left its home garrison at Wuppertal and assembled in the Euskirchen area. Note the changed tactical markings: a new style that featured a thin white outline with a black core. Their position was also changed to three places on the hull/superstructure, instead of the previous four places on the turret. (*AC*)

Below: PzKpfw 35(t)s of Kp.5/Pz.Rgt.11 during a spring training exercise in 1940 in the Westerwald area. The period of relative quiet on the Western Front allowed the newly formed division to perfect cooperation between tanks, motorised troops and artillery. (*AC*)

Above: This PzKpfw 35(t) belonged to the SS Totenkopf Div. Aufkl.Abt., Schw. Kp. Its crew are pictured carrying out maintenance tasks before the outbreak of the French Campaign. (*AC*)

Below: The crew of a 'Škoda' tank posing in their training uniforms in early 1940. The photograph was taken in front of the Paderborn garrison hospital (*Standortlazarett/Reserve-Lazarett*), a typical Wehrmacht medical facility of the time. These hospitals generally had a capacity of up to seventy-six beds, though on average housed around thirty-five patients at a time. They were intended to provide basic medical care and treatment for enlisted men and non-commissioned officers. (*AC*)

Above: A radio command tank rolls through the streets during a parade, warmly welcomed by local inhabitants lining the pavements, as it advances towards the western border with France. (*AC*)

Below: A Pz.Rgt.11 crew resting and carrying out maintenance tasks within a wooded area around Mayen in April 1940, just two weeks before the outbreak of the French Campaign. (*AC, photos possibly by Lt Friedrich Sender*)

The French campaign began on the morning of 10 May when 6.Pz.Div. advanced westwards in three march groups, led by *Oberst* Freiherr von Esebeck, commander of the 6th Rifle Brigade; *Oberst* von Ravenstein, commander of Schüt.Rgt.4; and *Oberstleutnant* von Seckendorff, commander of the 6th Motorcycle Battalion. A fourth group, comprising the light columns and the combat train, was under the command of Major Dr Topf.

Pz.Regt.11 began the campaign with 117 PzKpfw 35(t) tanks and ten PzBefWg 35(t) command tanks, attached to the regimental headquarters, along with Pz.Abt.65's forty PzKpfw 35(t) tanks and four PzBefWg 35(t)s. While the Czech-made tanks formed the backbone of 6.Pz.Div., it was also equipped with sixty light PzKpfw II and thirty heavy PzKpfw IV tanks.

General Reinhardt's units advanced through the central parts of the Ardennes, where the terrain was particularly difficult. Due to the limited number of roads, Reinhardt had assigned 6.Pz.Div. to take the lead. However, traffic jams delayed the armoured division and these delays cascaded through Kempf's division, preventing it from reaching its intended objective on 10 May. Attempts to make up for lost time on 11 and 12 May were hindered by fuel supply issues, so that 6.Pz.Div. finally crossed the Luxembourg border near Vianden on 12 May, reaching the Belgian border later that day at 4 pm. Crossing into Belgium, the tanks advanced through rolling grasslands that had been mined the previous winter. To the surprise of a Belgian officer, who had already been captured, the mines were reportedly rendered ineffective by the harsh weather conditions. By dusk that same day the 1st Platoon of the 1st Company, Pz.Abt.65, was leading the march, followed by the motorised infantry and, finally, the combat engineers with their pneumatic boats. The column advanced with all its lights on.

During the first two days of the French campaign, Kempf's men had faced more difficulties from traffic jams and narrow, winding roads than from enemy combat units. However, strong French resistance was soon to follow.

THE BATTLE OF MONTHERMÉ

On the night of 12/13 May 6.Pz.Div. conducted reconnaissance in the area between the Meuse river and the Franco-Belgian border. It quickly became clear that the area was undefended, as the French forces were positioned on the western bank of the Meuse in Monthermé. This small town was located in a narrow, gorge-like valley, forming a sweeping curve in the shape of a peninsula. It was protected by extensive barbed-wire entanglements along the river's edge on the town side and by improvised strongholds made of fortified houses. The French had also blown the bridge over the Meuse that led to the town.

At 3 pm on 13 May a thin haze enveloped the lowlands of the Meuse river as German troops from the 11th Company of the 4th Rifle Regiment (III./Schüt.Rgt.4), under *Oberstleutnant* Häfer, reached the heights overlooking Monthermé. At that time sporadic French artillery fire was falling in the area occupied by the German troops. German artillery (Art.Rgt.76, commanded by *Oberst* Werner Forst) concentrated fire on Monthermé until 4 pm, when General Kempf decided to cross the Meuse. There was no alternative but to attack with infantry, utilising the limited resources available

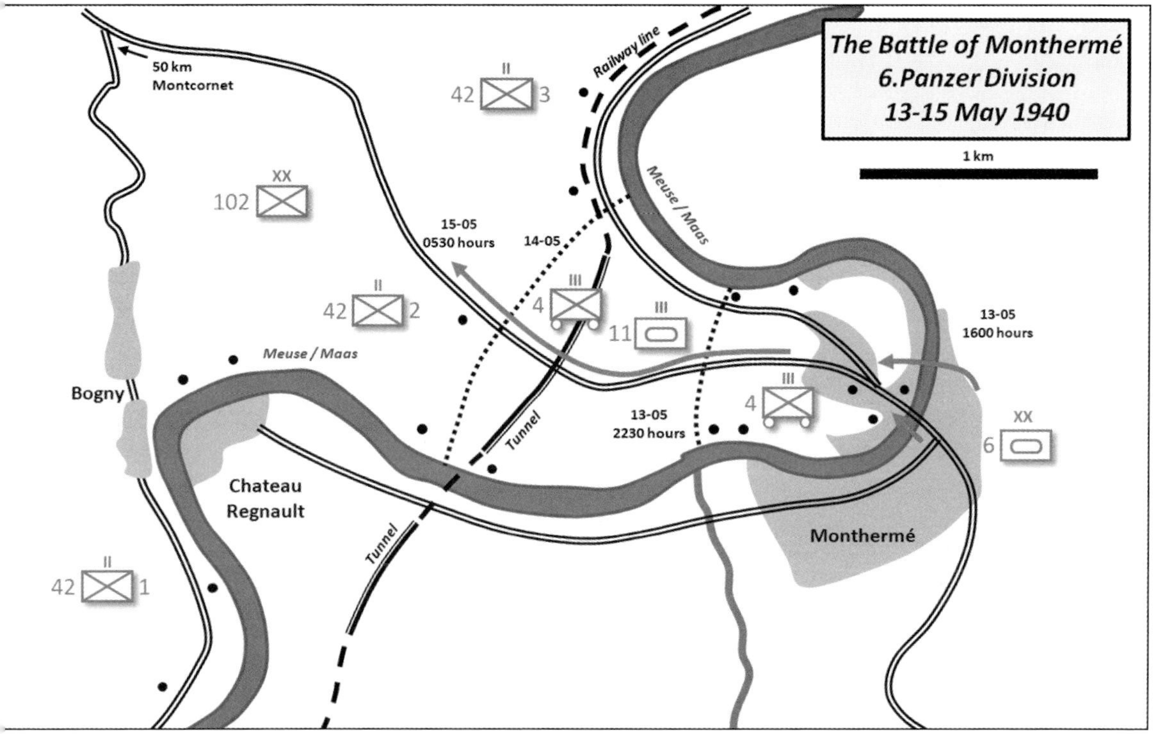

Above: The Battle of Monthermé, 13–15 May 1940.

Below: Monthermé was located on the Meuse river, nestled between Namur and Sedan. In the vicinity of this small town, the mountains force the Meuse into a narrow, gorge-like valley that forms a sweeping curve, resembling a peninsula. At the base of the steep descent from the hills to the river, a bridge crossed the Meuse into Monthermé, which had been partially destroyed by retreating French forces. Along the river's edge many of the houses were converted into makeshift forts. South of Monthermé lay a large wooded area. (*AC/Postcard*)

Standing beside a 'Skoda Panzer', Colonel Koll, commander of Pz.Rgt.11, observes Monthermé, assisted by Captain Saalbach, who stands by his side. (*AC, photo possibly taken by Lt Friedrich Sender or Eric Borchert*)

from the divisional engineering battalion for the crossing. The tanks were to provide fire support from the riverbank. Their 3.7cm guns were not very effective against enemy bunkers and machine-gun nests, but their shells caused the walls of houses to collapse, and flames from the fires set the buildings ablaze.

The Meuse river was not particularly wide, but the banks were steep and craggy, protected by barbed-wire obstacles. Despite these challenges, preparations for the attack continued. A few kilometres east of Monthermé engineers inflated rafts, while tank commanders scouted for firing positions that allowed them to cover key sectors on the western bank. The attack was to be carried out by III./Schüt.Rgt.4. The boats were brought forwards as quickly as possible, and the first groups hurried across the river. As they crossed, a series of small skirmishes broke out, with platoons and squads fighting independently as they encountered French defensive positions. Resistance came from the troops of the 42nd Demi-Brigade (*Demi-Brigade de Marche de Chasseurs*, or DBMC), equivalent to a German regiment, composed of two thousand, eight hundred French soldiers and four hundred Madagascan soldiers, organised into two battalions. These forces belonged to the 102nd Fortress Division (*Division d'Infanterie de Forteresse*).

Fortunately for the Germans, their engineers, while inspecting the blown bridge over the Meuse, discovered that the twisted metal of the destroyed structure was snagging the empty rafts as they floated downstream. Once some German tanks had blasted the casemates covering the bridge wreckage, they were able to tie the dinghies together into a makeshift footbridge.

At this point General Kempf ordered some of the tanks to cross the river via a ford that had been discovered earlier. One tank strayed from the prescribed route and sank up to its turret, but was later recovered by a heavy tractor. Shortly thereafter, German Pioneers, barely 300 metres upriver from the destroyed bridge, prepared rafts that could be used to ferry across heavy weapons, artillery pieces and light armoured reconnaissance vehicles, and then started to set up a pontoon bridge. Throughout the night French artillery fired at the bridge site, damaging the footbridge, and machine-gun exchanges took place. This did not stop the Germans from bringing up another battalion to support Höfer's weary troops. By 7 pm, after 3 hours of fierce fighting, the commanding heights on the isthmus had been cleared.

The following day, 14 May, the French continued to bombard the German positions with seemingly endless shell and machine-gun fire. Meanwhile, German artillery continued to harass the French defenders, who held their ground stubbornly until noon, but eventually began to be pushed back, primarily due to dwindling ammunition supplies. Despite this, the Germans were unable to advance beyond a bunker line at the base of the river loop. By this point, 6.Pz.Div. had lost around 150 men, 10 per cent of whom were killed in action.

The low water level in the Meuse enabled German engineers to use elements of the destroyed bridge to build a footbridge, with pontoons attached to its steel structure. (*AC*)

Above: On 14 May the German engineers built rafts using sections of the bridging equipment class B (Brückengerät B), which were utilised for ferrying the tanks, heavy weapons, artillery pieces and light armoured reconnaissance vehicles across the Meuse at Monthermé. Brückengerät B enabled the formation of several types of ferry, either rowing or motor-powered, in 4-, 8- and 16-ton classes, and could also be employed in auxiliary roles such as temporary or emergency bridging where pontoons were not required. (*AC*)

Below: Finally, a pontoon bridge was successfully constructed in front of Rue du Port. This structure was sturdy enough to support the weight of heavily loaded 35(t) tanks, each equipped with numerous jerry cans filled with fuel, ensuring they could continue to advance. (*AC*)

During the night of 14/15 May the pontoon bridge at Monthermé had been completed and some tanks from Pz.Regt.11 were brought forwards to back up the infantry. Early in the morning German infantry launched another attack, supported by some of their armoured vehicles, and finally managed to overcome the French defences. By the evening, the 102nd Fortress Division had practically disappeared, and Kempf's 6.Pz.Div. broke through into open country. In the fighting that led to the eventual success at Monthermé, the infantry component of 6.Pz.Div. played the most crucial role, with the tanks acting primarily in a support role. Given the terrain, the Germans had little choice but to rely on their infantry to push forwards.

THE ADVANCE ACROSS FRANCE

After breaking through the French defence lines, Kempf's armoured forces spent some time scouting the difficult, wooded terrain that lay before them. By 9 am German tanks were already moving towards Charleville. Although there were some skirmishes in the woods, nothing could halt the German spearheads. The remains of the 42nd Demi-Brigade fought valiantly, but since the area behind their positions was largely undefended, after a delayed start the Germans were able to advance rapidly.

The German tank force was directed westwards towards Montcornet via Liart, and by 8 pm on 15 May the objective was reached, after covering 65 kilometres in a single

A PzKpfw 35(t) from the HQ of Pz.Rgt.11 pictured in Place Ducale in the city of Charleville-Mézières, the first major French city encountered after crossing the Meuse at Monthermé. The photo was taken at mid-day on 16 May 1940. (*AC, photo possibly taken by Lt Friedrich Sender or Eric Borchert*)

day. The French defence crumbled as non-motorised units were swiftly overtaken and decimated by forces from both Kempf's division and General Kuntzen's 8.Pz.Div., including the French 61st Infantry Division to the north of Monthermé. By midnight on the 15th, German forces had obliterated the French XXXXI Corps, creating a vacuum in front of General Reinhardt's XXXXI Corps.

In an attempt to halt the German advance, the French deployed units of its 2nd Armoured Division (*2e Division Cuirassée de Réserve*, or 2e DCR) into the Aisne region. However, the deployment was chaotic due to the rapid advance of the enemy. French tank units were scattered at various locations, including Etreux, Saint-Quentin, La Capelle and Hirson, with orders to plug the gap between the Ninth and Second Armies. The irregular stream of vehicles, soldiers and units from 2e DCR—spread across a 40-kilometre stretch—was tasked with defending the Oise river and the Sambre-Oise canal at all costs.

In the early hours of 16 May German Army Group A headquarters was surprised to learn that 6.Pz.Div. had already reached Montcornet. General Rundstedt immediately became concerned, as the southeastern flank of his three-corps Panzer wedge was now dangerously stretched across 89 kilometres from Montcornet to Stonne. He feared that only the 19 kilometres around Stonne, south of Sedan, were properly defended. Despite this, General Reinhardt ordered the pursuit of the defeated enemy to continue

Soldiers of the 1st Mountain Division (*1.Gebirgsdivision*) march past tanks of 6.Pz.Div. on 15 May, advancing north along the main road from Bans Jakob to Monthermé. (*AC, photo possibly taken by Lt Friedrich Sender*)

At dawn on 16 May Pz.Rgt.11 took up positions in the village of Brunehamel and responded with force to a retreating French column coming from Mont-Saint-Jean. The fighting was intense and lasted for over an hour before the gunfire ceased, with hundreds of French troops taken prisoner and brought to the village square. (*AC, photo possibly taken by Lt Friedrich Sender or Eric Borchert*)

on 16 May. As a result, 6.Pz.Div. was instructed to advance as quickly as possible towards the Oise river, aiming to reach the crossing points at Etreaupont and Marly. General Kempf contacted Colonel von Esebeck and instructed him to push forwards rapidly towards Guisé with his Battle Group (*Kampfgruppe*, or KG). Oberleutnant Bäke and his Kp.1/Pz.Abt.65 in the vanguard would lead the formation.

From the moment the French lines were breached, 6.Pz.Div. began operating in ad hoc, flexible battle groups, composed of infantry, armour, artillery and support elements, which were capable of quickly carrying out specific missions and/or attacking tactical targets.

On 16 May the divisions of Hoth's, Reinhardt's and Guderian's Panzer corps raced forwards on a 56km-wide front, from Beaumont to Hirson and Montcornet. This rapid advance caused the French 9th Army, cut off from its neighbours to the north and south, to disintegrate quickly.

The night march became dangerous when the German tanks approached Falvigny, a suburb of Guisé on the River Oise, which was defended by a few French Char B1-bis heavy tanks. As the PzKpfw 35(t) tanks rumbled forwards, the French tanks opened fire from positions at the edge of town. The 3.7cm guns of the Czechoslovak tanks were unable to penetrate the frontal armour of the French machines, but the Germans managed to disable several of them by targeting the gap between the turret and the hull, jamming the turrets. It took several hours of intense fighting, with the tanks providing supporting fire, before the French troops in Guisé surrendered. Pz.Abt.65 had achieved its first major success of the French campaign, destroying or neutralising three heavy tanks, four anti-tank guns and a large number of trucks. Once the combat ended, 6.Pz.Div. continued its advance, and elements of Kampfgruppe von Esebeck captured the bridges at Macquigny and Hauteville intact. Meanwhile, Kampfgruppe von Ravenstein, accompanied by the divisional commander, arrived at Grigny.

On the evening of 17 May the forces of 6.Pz.Div. in the area of Hauteville-Neuvillette faced an attack by heavy French tanks, which they were unable to handle effectively. One 3.7cm PaK 35/36 gun of the 41st Anti-tank Battalion fired no fewer than twenty-six shots at an attacking French tank before hitting both its tracks and immobilising it. General Kempf immediately requested the deployment of 8.8cm anti-aircraft guns, which had been used with success as anti-tank weapons from the early days of the campaign. By nightfall, 6.Pz.Div. had secured two bridgeheads across the River Oise to the southeast of St Quentin and was racing northwestwards towards Cambrai.

On 18 May Kampfgruppe von Ravenstein assaulted Le Catelet, capturing the General Staff of the 9th French Army inside a hotel in the centre of town. If they had arrived just half an hour earlier, the success would have been even more significant as Marshal

The fast-moving German columns were unstoppable. By the morning of 15 May, just five days after the outbreak of hostilities, French Prime Minister Paul Reynaud informed Winston Churchill, 'We are beaten, we have lost the battle.' By 16 May, Panzer 35(t)s had been photographed at Origny-Sainte-Benoîte, already having crossed to the far side of the Oise River. (*AC*)

While on the move, the Czech tanks' guns and machine guns were covered to protect them from dust. By 1940 the original front reflector on the LT vz. 35s had been removed and replaced with a special Notek light mounted on the left fender. Its mushroom-like shape was designed to reduce light exposure and improve concealment. (*AC*)

Pétain and General Giraud, the commander of the 9th Army, would also have been captured. By the end of the day the bridgehead was securely in German hands. There was little cause for concern, as the French had no intention of launching a counterattack or offering any further resistance. They had been thoroughly demoralised by the loss of their headquarters staff and the rapid advance of the German forces.

Continuing their advance with Kampfgruppe von Esebeck at the forefront, German tanks reached a crucial fork in the road just 10 kilometres from Cambrai, establishing

A lone PzKpfw 35(t) makes its way back towards Nivelles in Belgium, trundling steadily past a truck column advancing into France. (*AC*)

another bridgehead near Banteux. The swift advance had bypassed many French units, and as night fell enemy forces appeared *behind* 6.Pz.Div., leading to several skirmishes.

On 19 May 6.Pz.Div. destroyed the last remnants of the French 2e DCR at Le Catelet and captured the headquarters of the 9th Army just before midnight. Army commander General Giraud was captured the following morning. He had been cut off while en route to his army and sought refuge in a barn, which, unfortunately for him, was chosen as the location for a field kitchen belonging to Pz.Regt.11. General Giraud was captured by a cook from the 7th Tank Company. That night, the Germans also secured bridgeheads across the Canal du Nord at Flesquières and Havrincourt, located on the historic Cambrai battleground of 1917.

On 20 May, parallelling Guderian's thrust, Kempf's 6.Pz.Div. captured Doullens, completely annihilating the 36th British Brigade. Pz.Abt.65 engaged British tanks for the first time, destroying several of them. However, many German tanks were lost and the German infantry also suffered casualties. After breaking the British resistance, the German vanguard reached Rougefay, just 20 kilometres from the coast. By this point, in one sweeping move three Panzer divisions had eliminated a British infantry division and decisively altered the Allies' situation. The already dire Allied strategic position became catastrophic. The tip of the German Panzer wedge had reached the sea, cutting off the northern Allied forces from the rest of the armies deployed in central France. After a 350-kilometre advance in just nine days, 6.Pz.Div. was reduced to seventy PzKpfw 35(t)s and nine PzBefWg 35(t)s still operational, with thirty-nine PzKpfw 35(t)s and two PzBefWg 35(t)s having been written off as total losses.

As part of the German attack on Calais, which officially began on 22 May, 6.Pz.Div. turned north on 21 May with orders to establish bridgeheads along the Aa river. It reached the river with little opposition, and the St Omer–Calais rail line was cut near Setques. Orders were also issued for bridgeheads to be established across the d'Aire canal, just east of Arques and St Omer, for 23 May. However, these orders did not reach 6.Pz.Div. until 6.20 am on the 23rd, by which time Kampfgruppe von Esebeck was already advancing on Calais. Despite this, the battle group changed direction and successfully captured the day's objective, St Omer. Several French armoured cars and light tanks attempted to defend the city but were mostly destroyed by German tanks.

By this point, 6.Pz.Div. was directly threatening Hazebrouck and Cassel. It seemed that little could prevent a total disaster for the BEF. However, at 12.45 pm on 24 May General von Rundstedt ordered General Günther von Kluge's Fourth Army to halt the German advance. This order was later confirmed by Hitler. Known as the 'Hitler halt order', it allowed Lord Gort, commander of the BEF, to manoeuvre his forces, strengthen them and create the 'Dunkirk Corridor', which enabled the British to reach the evacuation beaches at Dunkirk.

The 'halt order' was rescinded on 26 May, but by then the British 145th Infantry Brigade had arrived at Cassel and Hazebrouck, securing the western flank of the BEF and placing both towns in a state of defence. The British defenders at Cassel—including two infantry battalions, supported by the 209th Battery, 53rd Anti-Tank Regiment, with fifteen 2-pdr guns, and a battery of four 18-pdrs from the 5th Regiment, Royal Horse Artillery—were well prepared for the upcoming battle.

A photo taken in the field near the Cassel perimeter, after the 'Halt' order was issued by Hitler on 24 May, saving most of the BEF. (*AC*)

On 26 May 6.Pz.Div. was ordered to resume its attack on Cassel, but the British had transformed this small town into a stronghold. The terraced terrain provided a significant advantage for the defenders. (*AC*)

Above: A PzKpfw 35(t) destroyed by British anti-tank fire at the junction of the Route d'Oxelaëre and the Sainte-Marie-Cappel road leading to Cassel. (*AC*)

Below: The PzKpfw 35(t)s were better suited to street fighting than the French tanks, due to their smaller size, while their 3.7cm gun was deadly at short range even for the heaviest Char B1-bis. (*AC*)

Above: A pair of PzKpfw 35(t)s resting by the side of the road as wheeled vehicles pass by. Note the additional 20-litre jerry cans mounted on the fenders, a necessity during fast, long marches when refuelling/rearming from regular supply units was seldom an option. (*AC/PD*)

Below: The specialised clothing of German Panzer troops (*Sonderbekleidung*) consisted of a black beret, short double-breasted jacket, and straight trousers, designed to conceal oil stains. Worn with a mouse-grey shirt and black tie, the uniform prioritised practicality. The padded beret was replaced by a side cap in 1940. The close-fitting jacket, with broad lapels and minimal external features, allowed ease of movement within armoured vehicles. Trousers were loose and functional. The black uniform was worn only on vehicle duty; otherwise, standard field-grey dress or overalls were used. (*AC*)

6.Pz.Div. vs. the BEF

On 27 May 6.Pz.Div. resumed its advance to capture Cassel. Kampfgruppe von Esebeck was tasked with the initial attack on the town from the south and east, apparently with limited infantry support. As the German tanks made their way towards the grounds of the Château Masson, it became clear that their aim was to force their way onto the low saddle of land connecting Mont des Récollets with Cassel. As the battle unfolded, British anti-tank gun crews found no shortage of targets.

According to British reports, about forty tanks were seen approaching Cassel at 10.30 am. Some of the tanks were described as 'medium light' and others as 'medium heavy', suggesting the presence of a mix of PzKpfw 35(t)s and PzKpfw IVs. The British gunners inflicted heavy losses on the German armour, with the number of destroyed tanks estimated at eighteen by 3 pm. However, the actual number of destroyed vehicles was likely lower, as indicated by post-battle German reports. Still, the losses

Above: The crew of a German 'Škoda' tank posing for a photograph wearing the traditional black uniforms and berets introduced for tank crews in the mid-1930s. The beret began to be phased out in favour of the side cap during the French campaign, although at that stage both types of headgear remained equally popular among armoured units. (*AC*)

Opposite above: PzKpfw 35(t) (tactical no. 514) of Kp.5/Pz.Rgt.11 during a halt. Notable is the signal flag (yellow with a black cross) hanging from the antenna, indicating that other vehicles are to follow this one. (*AC*)

Opposite below: Battle Trail Map, 1940: *Fall Gelb* ('Case Yellow')—the first phase of the French campaign.

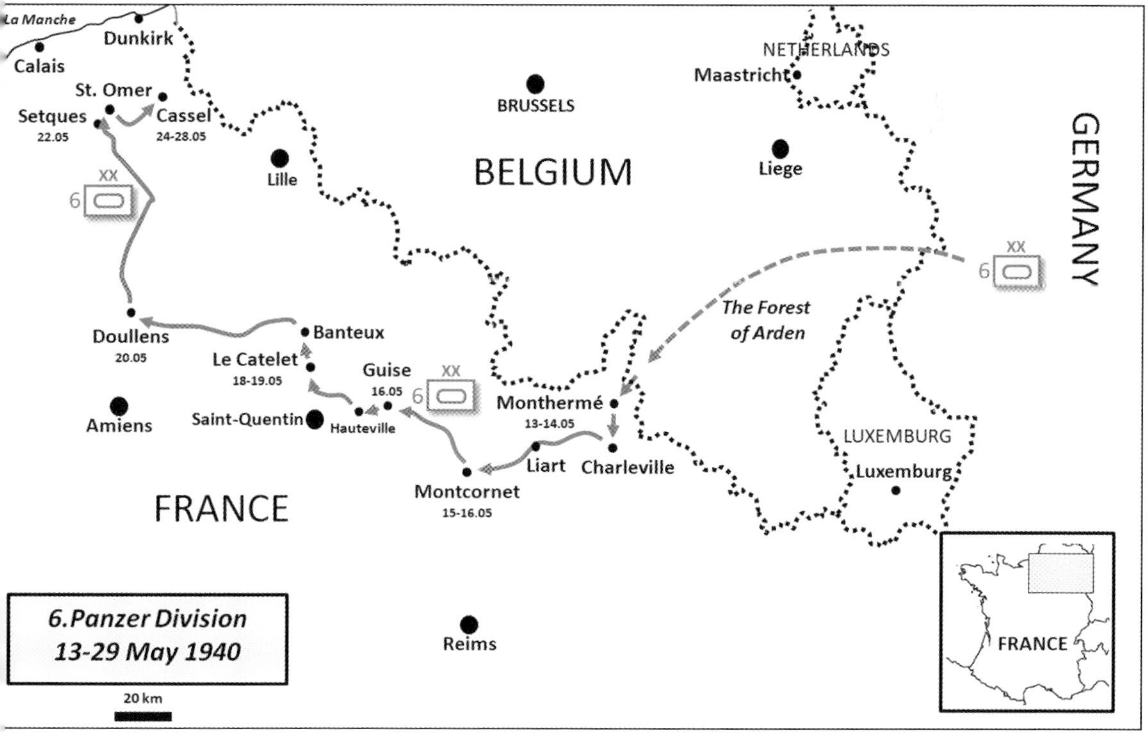

La Manche
Dunkirk
Calais
St. Omer
Setques
22.05
Cassel
24-28.05
NETHERLANDS
Maastricht
BRUSSELS
GERMANY
6 XX
Lille
BELGIUM
Liege
Doullens
20.05
Banteux
Le Catelet
18-19.05
Guise
16.05
6 XX
Amiens
Saint-Quentin
Hauteville
Monthermé
13-14.05
The Forest
of Arden
6 XX
LUXEMBURG
Liart
Charleville
Luxemburg
Montcornet
15-16.05
FRANCE
Reims
6. Panzer Division
13-29 May 1940
20 km
FRANCE

were significant. Captain Quartermaster Randolph Brasington reported that at least eight or nine tanks were knocked out in the 2nd Infantry Battalion's area, which he attributed solely to the work of the 0.55 Boys anti-tank rifle, which was effective against light armour a a range of 100 metres. If the tanks claimed to have been destroyed by the gunners and the men of the 4th Infantry Battalion are added, the total number of destroyed tanks rises to over forty, though this figure may be overly optimistic.

The German losses had to be significant, though, as on the following day Battle Group von Esebeck, which had led the advance on 27 May, was assigned a secondary role in support of Kampfgruppe Koll's assault. By the time Koll approached Cassel, he had an armoured force consisting of twenty PzKpfw IIs, twenty-five PzKpfw IVs and seventy PzKpfw 35(t)s. Koll initiated his attack at 10 am. While British battalions on both flanks were delayed by outposts, around two dozen tanks advanced from the south. The battle soon turned into a contest between British anti-tank guns and

Above: The PzKpfw 35(t) was less familiar to German pilots than were German-origin tanks, so to protect them from accidental friendly fire all of them were marked with red flags bearing swastikas. (*AC/PD*)

Opposite above: This French Char B1-bis heavy tank (named Ouragan), from the 8th Tank Battalion, was disabled by PzKpfw 35(t)s of Pz.Abt.65 at Guisé on 16 May. (*AC*)

Opposite below: The victory came at a cost; several 'Škodas' were knocked out, but once the combat ended, 6.Pz.Div. continued its advance. (*AC*)

CAFÉ DE LA GARE

the German tanks' main guns and machine guns. British 25mm and 2-pdr anti-tank rounds bounced off the PzKpfw 35(t)s' 25mm front armour, until the gunners adjusted their aim to target the tank tracks or waited for the tanks to pass and then hit the 16mm side or 15mm rear armour. By the end of the day the 209th Battery claimed to have destroyed dozens of tanks, although the actual number of knocked-out vehicles is uncertain. At midnight Koll called off the assault, and the surviving Panzers were withdrawn.

While most of the tanks were engaged at Cassel, part of Pz.Abt.65 drove towards the French fortifications on the Belgian border. The rear positions, which were largely

Above: A PzKpfw 35(t) leading a column, followed by a *Fahrschulwanne* (a turretless version of the PzKpfw IB used to train tank drivers) purposed either as an ammunition trailer or as a light support vehicle for the divisional workshop. It could be used for transporting spare parts and tools, critical to support front-line armoured units during fast-paced operations. (*AC, photo possibly taken by Lt Friedrich Sender*)

Opposite above: Upon entering French cities, PzKpfw 35(t)s were typically assembled in large main squares—the only urban spaces big enough to accommodate dozens of armoured fighting vehicles. (*AC*)

Opposite below: A PzKpfw 35(t) is followed by a PzKpfw II, accompanied by a German army bicyclist. Bicycles presented real advantages for rapid movement, especially in Western Europe, where the dense network of paved roads allowed for swift and silent travel. Bicyclists often served as reconnaissance troops scouting ahead of advancing units in areas where motorised transport was impractical or too conspicuous. (*AC*)

unmanned, were passed with minimal resistance. The Panzers then reached the line of undefended bunkers, destroying several before encountering enemy tanks that opened fire. Several enemy tanks were knocked out by the PzKpfw 35(t)s, proving once again that the Czechoslovak guns could destroy an enemy tank with a single shot.

At dawn on 28 May Reinhardt's corps advanced to Hazebrouck and Cassel, aiming to cut off the French and British retreat. The next day Kampfgruppe von Ravenstein cut the road from Poperinge to Proven, where contact was first made with the infantry of Army Group B. However, the remnants of the British division made a determined last stand on high ground at Mont des Cats, which allowed the 2,500-strong remnant

Above: A PzKpfw 35(t) of Kp.7/Pz.Rgt.11 during a brief pause in battle. Due to the tank's inadequate ventilation system, the interior quickly filled with gunfire fumes when in action; to counter this, crews were often forced to open the turret hatch during lulls in the fighting to air out the fighting compartment. (*AC*)

Opposite above: Throughout the entire French campaign, rapid river crossings played a crucial role in the success of the German advance. Whether by seizing intact, structurally sound bridges before they could be destroyed by retreating forces, or by swiftly constructing temporary bridges under fire, German engineering units ensured the momentum of the Panzer divisions was maintained. (*AC*)

Opposite below: This PzKpfw 35(t) of Kp.3/Pz.Abt.65 is identifiable by its unique emblem—the Lion, likely the Lion of Berg from the Wuppertal coat of arms, representing the region that hosted 6.Pz.Div. during peacetime. The origin of the emblem may, however, be simpler, as Kp.3/Pz.Abt.65 was commanded by Hauptmann Erich Löwe, whose surname translates as lion. (*AC*)

of the 5th Brigade to retreat northwards through Watou. Meanwhile, 6.Pz.Div. and the Leibstandarte-SS Adolf Hitler overwhelmed the British 144th Brigade's defence of Wormhoudt and encircled the 145th Brigade in Cassel. After a fierce defence of the town, the British survivors attempted to break out towards Dunkirk but were trapped by Battle Group Koll near Droogland, despite having tank support.

Once the battle with the British was over, many tanks lay destroyed and burning on the battlefield. The British brigade commander, forty officers and nearly two thousand men were captured, most of them wounded. The Germans' spoils for the day included sixty tanks, five armoured cars, ten artillery pieces, eleven anti-tank guns, thirty-four cars and 233 trucks. With this, the first phase of the French campaign came to an end.

'FALL ROT'

Along with the rest of XXXXI Corps, 6.Pz.Div. was now placed directly under the command of General Guderian. His Panzergruppe assembled in the Charleville area in preparation for the second phase of the French campaign, called 'Fall Rot' (Case Red), which aimed at advancing into southern France. In preparation, 6.Pz.Div. took up positions in the Monthermé-Rozoy area. At this stage, Pz.Rgt.11, with Pz.Abt.65, had seventy-six PzKpfw 35(t) tanks and eight PzBefWg 35(t) vehicles operational, including replacements that had been issued to the units.

Army Group A, under General von Rundstedt, was scheduled to attack on 9 June. Meanwhile, 6.Pz.Div. remained on high alert, waiting for the 86th Infantry Division to cross the Aisne river and establish a crossing point for the tanks. When the infantry failed to achieve this objective, Guderian was forced to move XXXXI Corps into positions behind his XIX Corps, west of Rethel, where the Aisne had been successfully crossed. On the first day of the attack, 3.Pz.Div. established a bridgehead on the far side of the Aisne, from which XIX Corps' 1.Pz.Div. and 2.Pz.Div. began advancing southwards; 6.Pz.Div. and 8.Pz.Div. were to follow on.

On 11 June Kampfgruppe von Ravenstein crossed the Aisne via a bridge built by the Pioneers. Near Machault, it encountered a strong enemy defensive position, which included a significant concentration of artillery. Kampfgruppe von Esebeck faced a similarly strong force near Semide and was forced to go on the defensive. Colonel von Ravenstein ordered *Oberstleutnant* Koll to lead an attack with Pz.Abt.65 and II./Pz.Regt.11, followed by the motorised rifles of II./Schütz.Rgt.4 in their half-tracks. The infantry would dismount at the breakthrough point and continue the fight on foot.

The tanks advanced towards the enemy positions through a long, shallow valley, remaining out of sight of the enemy. When the tanks emerged on the far side, French artillery fire intensified. However, the shells passed over the tanks and struck the ground behind them. The first Panzers, on the right and left, engaged the forward enemy positions. Machine guns rattled as the infantry dismounted. The tank gunners focused their fire on the enemy machine guns, silencing them with bursts of gunfire. The last of the enemy resistance seemed to be broken—but suddenly heavy guns opened fire on the tanks, and General Kempf ordered the attack to halt. His forces were instructed to take up defensive positions in their current favourable location. The tanks rolled behind a wood and vanished from the enemy's sight. The artillery fire that had halted 6.Pz.Div.'s attack ceased about an hour after midnight.

The enemy forces withdrew undetected during the night. When the German attack resumed on the morning of 12 June, there was no opposition. Two hours later, the day's objective of Somme-Pys was reached, and the town itself was free of enemy forces.

By noon, Kempf had reorganised his division. Spearheading the attack now was Kampfgruppe von Esebeck, with II./Pz.Rgt.11 forming the tip of the spear. After advancing 3 kilometres, they encountered a strong defensive position at the edge of the Chalons-sur-Marne troop training grounds, which halted their progress. The next attack, however, launched on the morning of 13 June, broke through, and the German forces quickly moved through the wooded terrain of the Chalons camp.

On 14 June, while German troops were advancing into Paris, 6.Pz.Div. found itself fighting in a densely wooded area near St Mard, which was poorly suited to tank operations. The vanguard repeatedly encountered French colonial troops, who fought stubbornly and tenaciously. Fortunately, the 17th Infantry Division arrived quickly and relieved 6.Pz.Div. for the next phase of the attack.

On 15 June the Rhine–Marne canal was crossed, but the advance was again halted by French troops. During the night more than fifty soldiers from the 12nd Senegalese Tirailleur Regiment (*Régiment de Tirailleurs Sénégalais*), who had been taken prisoner, were murdered by soldiers of 6.Pz.Div. in a forest near Brillon-en-Barrois.

Épinal—The Last Battle in France

On 16 June 6.Pz.Div. changed direction. Following 1.Pz.Div., and covering more than 100 kilometres in a single night, the tanks advanced through Langres to Jussey, where the 57th Reconnaissance Battalion had established a bridgehead. At Fontenoy-le-Château German infantry encountered the first opposition, which was quickly overrun. In Bains-le-Bains and at Rasey the resistance grew heavier, requiring the deployment of tanks to break through. Finally, 6.Pz.Div. reached the outskirts of Épinal, but its first attempt to capture the city in a *coup de main* failed.

The city was defended by the 46th Infantry Division Reconnaissance Group (*Groupe de Reconnaissance de Division d'Infanterie*, or GRDI), armed with only two 25mm anti-tank guns. The French forces had dug in, fortifying houses and creating firing slits in the walls to cover the buildings' flanks; they intended to hold the Germans at the river line, with the bridges protected by mines.

At 6 am on 19 June the Germans launched an attack but it was halted by the anti-tank guns. Two tracked vehicles were hit and set ablaze. A PzKfz 35(t) tried to approach the quay; coming under fire from the anti-tank guns, it briefly returned fire with its 3.7cm gun and then spun in place and retreated behind a building. Ten minutes later, another Czechoslovak Panzer cautiously descended Leopold-Bourg Street and stopped in front of the Peiffer house on Quai Boyé. The tank halted beside the river and began firing at the buildings again. After six or so rounds, it lurched forwards and crossed the bridge, avoiding the mines laid there, but was then hit by a French shell and caught fire.

In response, the Germans brought up some Stug IIID assault guns from the 660th Assault Gun Battery to provide supporting fire, which proved to be decisive. Unable to respond effectively, the French troops began to fall back, abandoning their positions. I./Schut.Rgt.4 pushed through Epinal towards the fortress, which, following negotiations, surrendered at noon the next day with full military honours. The garrison of Fort Longchamps marched out past an honour guard of 6.Pz.Div. tanks, and the French flag was hauled down as the Reich war flag was raised over the fortress. Over ten thousand prisoners of war, along with large quantities of weapons, equipment and supplies, were captured.

On 21 June Pz.Rgt.11, which had been reinforced during the second phase of the French campaign, had sixty-eighty PzKpfw 35(t) and eight PzBefWg 35. tanks operational, only slightly fewer than at the start of the campaign. Data on the strength of Pz.Abt.65 are not available, but it is likely that its strength was also close to its initial state at the start of the campaign.

On the evening of 22 June 1940 a ceasefire was signed in the forest of Compiègne. At 1.35 am on 25 June the message 'Stand down!' was sent to all German armed forces from the Channel coast to Switzerland.

On 26 June 6.Pz.Div. held a large field parade, and on 3 July it moved into its peacetime garrison. During the French campaign, 6.Pz.Div. had suffered a total of 2,140 casualties, including soldiers killed, wounded or lost due to illness. This total included 108 officers. By the end of May 1940 a total of forty-five PzKpfw 35(t) tanks, including PzBefWg 35(t) vehicles, had been written off as unrepairable. An additional seventeen machines were lost in June 1940. Considering these heavy losses, the fighting in France could hardly be described as an 'easy campaign'. By 20 June

Battle Trail Map, 1940: *Fall Rot* ('Case Red')—the second phase of the French campaign.

Above: A PzKpfw 35(t) passing a 10.5cm le.FH 18 light howitzer, the standard artillery piece of the Wehrmacht, adopted for service in 1935 and used by all divisions, including Panzer divisions. The le.FH 18 featured a superior calibre compared to its early-war opponents and performed effectively as supporting artillery for tank formations, thanks to its motorised traction provided by half-tracks. (*AC*)

Below: Although the German invasion of France in 1940 was spearheaded by Panzer divisions, the majority of the Wehrmacht advanced on foot, with horse-drawn transport still playing a dominant logistical role. By 1940 German superiority was not primarily due to the number or technical quality of their tanks, but rather stemmed from superior tactics, effective command structures and advanced communication systems that enabled rapid coordination and exploitation of breakthroughs. (*AC*)

1940, due to the replacements issued to 6.Pz.Div. during the campaign, only eleven PzKpfw 35(t) tanks remained available at the *Heereszeugamt* in Magdeburg for further replacements.

In post-combat assessments, the overall performance of the PzKpfw 35(t) was rated as satisfactory. However, several critical shortcomings were identified. The optical equipment, particularly the vision devices for both the commander and the driver, as well as the gun sight, were deemed inadequate for effective battlefield observation and target acquisition. Furthermore, the vehicle's armour protection, especially the frontal armour, was assessed as insufficient. It was noted that at close range the frontal plates were vulnerable even to light anti-tank weapons, including the French 2.5cm anti-tank gun. Against the 7.5cm guns fielded by British and French forces, the armour offered little to no effective protection.

Above: The final major objective of the campaign for the PzKpfw 35(t)s was the capture of the fort at Épinal, located on the Moselle river. On 18 June 35(t)s approached the high ground outside Épinal. (*AC*)

Opposite above: During the night of 19/20 June advanced elements of 6.Pz.Div., including a patrol of engineers from Pioneer Battalion 57, entered Épinal. There, the German engineers fought their final significant battle over one of the bridges on the Moselle, which was fiercely defended and prepared for demolition. (*AC*)

Opposite below: A destroyed PzKpfw 35(t) at the corner of Quai Louis Lapicque and Rue de Léopold Bourg in Épinal. It was knocked out on 19 June by a 25mm anti-tank gun of the 46e GRDI. (*AC*)

In August, while preparations for a potential invasion of England continued, a major reorganisation of the *Panzerwaffe* began. As part of this restructuring, 6.Pz.Div. was 'coupled' with the 16th Infantry Division. The tank regiments of 6.Pz.Div. retained much of the same structure and strength as it had at the beginning of the war. It comprised three battalions (I./Pz.Rgt.11, II./Pz.Rgt.11 and Pz.Abt.65), each equipped with its own headquarters, six light companies (each with twenty-two PzKpfw 35(t) tanks), and three medium companies (each with fourteen PzKpfw IV and five PzKpfw II tanks). In total, the regiment had 239 tanks, including the headquarters sub-units at battalion and company levels.

During the French campaign, the tank repair company in Pz.Rgt.11 (Pz.Werkst. Kp.11) reported that they had carried out nearly four hundred field repairs on various PzKpfw 35(t) tanks. After the campaign ended, twenty-one PzKpfw 35(t)s were loaded onto railcars and sent to Germany for major repairs. In the weeks that followed, recovery units collected a number of severely damaged PzKpfw 35(t) tanks from the battlefields and sent them to Germany for overhaul. This effort resulted in the number of combat-ready Czechoslovak tanks in both line units and depots being brought up

Above, opposite above and opposite below: After the French campaign, specialised recovery teams were dispatched to search the battlefields for knocked-out PzKpfw 35(t) tanks. Their mission was to locate and retrieve even heavily damaged vehicles. Tanks that could potentially be repaired were collected and prepared for transport, while those judged beyond recovery were stripped of any usable parts on site. This approach ensured that valuable components were salvaged and contributed to maintaining the operational strength of 6.Pz.Div. prior to Operation Barbarossa. (*AC*)

to 190 by the end of 1940. By 3 October 1940 6.Pz.Div. was back up to its authorised strength, as the last batch of fourteen overhauled PzKpfw 35(t) tanks arrived.

PzKpfw 35(t) in SS Totenkopf Division

In fact, 6.Pz.Div. was not the only German unit equipped with PzKpfw 35(t) tanks during the French campaign. Six of these machines were also assigned to an armoured platoon in the heavy weapons company (*schwere Kompanie*) of the Reconnaissance Battalion (*Aufkl.Abt.*) of the SS Totenkopf Division. This unit was sent into action in France, but little is known about its performance, aside from a brief report detailing an encounter with British Matilda tanks near Arras on 21 May 1940, when the German tank platoon, led by *SS-Oberscharführer* Werkmeister, engaged British forces north of the Mercatel-Ficheux/Arras-Bucquoy crossroads. In the ensuing tank duel the Germans lost two tanks and were ultimately forced to withdraw.

Above: A PzKpfw 35(t) of Kp.7/Pz.Rgt.11 abandoned in the main square of an unknown French city. This tank had sustained only light damage, making it possible for it to be recovered, repaired and returned to full operational service. (*AC*)

Opposite above: A PzKpfw 35(t) fording a shallow river. Such manoeuvres allowed German armoured units to maintain momentum through enemy territory, especially when bridges were destroyed or unavailable. (*AC/PD*)

Opposite below: Tanks of PzAbt.65 welcomed by citizens of their home garrison city upon returning from the French campaign. The lead tank in the column belongs to Kp.1/Pz.Abt.65, commanded by *Leutnant* Scheibert. (*AC, photo possibly from the collection of Lt Friedrich Sender*)

The Russian Front (1941)

In September 1940 6.Pz.Div. was transferred to West Prussia, where it became part of XVI Army Corps under the Eighteenth Army. Brigadier General Landgraf assumed command of the division. Previously, he had led 4.Pz.Div. during the French Campaign and was awarded the Knight's Cross on 16 June 1940 for his achievements. For the following twelve months 6.Pz.Div. did not participate in any further operations in the European theatre. During this time both Pz.Rgt.11 and Pz.Abt.65 were replenished and intensively trained through exercises and war games in preparation for their next major campaign—this time in the East. Russia was the next target.

The regiment fielded a total of 238 tanks, including 160 PzKpfw 35(t)s, eleven PzBefWg 35(t)s, forty-seven PzKpfw II light tanks, and twenty short-barrelled PzKpfw IVs (although estimates for the latter vary between twenty, thirty or even forty-two, depending on the source). Just before the invasion, 6.Pz.Div. assembled in the area around Osterode (Ostróda), Riesenburg (Prabuty) and Deutsch Eylau (Iława), having previously occupied the surrounding region. The build-up for the attack involved four successive night marches, which proved difficult due to the massive concentration of troops from Army Group North and their overlapping movement routes near the border.

The division was only permitted to occupy its actual assault positions during the night of 21/22 June 1941. The initial tactical deployment for the attack was based on two Kampfgruppen of unequal strength: on the right, the weaker Kampfgruppe von Seckendorff was tasked with spearheading the assault and opening the road to Kangailai. On the left, the stronger Kampfgruppe Raus, which included Pz.Rgt.11, was to follow up with a powerful thrust, breaking through Soviet border fortifications and continuing the advance as ordered.

By the evening of 21 June divisional headquarters had been established at Szugken. After a brief artillery preparation at 3.05 am on 22 June, 6.Pz.Div. crossed the Soviet border south of Tauroggen, encountering only light infantry resistance, and captured a critical bridge across the Sesuvis river at Kangailai.

On the second day of combat, following the deep breakthrough at the frontier, both Kampfgruppen advanced rapidly eastwards. Their goal was to prevent Soviet forces from establishing defensive positions along the Raseiniai Heights and to secure control of the important Dubyssa river sector. The Soviets had planned a systematic ambush in the Raseiniai area to delay the German tanks, since German presence there threatened not only the town itself but also the rear of the Soviet forces engaged in combat further south.

Assault on Raseiniai and the Soviet Counteroffensive

On the morning of 23 June 6.Pz.Div. launched its assault on Raseiniai, capturing the town by the afternoon. To enable attacks in multiple directions, the division had been divided into two Kampfgruppen. Kampfgruppe von Seckendorff advanced to the east and northeast of Raseiniai, successfully crossing the Dubysa river at two separate points and establishing bridgeheads on the eastern bank. Further north, near the settlement of Bedančiai, Kampfgruppe Raus seized an intact bridge over the Dubysa and also established a bridgehead on the far side.

While the Germans were enjoying their initial tactical successes, the Soviet High Command ordered the 3rd Mechanised Corps, under Major General Alexei Kurkin, to counterattack and push the enemy back across the Dubysa. The Soviet corps was nominally composed of three divisions, totalling around thirty-two thousand soldiers, 670 tanks and 224 armoured cars. However, only the corps headquarters and the 2nd Tank Division were sent to Raseiniai—the other two divisions were held back by the Northwestern Front to defend separate sectors.

The 2nd Tank Division was regarded as one of the most capable armoured formations in the Red Army. It was equipped with fifty-seven of the new heavy KV tanks, named after the prominent Soviet military officer and politician Kliment Voroshilov. The KV-1, weighing 43 tons, featured 75mm of armour on all sides and up to 90mm at the gun mantlet. The even more massive KV-2, at 52 tons, had armour thickness up to 110mm and was fitted with an enormous turret housing a 152mm howitzer, designed primarily for bunker-busting. The KV-1, in contrast, was armed with a 76.2mm gun. In addition to its KV tanks, the 2nd Tank Division also fielded

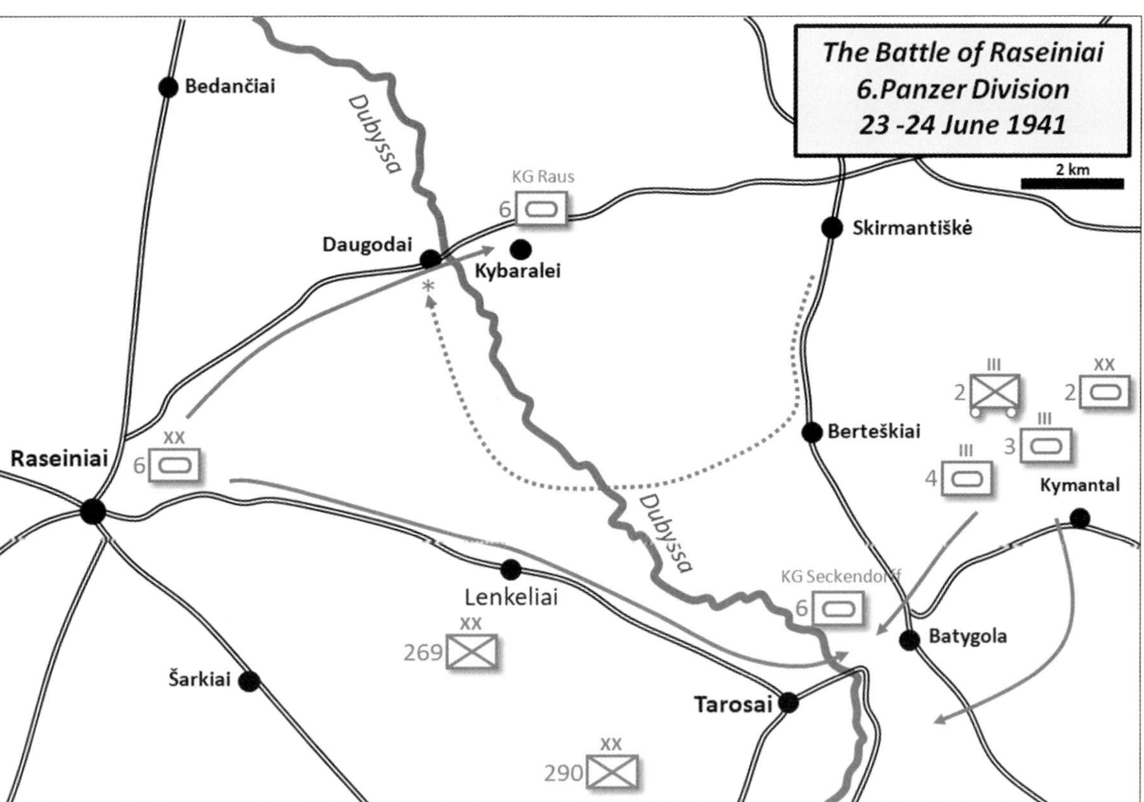

The Soviet 2nd Tank Division attacked KG Seckendorff's bridgehead over the Dubysa river, overrunning the German units and forcing them to retreat. A small group of Soviet tanks, including three KVs, crossed the river at an unguarded point and advanced towards Raseiniai. Two were immobilised by German heavy artillery firing at close range, but one KV-2 managed to reach the road supplying KG Raus before running out of fuel. Attempts to destroy it with light anti-tank guns failed, but 8.8cm Flak guns eventually succeeded.

Above: A PzKpfw 35(t) passing a KV, a heavy Soviet tank weighing around 43 tons, featuring up to 75mm of armour on all sides and up to 90mm on the gun mantlet, and armed with a 76.2mm gun. Although lighter and less heavily armed than the super-heavy KV-2, the KV-1 was deadly enough to eliminate all German tank models operating during the summer of 1941. (*AC/PD*)

Below: A German tank crewman of Kp.7/Pz.Rgt.11 inspects a Soviet BT-series tank that was knocked out by a PzKpfw 35(t). (*AC, photo possibly from the collection of Lt Friedrich Sender*)

twenty-seven medium T-28 tanks and 147 light tanks (BT-7s and T-26s). The light tanks were more vulnerable, possessing thinner armour and lighter armament than the PzKpfw 35(t) tanks. Fortunately for the Germans, the Red Army was still undergoing rearmament and reorganisation, and many Soviet tanks—including the KVs—were sent into combat equipped only with high-explosive shells, as armour-piercing ammunition had not yet reached the front lines.

The approach of the Soviet armour towards Raseiniai did not escape the attention of German aerial reconnaissance. However, at that critical moment only motorcycle reconnaissance units from 6.Pz.Div. were positioned on the eastern bank of the Dubysa—a force hopelessly outmatched by the advancing Soviet tanks.

On the morning of 24 June the German southern bridgehead came under heavy attack from the 2nd Tank Division, whose objective was to retake Raseiniai and push 6.Pz.Div. off the plateau. The Soviet assault was spearheaded by KVs, which penetrated deep into the German positions in the extended bridgehead.

Approximately a hundred tanks from Pz.Rgt.11—one-third of them PzKpfw IVs and the remainder PzKpfw 35(t)s—were assembled for a counterattack. Some of these engaged the advancing Soviet KV heavy tanks head-on, but the effort proved futile. The frontal armour of the KVs rendered the German anti-tank weapons largely ineffective. Meanwhile, the lightly armoured PzKpfw 35(t)s began to suffer losses. Under intense fire, they were forced to retreat into cover to avoid total destruction. One such tank became mired in a marshy pool. Moments later, a KV tank—without hesitation—rolled over the immobilised vehicle, crushing it beneath its massive treads.

Though the Soviet tanks suffered little to no damage from Pz.Rgt.11's brief counterattack, the action did force them to halt and disperse to respond. This disruption caused the Soviet advance to lose momentum and cohesion. The tide turned when the German forces brought in heavier firepower. The Soviet tanks were eventually halted by a combination of direct fire from 100mm artillery batteries, 88mm Flak guns, used in a ground-support role, and anti-tank mines laid by pioneer engineers. These defences inflicted significant losses on the Soviet armour and brought their offensive to a standstill.

At the same time, the second German bridgehead over the Dubysa river came under attack. Though most of the attacking Soviet units were scattered and disorganised, one KV tank, manned by a determined crew, managed to break through German lines and block a critical supply route. Despite repeated attempts to destroy it—using anti-tank guns, PzKpfw 35(t)s and mines—the massive KV withstood everything thrown at it. German tanks reportedly attacked it from three sides, yet the behemoth held its position for two full days, effectively stalling all German movement. When the KV was finally taken out by 8.8cm rounds, the German crews discovered that the 3.7cm shells fired by the PzKpfw 38(t)s had left no visible marks on its armour. Deeply impressed by the bravery and determination of the enemy crew, German troops buried the fallen Soviet tankers with full military honours.

With the obstruction removed, Kampfgruppe Raus launched a renewed assault. Breaking out from the bridgehead, it advanced southwards along the eastern bank of the Dubysa river, executing a bold manoeuvre that cut off the retreat of the Soviet 2nd Tank Division. According to German war reports, in the sector of 6.Pz.Div. alone,

Above: Tanks of Pz.Rgt.11 passing through the village of Lubāna in Latvia as they advanced towards the Soviet border. In many parts of Latvia the local population initially greeted the German forces as liberators. This reception was shaped by widespread resentment towards the Soviet occupation that had begun in 1940, marked by political repression, deportations and the dismantling of local institutions. (*AC/PD*)

Below: For long marches, the 35(t)s were equipped with additional jerry cans mounted on the rear hull and track fenders, which were not removed even when entering combat. This arrangement made the 'Škodas' particularly vulnerable to enemy fire, even from small-calibre weapons, if accurately aimed. (*AC/Postcard*)

Above: Crew members pausing in a Latvian village recently taken by German troops. (*AC*)

Below: By July 1941 the Red Army possessed approximately four hundred T-28 multi-turret tanks, designed in the 1930s as infantry support vehicles intended to break through fortified defences. The T-28 featured several advanced elements for its time—such as multiple gun models, radios and an anti-aircraft gun—although its suspension and overall layout were outdated by the outbreak of the Soviet-German war. The majority of these tanks were lost within the first two months of the invasion, many abandoned due to mechanical breakdowns. (*AC/PD*)

Above: A PzKpfw IV (Kp.6/Pz.Rgt.11) follows two PzKpfw 35(t)s as they reconnoitre the terrain ahead of the advancing battle group. The short-barrelled Panzer IVs, equipped with 7.5cm guns, were designed to suppress bunkers and machine-gun nests. While the lighter 35(t) s attempted to outflank enemy positions, the Panzer IVs were tasked with crushing resistance head-on. (*AC/PD*)

Below: The heavily loaded 35(t)s, burdened with jerry cans, spare parts and other supplies, resembled supply trucks more than front-line combat vehicles. (*AC*)

125 Soviet tanks were destroyed or disabled during the fighting—including twelve to fourteen KV-1s. In contrast, 6.Pz.Div. recorded 197 casualties (including fifty-five dead, 124 wounded and eighteen missing), and just four tanks lost beyond repair (three PzKpfw 38(t)s and one PzKpfw IV), although many were damaged. That night the division regrouped, its forward elements already preparing to resume the offensive on 26 June.

ADVANCE TOWARDS THE STALIN LINE AND THE LATVIAN–RUSSIAN BORDER

On 26 June 6.Pz.Div. resumed its offensive with the objective of advancing through Lithuania, Latvia and Estonia towards Leningrad. The exhausted Soviet forces were retreating towards the Dvina river, and German progress was hindered primarily by difficult terrain, extreme heat and thick clouds of dust rather than by any organised enemy resistance.

On 29 June, facing only scattered opposition, Kampfgruppe Raus successfully established a 10km-deep bridgehead across the Dvina river near Livani, south of Dubna. This bridgehead was steadily expanded both northwards towards Rudzeti and to the south of the town, enabling the full division to cross and regroup on the northeast bank of the Dvina in preparation for the next phase—an advance towards the pre-Molotov-Ribbentrop Pact Latvian–Soviet border.

By 2 July the division had reached a forward line stretching approximately from Zobleva to Birzi, encountering no major Soviet formations, but dealing with frequent skirmishes and rearguard actions by retreating Red Army elements. Despite the initial rapid progress, the division's spearhead units, led by PzKpfw 35(t)s, were soon forced to navigate marshy, treacherous terrain that significantly slowed their advance.

On 4 July forward elements of the division encountered increasing Soviet resistance near the Russian border as they manoeuvred to establish assembly areas for the attack on the Stalin Line—a fortified defence belt of reinforced concrete pillboxes and bunkers. The Soviets launched a surprise armoured counterattack just east of Baltinava, temporarily threatening the German advance. After restoring the situation, 6.Pz.Div. resumed its drive towards the fortified frontier.

The Stalin Line proved to be a formidable obstacle. The Soviets defended every pillbox tenaciously and the German assault bogged down in front of the main bunker line. These fortifications had to be cleared one by one, in brutal close-quarters fighting using stormtrooper tactics, engineer support and anti-tank weapons. Only by the late afternoon of 6 July did the breakthrough succeed—after more than 15 hours of continuous combat and the capture of over twenty bunkers.

Following the breakthrough, the division advanced into the eastern section of the Ostrov bridgehead, which was to be expanded for further operations. The subsequent fighting between Ostrov and the Luga river was marked by continuous combat, often lasting through the night. The Red Army fought a determined delaying action, aided by increasingly difficult terrain—deep mud, forests and swamps—as well as by sudden changes in the division's operational direction, as dictated by higher command.

Above: A PzKpfw III of Kp.7/Pz.Rgt.11 and a heavy PzKpfw IV of Kp.6/Pz.Rgt.11 carrying infantry as they advance in support. The Germans began transporting infantry on tanks only after the start of the campaign in the Soviet Union, whereas the Red Army had been practising the use of 'desant' tactics since the 1930s. (*AC*)

Below: As the armoured columns of 6.Pz.Div. advanced towards Leningrad, they moved past expansive grain fields that were still waiting to be harvested. Traversing this type of open landscape necessitated protective cover on the flanks, a task that fell to the accompanying infantry. (*AC/PD*)

Above: Tanks from Pz.Rgt.11 in the assembly area prior to the attack. Seated on the front armour of a PzKpfw 35(t) are three crew members, each holding the rank of lance corporal. They wear the classic black uniforms of the armoured units along with green-grey side caps, replacing the distinctive black berets that were eventually considered impractical. Notably, they are wearing long infantry boots, an unexpected choice for tank crews. (*AC*)

Below: On Russian dirt roads, where shallow streams intersected the route, bridges were rarely constructed. Instead, simple clearings were created by laying logs along the streambed to keep vehicles from becoming bogged down in the mud. Thanks to their light weight and ability to ford water up to 80–90 centimetres deep, the 'Škoda' tanks could typically traverse these makeshift crossings at a slow, steady pace. (*AC*)

Above: German soldiers of 6.Pz.Div. hitch a ride on a 'Škoda' tank in the Western Dvina river region (Belarus), summer 1941. Prior to Operation Barbarossa, the vehicle was modified with a pair of spare road wheels and a large stowage box mounted on the left front fender—field adaptations typical of long-range operations in the East. (*AC*)

Below: With the onset of autumn's rapidly falling temperatures, the tank crews were given standard-issue greatcoats. However, these garments offered little protection against the brutal, freezing conditions of the Soviet winter. (*AC*)

On 10 July 6.Pz.Div. suffered its first tactical setback since crossing into the Soviet Union when its attack on the Jamkino road triangle failed to achieve its objective. The Soviets offered stubborn resistance, skilfully using the dense forests and undergrowth to launch repeated counterattacks, often supported by tanks. The main obstacle, however, was the reappearance of Soviet KV heavy tanks, which had not been encountered since the fighting at Raseiniai. These tanks were employed as mobile bunkers—each escorted by two or three lighter tanks and supported by an infantry platoon tasked with protecting the heavy vehicle. This made it impossible for German infantry to approach and destroy the KVs with close-assault weapons, forcing them to engage from a distance. But at Jamkino, the division lacked 8.8cm Flak guns, which had previously proved effective against heavy armour. As a result, the German troops were forced to improvise under fire, experimenting with alternate methods of neutralising these 'roving bunkers'.

COMBAT LESSONS AND THE DRIVE TOWARDS THE LUGA RIVER

The first two weeks of fighting against Soviet armour revealed several critical lessons for 6.Pz.Div. The 3.7cm gun mounted on the PzKpfw 35(t) was highly effective against obsolete Soviet tank types such as the T-26 and BT-7. It could also immobilise a T-34 with a hit to the tracks or vision devices, but lacked the penetrating power to defeat the T-34's sloped armour. The heavy KV-series tanks proved virtually indestructible. Only concentrated fire at very close range—especially targeting turrets or running gear—had a chance of disabling them, often merely by jamming the turret or breaking the tracks. Even the PzKpfw IV, armed with the low-velocity 7.5cm, was ineffective against the KV. With a muzzle velocity of just 420m/s, it could only penetrate 41mm of armour at medium range, insufficient to deal with the KV's frontal protection.

Faced with this challenge, 'Škoda' tank commanders had to rely on superior tactics, enhanced by effective radio communication, excellent optics and close coordination with anti-tank and anti-aircraft units—particularly the powerful 8.8cm Flak guns, which proved to be one of the few reliable means of destroying Soviet heavy armour.

On 11 July 6.Pz.Div. was ordered to suspend its eastwards advance towards Porkhov and Dno, and instead to assist 1.Pz.Div., which had encountered strong Soviet resistance near Novoselye while advancing along the Leningrad–Pskov highway. The movement of Kampfgruppe Raus to this new sector turned into an arduous march across sandy and swampy terrain, and over wooden bridges that frequently collapsed under the weight of even the light PzKpfw 35(t) tanks.

On 12 July the German advance detachment struck the flank of the Soviet forces defending the highway. These troops had been reported the day before to be stationed south of a narrow, swampy stream. A brief but intense engagement followed, including close-range tank combat. The Germans succeeded in pushing the Soviet flank guard back across the stream. During the fight the Germans encountered Soviet T-37 amphibious tanks for the first time. Six of them were destroyed at close range—three on land and three while attempting to cross the stream—by anti-tank and tank fire from German positions in the woods.

Above: After breaking through the Stalin Line on 6 June, 6.Pz.Div. advanced towards Ostrov. The Soviets offered stubborn resistance, deploying KV tanks used as mobile bunkers. Although these heavy machines were difficult to destroy, many were eventually abandoned by their crews due to a lack of fuel. (*AC*)

Below: A Panzer 35(t) from *Kp.1/Pz.Rg.11* lies immobilised in the autumn of 1941, already stripped for spare parts. The mechanically complex and maintenance-sensitive design of 'Škodas' proved ill-suited to the extreme conditions of the Eastern Front, leading to frequent breakdowns and the widespread practice of cannibalising damaged vehicles to sustain operational strength. (*AC*)

A German light truck stranded in a roadside drainage ditch awaits recovery by a 35(t) from Kp.1/Pz.Rg.11. In the absence of tracked recovery vehicles, tanks were sometimes pressed into service for towing, especially during the autumn mud season. (*AC*)

After this sharp clash the main German assault collapsed the Soviet flank, and, once German tanks smashed into their rear, the entire Soviet position disintegrated.

The next day, Kampfgruppe Raus received new orders: to march north and capture the bridge over the Plyussa river at Lyady and establish a bridgehead on the far bank. The unit covered 59 kilometres in 9 hours, averaging just over 6.5km/h. The bridge was seized in a bold surprise attack by a lieutenant of the advance guard, who acted without waiting for orders. Thanks to his initiative, the 150m-long, 10m-high bridge fell into German hands intact and without a fight.

Seizing the moment, Kampfgruppe Raus was immediately tasked with advancing to capture the two large wooden bridges over the Luga river near Porechye, known as the 'Gateway to Leningrad'. The objective lay over 100 kilometres away, across difficult swampy roads and several river crossings. Despite these challenges, the spearhead of 6.Pz.Div. managed to capture the burning Dolgaya bridge without resistance. German engineers succeeded in extinguishing the flames, preserving the crossing. From there, the Kampfgruppe advanced towards the crucial Luga river bridges, positioning themselves for the next thrust towards Leningrad.

Above, below and opposite above: These three photographs feature command tanks (PzBefWg 35(t)s), distinguished by their prominent frame antennas. This specialised communication gear allowed the crews to maintain contact not only with several armoured battle groups operating at distances of 20 to 30 kilometres apart, but also with the infantry units advancing in their wake. During the summer of 1941 combat on the Eastern Front was marked by rapid, large-scale manoeuvres, with both German and Soviet forces struggling to establish a continuous front line. In such a fluid and dynamic battlefield environment, the ability to coordinate movements and relay orders quickly became essential. As a result, effective radio communication proved to be a decisive factor in the success of both offensive thrusts and defensive actions. (*AC*)

THE SEIZURE OF THE LUGA RIVER BRIDGES AND THE BATTLE FOR PORECHYE

The assault was spearheaded by commandos from Lehr-Regiment 'Brandenburg' z.b.V. 800, an elite *Abwehr* unit specialising in commando raids, sabotage and deception, often using disguises to infiltrate enemy lines. For this mission, the commandos operated a captured BA-10 armoured car, crewed by three Russian-speaking 'Brandenburger' operatives dressed in Soviet uniforms. They were followed by a ZIS truck filled with additional commandos. Upon arrival, they leapt from the vehicles, eliminated the sentries and cut the detonation wires linked to explosives rigged on the bridge's supporting pillars. Following closely behind were German tanks, which rapidly advanced, reaching the river crossings and rolling over the intact bridges. Once across, they quickly neutralised the large Soviet log bunkers positioned on the northern bank of the Luga river.

Within 30 minutes, the spearhead of 6.Pz.Div. had seized not only both Luga river bridges but also the road junction at Ivanovskoye, without encountering organised resistance. The Brandenburgers then rushed forwards and captured the Ivanovskoye dam, again meeting no serious opposition. During the occupation of Ivanovskoye, a captured Soviet prisoner revealed the existence of a nearby airfield in the village of Yastrebina. Acting immediately on the intelligence, five PzKpfw 35(t)s launched a surprise raid, driving through the hangars and over aircraft parked on the ground, destroying many before any could take off.

After three days and nights of gruelling operations through swamps, sand and rivers, Kampfgruppe Raus had advanced nearly 200 kilometres and captured what the Germans referred to as the 'Gateway to Leningrad', now just 105 kilometres from the city. But although Kampfgruppe Raus had successfully captured the Porechye bridgehead, a question remained—could it hold the position alone until the rest of 6.Pz.Div. arrived? Anticipating a Soviet counterattack, the Germans hastily prepared defensive positions around the small bridgehead.

The Soviets struck on the morning of 15 July, launching an assault supported by tanks in an attempt to recapture both Luga bridges. Advancing in wedge formation, the Soviet armour pushed towards the German line—until it entered a carefully prepared kill zone, where 8.8cm Flak guns and 10cm artillery opened fire from ambush positions at a range of only 500 metres. As the Soviet attack ground to a halt under the intense fire, thirty tanks from Pz.Rgt.11 launched a counterattack, charging

Above: A temporary staging area for the headquarters of II./Pz.Rgt.11 set up in the field. In the densely forested region, suitable locations for establishing such command posts were scarce, as villages were few and far between. As a result, the headquarters staff often had to improvise, selecting clearings or other open spaces within the woods to organise their operations, coordinate unit movements and relay orders to the front lines. (*AC*)

Opposite above and opposite below: German armoured battle groups typically advanced along main roads, many of which were unpaved and cut through dense forests and marshy terrain. These routes were frequently interrupted by numerous rivers, further hindering the pace of the advance. Most of the bridges encountered along these roads were wooden constructions, originally intended to support vehicles weighing no more than 5 tons. Despite these limitations, the lighter 'Škoda' tanks often attempted to cross these fragile bridges, which occasionally resulted in the structures collapsing under their weight. In contrast, the heavier PzKpfw IV tanks had to halt and wait for engineers to reinforce the bridges with temporary supports before they could safely proceed. (*AC*)

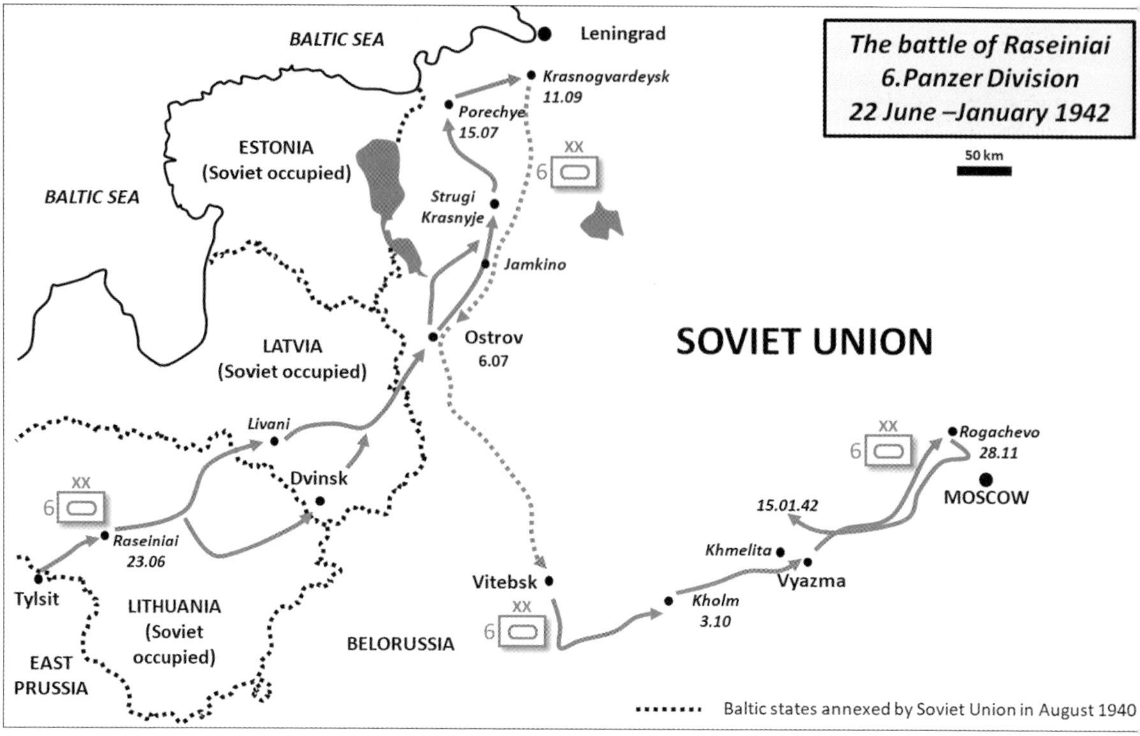

Above: Battle Trail Map: 6.Pz.Div. during Operation Barbarossa, 1941–1942.

Below: A PzKpfw 35(t) of Kp.5/Pz.Rgt.11 being transported on an Ah.115 flatbed trailer towed by a 9-ton tracked tractor. While this method conserved the tank's engine wear and tracks, it was rarely practical under fast-moving Soviet front conditions as the tractor could not keep pace with advancing tanks. This photo was likely taken during the redeployment from the Leningrad Front to Army Group Centre, now positioned for the planned advance on Moscow. (*AC*)

Travelling over unpaved, sandy Soviet roads posed a constant challenge for German crews. The combination of dust and summer heat often forced all crew members—except the driver—to ride on the outside of their vehicles, exposing them to the risk of enemy ambushes. (*AC*)

forwards with all guns blazing. They disabled several more Soviet tanks and dispersed the accompanying infantry, regaining control of the battlefield.

Over the following two days heavy fighting raged around the bridgehead. Despite putting up strong resistance, the Germans were increasingly hard-pressed, particularly by the KV heavy tanks, which the PzKpfw 35(t)s were virtually powerless to stop.

Reinforcements finally arrived on 19 July, but the following day the Soviets launched another fierce assault—again employing KV tanks, these driven by civilian mechanics from the Leningrad Tank Factory, straight off the production lines. A violent firefight erupted, with waves of lighter Soviet tanks following the KVs clashing against German armour. Losses were sustained on both sides. The breakthrough was achieved only when German tanks forced their way through after Soviet engineers cleared the battlefield of wrecked tanks, opening a gap.

Although the battle was won, the full strength of 6.Pz.Div. did not arrive until several days later. Over the next three weeks (20 July–13 August), the division endured its first prolonged standstill, engaging in costly positional warfare under difficult conditions.

On 24 July, due to high losses and mechanical breakdowns, Pz.Rgt.11 was reorganised from three to two battalions. Maintaining three had become impossible due to a shortage of replacement tanks. It could be said that the drive from the German border to the Luga river had cost the division the equivalent of an entire Panzer battalion. Notably, technical failures far outnumbered combat losses.

By 27 July the Soviet attacks against the Porechye bridgehead had gradually diminished, reduced to sporadic artillery bombardments and air raids. This relative pause allowed 6.Pz.Div. to regroup, resupply and prepare its tactics for the next breakout attempt. This came on 9 August, when the division launched an offensive from the Luga river bridgehead along the Porechye–Yurky road. The initial assault failed to breach the Soviet lines but the attack resumed the following day and by nightfall the Germans had finally penetrated the Soviet defensive positions, opening the way for further advances towards Leningrad.

THE FINAL PUSH TOWARDS LENINGRAD

Between 13 August and 7 September there was a gradual slowing of the German advance towards Leningrad, and the offensive eventually bogged down in front of the city's outer fortifications. This period saw a shift from rapid, mechanised warfare to positional fighting, characterised by limited gains and escalating resistance. The German advance was hampered not only by fierce Soviet resistance, but also by the extensive use of landmines, which caused significant damage to the lightly armoured PzKpfw 35(t) tanks. On a single day—16 August—engineers had to clear more than two thousand mines in 6.Pz.Div.'s sector alone. By this point in the campaign, Pz.Rgt.11 had lost no fewer than forty-seven PzKpfw 35(t)s, primarily due to mechanical breakdowns and combat losses.

A PzKpfw 35(t) of Kp.7/Pz.Rgt.11 during a rest stop, with a heavily loaded engine deck. The added gear hampered quick engine access, but was necessary as fast-moving battle groups often operated without dedicated technical support, carrying essential supplies themselves. (*AC*)

Above: A column of Škoda-built tanks en route from the rear areas to the front-line assembly zones, moving without accompanying infantry. While the absence of cover increased their vulnerability to ambushes, the priority was speed and rapid deployment. (*AC*)

Below: Close view of the extra fuel storage—eleven 20-litre jerry cans—and personal crew equipment carried on long marches by 35(t)s. Note the fascine (bundle of sticks) mounted on the rear; these were used by the tank crews to create 'corduroy roads' (*cardstrasse*) for crossing marshy terrain. (*AC, possibly from the collection of Lt Friedrich Sender*)

Above: Tank crew members from Pz.Rgt.11 inspecting a T-26, which had been abandoned by its Soviet crew. The T-26, particularly this 1936 variant, was one of the few Soviet tanks in service that was notably less well armed than the German 'Škoda' tanks. (*AC*)

Below: From 1933, the T-26 was produced in several different models, each featuring gradual improvements in turret design and armament. In this photograph, taken in the summer of 1941, the lead tank is a T-26 M1936, identifiable by its straight-sided turret. Following behind is an M1939, which features sloped turret sides that increased the effective thickness of its armour. (*AC*)

The KV-2 heavy tank, equipped with additional armour screens (referred to as 'KV z ekranami'), represented a significant advancement in Soviet armoured protection following the outbreak of the war. Thanks to these enhancements, the KV-2 was capable of withstanding even direct hits from the formidable 8.8cm calibre guns, which were considered the most powerful anti-tank weapons in the German arsenal at that time. (*AC*)

A renewed offensive against Leningrad was launched on 9 September, with the SS Polizei Infantry Division attacking Krasnogvardeysk on 6.Pz.Div.'s right flank. On its left flank, the recently redeployed 1.Pz.Div. and the 36th Motorised Infantry Division joined the assault. During the night of 11/12 September the battered Soviet infantry managed to evacuate Krasnogvardeysk under cover of darkness. They successfully withdrew and regrouped with strong rear guards on elevated ground between Krasnogvardeysk and Pushkin.

By 13 September 6.Pz.Div., committed to an encircling manoeuvre via Posyolok Taytsy, had begun pivoting into the rear of the Soviet defensive line—the so-called Leningrad Line. Sensing the threat, Soviet forces launched a counterattack from Pushkin, targeting the vulnerable German rear. The only immediate support for the German rear guard—a lone infantry battalion—was a single battery of 8.8cm Flak guns and II./Pz.Rgt.11, equipped exclusively with PzKpfw 35(t)s.

The vanguard of the Soviet assault—over fifty KV heavy tanks—advanced swiftly along a narrow strip of solid ground flanked by swamps. As they spread out and moved forwards, the lead elements suddenly came under intense fire from Panzerjäger Abt. 616, which had just arrived with twenty-seven heavy anti-tank guns. In the ensuing ambush, fourteen Soviet tanks were destroyed in short order, forcing the rest of the Soviet armoured column to halt abruptly. Soon after that, the rest of Pz.Rgt.11 was brought into action. In quick succession, Panzer regiments from the neighbouring 1.Pz.Div. and 8.Pz.Div. arrived and launched flanking and rear attacks against the Soviet force. Under the combined pressure, the Soviets retreated. The road to Leningrad appeared nearly open.

However, on 14 September 6.Pz.Div. received sudden orders to abort its Leningrad offensive. Instead, it was to begin redeploying by rail in the direction of Luga-Pskov, followed days later by a gruelling march through Nevel, covering nearly 1,000 kilometres to link up with Panzer Group 3 of Army Group Centre, now poised to advance on Moscow.

At this point, Pz.Rgt.11 retained only 104 operational PzKpfw 35(t)s out of the original 160, along with four PzBefWg 35(t) command tanks—a clear indicator of the toll exacted by both the terrain and prolonged combat.

The October Offensive and the Collapse before Moscow

The final German offensive toward Moscow—Operation Typhoon—began on 2 October 1941. During its initial phase, 6.Pz.Div. advanced over 30 kilometres, swiftly reaching the upper Dnepr river, where it seized two key bridges in a *coup de main*. This bold move cut off those Soviet forces still positioned west of the river and cleared the way for Panzer Group 3 to continue its thrust eastwards.

On 3 October, as 6.Pz.Div. resumed its drive towards Kholm, Soviet forces launched a flank attack with approximately a hundred tanks, striking from the south towards the key road junction. Most of the Soviet armour consisted of medium tanks. In response, the Germans dispatched a single battalion of PzKpfw 35(t)s and the 6th Company (Armoured Personnel Carriers) from the motorised infantry. Despite the odds, this modest force held the Soviet advance long enough for German Flak and anti-tank guns to be brought up to form a defensive line between Kholm and the Dnepr bridges. After eighty Soviet tanks were knocked out, 6.Pz.Div. broke through the final Soviet fortifications on the eastern bank of the Dnepr. The Soviet tank thrust had only delayed the division by a few hours.

PzKpfw 35t of II./PzRgt.11 (tactical no. 721). A Soviet shell struck the tank, severing its track and damaging the front road wheel. Fortunately, the impact only resulted in the vehicle being immobilised, and all of the crew escaped without injury. Damage of this nature meant that the tank could be sent to a field repair shop, where it could be restored to operational condition. (AC)

Above: Wreckage of two PzBefWg 35(t) command tanks from the HQ platoon of Pz.Rgt.11 lies scattered across open ground. The tanks were apparently caught off guard by a Soviet anti-tank gun, which succeeded in destroying two German machines. (*AC*)

Below: Red Army soldiers inspecting a damaged and partially disarmed PzKpfw 35(t). (*AC/PD*)

Above: As the first Russian snowfalls arrived and temperatures dropped below freezing, the once-impassable muddy roads became navigable again. Nevertheless, the plummeting temperatures caused many tanks to become immobilised. Vehicles that broke down in the field were sometimes abandoned by their crews but kept under guard until technical assistance could arrive. (*AC*)

Below: The first Russian winter faced by the Wehrmacht was among the coldest of the twentieth century, with deep snow and extreme cold. (*AC*)

One of the major shortcomings of the PzKpfw 35(t)s in the harsh Russian winter conditions was their narrow tracks, which led to poor weight distribution over snow-covered terrain. As a result, they frequently became bogged down in the snow. (*AC*)

From Kholm, the division pushed forwards through Khmelita towards Vyazma, while its right flank—exposed and stretched over 40 kilometres—was attacked by hastily organised Soviet tank and rifle units, supported by medium artillery. However, the German response was devastating: a massive barrage from all available weapons annihilated the Societ attackers in just 20 minutes, leaving their tanks ablaze, their artillery batteries in ruins and their infantry swept away by intense machine-gun fire. Without slowing, the Panzer division continued its advance, and reached Vyazma on 10 October, linking up with Panzer Group 4's 10.Pz.Div., which had approached from the south. This manoeuvre completed the encirclement of approximately four hundred thousand Soviet troops.

Between 2 and 11 October the 5th Company of Pz.Rgt.11 lost eighteen out of its twenty-four 'Skodas'. The entire II./Pz.Rgt.11 had been reduced to the strength of a single, weakened company.

By 16 October the division reported only sixty operational tanks of all types. Less than two weeks later just thirty-four PzKpfw 35(t)s remained functional, with forty-seven more awaiting repairs or being cannibalised for spare parts.

The Soviet remnants withdrew eastwards, but pursuit became impossible due to the worsening weather. The infamous *rasputitsa*—'the season of bad roads'—descended. Deep mud immobilised entire units, destroyed vehicles and halted the German operations. The PzKpfw 35(t), with its small road wheels and complex leaf-spring suspension, proved particularly vulnerable: mud clogged the suspension, rendering many tanks useless.

In late October the situation deteriorated further as sudden frost froze vehicles solid. The cold caused track links and leaf springs to fracture, while the pneumatic systems of the 35(t)s failed altogether—any condensation in the lines froze, making the vehicles undrivable. Repairs required specialist workshops, which were often out of reach. In some cases 'Škoda' tank crews were forced to abandon their vehicles and travel on foot to reach friendly units or seek shelter from locals, surviving the mud and cold as best they could.

By 31 October the average operational lifespan of a PzKpfw 35(t) had reached 11,000 kilometres—well beyond its design limits without a major overhaul. Repairs could only be performed by cannibalising parts from other damaged vehicles, as no new spare parts were available. Of forty-one tanks awaiting repair, only ten were restored using salvaged parts.

By 27 November temperatures had dropped to -35 degrees Centigrade, freezing fuel, seizing engines and severely affecting front-line troops, who were still wearing lightweight uniforms, wholly unprepared for a Russian winter. Logistical failures meant winter gear stockpiled in Germany and Poland never reached the front lines. Nevertheless, on 28 November, during a heavy snowstorm, the division captured Rogachevo, a strategically important town just 30 kilometres from the Volga–Moscow canal. In some sectors German forces were now less than 20 kilometres from Moscow.

Two days later the last operational PzKpfw 35(t) in the division had to be destroyed. By early December 6.Pz.Div. stood a mere 14 kilometres from Moscow, and just 24 kilometres from the Kremlin. But then the unthinkable happened. A sudden drop in temperature and a massive Soviet counterattack by fresh Siberian troops smashed into the advancing Germans. The division's defensive perimeter—organised around the last five functioning tanks—held off the initial assault, allowing a partial disengagement. The withdrawal proper began on 6 December, reaching Klin within days. By mid-December the division had regrouped near Shakhovskaya, approximately 150 kilometres west of Moscow, for rest and refit.

On 2 December 6.Pz.Div. reported that the last operational company of Pz.Regt.11 was taken out of action, with no remaining functional PzKpfw 35(t)s or PzKpfw IVs. By 10 December the division still had fifteen PzKpfw 35(t)s, though none was operational, and seven PzBefWg 35(t) command tanks, of which only five remained functional. By this point a total of 142 PzKpfw 35(t)s and six command tanks had been written off.

Though Shakhovskaya held against multiple Soviet assaults, neighbouring units were forced to retreat when Russian tanks penetrated their lines. This meant 6.Pz.Div.'s position became untenable. On 15 January 1942 the division formally reported to LVI Panzer Corps: 'The division is no longer capable of operations. Reconstitution—not refitting—is required. However, this is not possible in the present area.'

Once the front had stabilised, 6.Pz.Div. was withdrawn and redeployed to the Rzhev sector, and then transferred to France in May 1942 for complete reorganisation, restaffing and re-equipment with modern, German-produced tanks. By November 1942 the division was fully rebuilt and combat-ready once again.

The Second Life of the PzKpfw 35(t)—*Mörserzugmittel* 35(t)

During the early months of Operation Barbarossa, no fewer than fifty PzKpfw 35(t) tanks that had sustained only light damage were recovered from the front and transported to the Škoda Works in Pilsen for evaluation. After thorough technical inspection, these vehicles were deemed unsuitable for further front-line service—even after potential refurbishment.

In March 1942 Weapons Testing Office No. 6 (*Wa Prüf 6*) of the German Army Ordnance Office (*Heereswaffenamt*) proposed repurposing the existing chassis as artillery towing vehicles. A prototype was developed by Alkett, after which Škoda was contracted to convert forty-nine tanks into *Mörserzugmittel* 35(t) tracked artillery tractors.

By late 1942 a total of thirty-seven conversions had been completed, with the remaining twelve finished by mid-1943. The conversion involved the removal of the turrets, which were subsequently reused in static defensive positions—*Panzertürme* ('turret bunkers')—installed in Denmark and Corsica. These retained their original 3.7cm anti-tank guns and coaxial machine guns.

To expand the internal space for the crew of the artillery tractors, the ball-mounted ZB machine gun in the front hull was also removed. The turret ring was sealed with

The *Mörserzugmittel* 35(t) was created by removing the tank turret from the original chassis, with the former fighting compartment covered by a simple frame and tarpaulin. Additional jerrycan racks were installed along both hull sides to extend the operational range—an essential modification for the long-distance marches typical of the Eastern Front. (*AC*)

Above: Additional jerry cans were also mounted inside the fighting compartment, replacing the original ammunition racks. The crew seats were also rearranged to accommodate the new internal layout. (*AC*)

Below: To enable the *Mörserzugmittel* 35(t) to tow the 21cm howitzer, it was fitted with a heavy-duty crossbeam welded to the rear hull plate. This towing fixture was designed to handle loads of up to 12 tons. (*AC*)

a canvas cover, and the vehicle's crew—now reduced to three men—relied entirely on personal small arms for defence, typically including MP 40 submachine guns and Walther P38 pistols.

The removal of the turret reduced the overall weight of the vehicle to approximately 10.5–11 metric tons. However, neither the armour protection nor the engine was modified. The *Mörserzugmittel* 35(t) was capable of towing at speeds up to 35km/h, with an average cross-country speed of approximately 12–15km/h.

At the rear, a heavy-duty crossbeam was welded onto the chassis' back plate, capable of towing loads of 12–14 tons. To improve operational endurance—especially across the vast expanses of the Eastern Front—external jerrycan racks were fitted on both sides of the hull, with space for four additional cans installed inside.

These adaptations enabled the *Mörserzugmittel* 35(t) to tow heavy artillery pieces such as the 21cm Mörser 18, a howitzer with a range of 16.7 kilometres. Due to its weight, the Mörser 18 had to be transported in two parts: the barrel and transport platform (approximately 10.5 tons) and the carriage (around 12 tons). Such howitzers were deployed in *schwere Artillerie-Abteilungen* (heavy artillery battalions), each consisting of three batteries, with two howitzers per battery, and up to twelve towing vehicles per battalion.

By mid-1942 the Wehrmacht had formed twenty-six such heavy artillery battalions, although only four are believed to have been equipped with the *Mörserzugmittel* 35(t). The remainder typically used the SdKfz 8 half-track or the *Mörserzugmittel* 35 R(f)—a similar artillery tractor derived from turretless Renault R-35 tanks.

The *Mörserzugmittel* 35(t) offered superior manoeuvrability compared to traditional tracked artillery tractors, thanks to its tank-based chassis and more advanced suspension system. (*AC*)

Precise documentation regarding the deployment of the *Mörserzugmittel* 35(t) is limited. However, available evidence suggests these vehicles may have been used during Operation Blue (*Fall Blau*) in the Caucasus in the summer of 1942, as well as on the Volkhov Front, where one of the artillery battalions was reportedly annihilated in February 1943.

Above: A 21cm Mörser 18 heavy howitzer in firing position, prepared for long-range bombardment. This dual-recoil artillery piece was one of the Wehrmacht's most powerful field weapons, capable of destroying fortified targets with high-explosive shells. (*AC*)

Below: Destroyed or abandoned *Mörserzugmittel* 35(t) vehicles lie scattered across a snow-covered landscape, likely on the Volkhov Front during the harsh winter of 1942/1943. A geometric symbol painted on the front armour (as seen in the inset photo) indicated the vehicle's unit assignment: a square for the 1st Battery, a circle for the 2nd and a triangle for the 3rd. (*AC*)

6

In Slovak Army Service

The Slovak Republic was established on 14 March 1939 following the disintegration of Czechoslovakia. Though nominally independent, the new state quickly became a satellite of Nazi Germany.

At its inception, the Slovak army inherited fifty-two LT vz. 35 tanks from the former Czechoslovak 3rd Mobile Division and the 3rd Armoured Regiment (PÚV-3) based in Turčiansky Svätý Martin. Nine additional tanks from the original inventory were undergoing warranty repairs at the Škoda Works at the time of the German occupation and were subsequently confiscated by the Wehrmacht. However, the Slovaks acquired another nine tanks from the 2nd Armoured Regiment (PÚV-2), which had retreated from Transcarpathian Ruthenia into Slovak territory.

Following the declaration of independence, all officers and soldiers of Czechoslovak origin were ordered to leave Slovakia, severely depleting the armed forces of experienced leadership and qualified technical personnel. After this purge, only ten officers, thirty-seven NCOs and 222 enlisted men remained at the PÚV-3 barracks—insufficient to operate a full armoured regiment. Due to the personnel shortfall, the Slovak tank force was initially restructured as an ad hoc armoured vehicle battalion. By September 1939 the unit was brought up to full strength using technical personnel transferred from the 1st and 5th Infantry Regiments. Despite this, technical staffing levels remained critically low. The Slovak command requested assistance from the Škoda factory, which sent a team of technicians to the battalion. Their support enabled the rapid restoration of all available tanks to operational status.

In the autumn of 1939 the battalion's structure was revised to include three light tank companies. However, this organisation was short-lived. Through the efforts of Major Tani (Čáni), the battalion was expanded and reclassified as a regiment.

As of January 1940 the armoured regiment consisted of two battalions. The 1st Battalion fielded two operational tank companies and one reserve company. Initially, the regiment followed Czechoslovak army standards, with tank platoons consisting of three tanks, and companies formed from five platoons. Later in 1940 a transition to the German model was implemented: platoons were increased to five tanks, while the number of platoons per company was reduced from five to three. This kept the total strength of a company at sixteen tanks, including the company commander's vehicle.

Training throughout 1940 proceeded under peacetime conditions. New drivers were first trained on tankettes, then LT vz. 34 tanks and finally on LT vz. 35s. The regiment

An LT vz. 35 fording a river during field exercises. 'Škodas' were capable of crossing water obstacles with depths of up to 80–90 centimetres without the need for special preparation. This capability allowed them to operate effectively in the narrow river valleys typical of the mountainous border regions of Czechoslovakia. (*AC*)

A company of LT vz. 35s awaiting orders to march. The last tank in the column (Serial no. 13.847) was delivered to PÚV-3 in March 1937 and remained in service with the Slovak Army following the partition of Czechoslovakia. (*AC*)

An LT vz. 35, with its machine guns removed, being used for driver training. This type of temporary disarmament—intended to preserve valuable equipment—was also a common practice in the German Panzer forces prior to the outbreak of the Second World War. (*AC*)

conducted training at the Bukovina training ground, with live-fire exercises held in the Oremov Láz area. Slovak armoured units also participated in ceremonial parades in Bratislava, Michalovce, Banská Bystrica and Martin. In one instance, four LT-35 tanks and four armoured cars were deployed to Handlová to suppress a miners' strike. However, the protest ended peacefully, and no action was required.

In 1941 a command platoon of three tanks was added to each tank company, increasing the total strength to nineteen tanks per company. At this time the regiment remained primarily equipped with LT vz. 35s and some obsolete LT vz. 34s. To address this, the armoured inventory was gradually supplemented with LT vz. 38 tanks and newly acquired LT vz. 40s (originally LLT tanks ordered by Lithuania but taken over by Germany and redirected to Slovakia). In October 1941 the armoured regiment was transferred from infantry command to the newly formed Motorised Troops Command, marking a further step in the modernisation and reorganisation of the Slovak armoured forces.

The Little War between Hungary and Slovakia (March 1939)

In mid-March 1939 Hungary seized the opportunity to reclaim parts of Carpathian Ruthenia, territories it had lost to Czechoslovakia after the First World War. The newly established Slovak Republic, recognising the imminent threat, mobilised an improvised defense force primarily drawn from the 17th Infantry Division and elements of artillery units. This ad hoc corps was equipped with nine LT vz. 35 light tanks and eight OA vz. 30 armoured cars. These vehicles had previously served in Carpathian Ruthenia and were interned by the Slovak army after retreating across the new border. However, before their abandonment, Czechoslovak crews had deliberately sabotaged the vehicles, leaving them in need of repair.

Hungary launched its invasion during the night of 22/23 March 1939, rapidly advancing to a line stretching from Remetské Hamre through Ruskovce, Jesenov and Bunkovce to Blatné Remety.

On the morning of 24 March a newly formed Slovak armoured car platoon departed Prešov. Due to a lack of repair facilities, the LT vz. 35 tanks could not be restored to operational condition in time, leaving the armoured car platoon as the only functional armoured unit available to the Slovak army. Upon arrival at the front, the platoon was ordered to conduct an immediate counterattack near Zavadka. However, the assault quickly stalled under intense machine-gun and artillery fire. The accompanying infantry was forced to retreat, and one OA vz. 30 was knocked out by an anti-tank gun. The withdrawal turned into a disorderly rout, but the arrival of reserves and experienced officers helped stabilise the situation.

Later that evening, another group of armoured vehicles reached Michalovce, dispatched by the Assault Vehicle Regiment. This reinforcement included four OA vz. 30 armoured cars and three LT vz. 35 tanks. The armoured cars were immediately sent to Gajdoš, with orders to halt the infantry's retreat and re-establish a defensive line—a mission they successfully completed.

By the morning of 25 March approximately fifteen thousand Slovak troops had assembled in Michalovce for a decisive counteroffensive. Supported by light tanks and armoured cars, Slovak forces successfully retook Zavadka, Fetisovce, Hnojné and both Vyšná and Nižná Revistia. Further advances were halted when a ceasefire agreement was signed later that day.

The brief but intense conflict, later known as the 'Little War', resulted in twenty-five Hungarian soldiers killed and fifty-six wounded, while Slovak losses included twenty-two killed and several dozen wounded. The Hungarians also captured 360 Slovak soldiers and 311 Czechs.

Above and left: An LT vz. 35 that came into Hungarian hands in March 1939 after being abandoned by retreating Czechoslovak forces near the town of Michalovce. The tank had suffered a fire—reportedly the result of a non-combat-related accident—during the chaotic withdrawal. It was eventually refurbished and brought into service with the Royal Hungarian Army. (*AC/PD*)

Above: A damaged OA vz. 30 armoured car captured by Hungarian forces during their counterattack at Ubrež, approximately 10 kilometres east of Michalovce, on 23 March 1939. The retreating crew had removed both machine guns before abandoning the vehicle. (*AC*)

Below: A platoon of Italian-built Ansaldo L3/35 tankettes of the Royal Hungarian Army photographed in Chust, Carpathian Ruthenia, on 16 March 1939. The crewmen are wearing M1937 brown leather protective helmets and M1935 leather tunics. (*AC/PD*)

A Hungarian soldier stands guard over an LT vz. 35 (serial no. 13.903), which was damaged by an anti-tank gun on 15 March 1939 near Fančíkova. The vehicle was later repaired and incorporated into Hungarian service. (*AC/PD*)

An LT vz. 35 in Hungarian service during field manoeuvres. The picture-in-picture shows the typical markings applied to this type: a white beam cross on a square black background painted on the hull side, along with a small Hungarian army emblem displayed on the turret sides. (*AC*)

Two LT vz. 34 tanks were lost during skirmishes: the first was destroyed by a Hungarian PaK 35/36 anti-tank gun, killing the driver and igniting the tank, while the second, tank no. 13.673, caught fire near Michalovce. The crew managed to escape, but the vehicle was abandoned. Both wrecks were later recovered by Hungarian forces and sent to the Škoda Works, now under German administration, for repair. Initially, Škoda demanded 645,000 Kč/Czechoslovak crowns (approximately 26,000 dollars) for the work. However, after Hungary secured a licence to produce the Turán tank, Škoda agreed to complete the repairs free of charge. The restored tanks were re-designated 1H-406 and 1H-407 and were used for training purposes at the Armoured Training Centre in Esztergom-Tábor until the end of 1943.

War with Poland (September 1939)

In September 1939 Slovakia committed a contingent of its armed forces to support the German invasion of Poland, partly in response to Poland's occupation of Czechoslovak territory during the Munich Crisis in September 1938. The invasion began at 5 am on 1 September 1939. Slovak forces, consisting of four infantry divisions and an armoured vehicle company, advanced into southern Poland with minimal resistance. The armoured element comprised a platoon of four OA vz. 30 armoured cars and a platoon of three LT vz. 35 light tanks. The defending Polish Karpaty army, responsible for the southern border, lacked any significant armoured units and possessed only limited artillery, leaving it ill-equipped to repel the Slovak incursion.

The 1st Slovak Division captured Zakopane and pushed approximately 30 kilometres north towards Nowy Targ before withdrawing back across the border on 9 September. Simultaneously, the 3rd Division coordinated its advance with the German XVIII Mountain Corps, following an axis through Jasło-Krosno-Sanok. Slovak units penetrated up to 90 kilometres into Polish territory, encountering only sporadic resistance. One notable incident occurred on 3 September, when a detachment of four OA vz. 30 armoured cars, accompanied by cavalry, entered the town square of Tylicz. They encountered unexpectedly strong Polish resistance and were forced to withdraw due to a lack of sufficient infantry support.

In response to early battlefield developments, on 5 September the Slovak High Command ordered the formation of a mobile, combined-arms task force, codenamed

Slovak LT vz. 35 tanks crossing what is likely the Jasiołka river, a few kilometres from the Polish town of Dukla, en route to Sanok during the 1939 invasion of Poland. (*AC*)

A Slovak LT vz. 35 (serial no. 13.834) manoeuvring through a wooded area during the invasion of Poland. The LT vz. 35 was capable of uprooting trees with trunk diameters of up to 35 centimetres. (*AC*)

A platoon of LT vz. 35 tanks passing through a Polish village, preceded by a staff car—likely a Tatra 57 model. A total of forty-five Tatra 57s and 243 of the upgraded 57a variant were produced for the Czechoslovak armed forces. (*AC*)

Kalinčiak. This unit initially consisted of a tank platoon with thirteen LT vz. 35 tanks, an armoured car platoon with six OA vz. 30 vehicles, and supporting elements including cyclists, cavalry and anti-tank detachments. On 7 September the *Kalinčiak* unit moved to Brekov, where it absorbed an assault vehicle company previously attached to the 2nd Division, increasing its armoured strength to nineteen LT vz. 35 tanks. The combined force was then repositioned from the Poprad-Brezno area to the Stropkov-Svidník sector.

Polish resistance faced by Slovak units was primarily composed of light infantry with limited anti-tank capabilities. By this stage, the Polish front was already collapsing under sustained German pressure. Consequently, Slovak tanks saw little direct combat. Their primary role became one of psychological impact and deterrence, providing mobile firepower and rapid exploitation potential. However, due to the swift German advance, few opportunities for independent offensive armoured operations presented themselves.

War with the Soviet Union (1941)

When Germany launched its invasion of the Soviet Union on 22 June 1941, the Slovak Republic joined the offensive under the terms of mutual alliance agreements. Slovakia thus became part of the German-led 'European Anti-Bolshevik Coalition', which also included Finland, Romania and Hungary.

To support the campaign, Slovakia assembled an improvised motorised formation known as the Rapid Group (*Rýchla skupina*, or RS), which included a small armoured detachment. By the morning of 25 June the Rapid Group was concentrated and ready to deploy to the front. It consisted of 1,910 personnel, artillery support and an armoured component comprising three OA vz. 30 armoured cars, forty-seven tanks (thirty LT vz. 35s, ten LT vz. 38s and seven LT vz. 40s), along with over 230 trucks and staff vehicles. Later that day, the Rapid Group crossed into Soviet territory via the German–Soviet demarcation line established after the partition of Poland on 17 September 1939. The first Soviet resistance was encountered near Wojtkowa, north of Krościenko, where the LT vz. 35 tanks made their combat debut. Although the Red Army was temporarily pushed back, the Rapid Group nearly lost an undamaged LT vz. 35 to Soviet forces; it was only saved by the quick thinking of its crew. Skirmishes continued in the area.

At 8 am on 27 June a platoon from the 3rd Tank Company advanced from positions near Trzcianiec but found that Soviet forces had withdrawn during the night. German units assumed the pursuit, and the Slovak tanks returned to their previous positions. Later that day the Slovak advance was redirected westwards, along the Kuzmina-Tyrawa/Wołoska-Załuż axis, towards the Molotov Line, a series of defensive bunkers armed with machine guns. Though still under construction, the line posed a significant obstacle. Slovak tanks, including LT vz. 35s, fired at the bunkers' embrasures, providing covering fire for infantry advances, albeit with limited effect.

When infantry failed to neutralise the defences, Slovak combat engineers advanced from the rear through wooded terrain. After several hours of fighting, nine of the thirteen bunkers near Załuż were captured. The remaining four were encircled and later secured on 3–4 July by Infantry Regiment 5 of the 2nd Division. With the fortified zone around Załuż breached, Slovak forces occupied Olchowce, Monastirzec and Tyrawa Wołoska by 7 pm, allowing the German 454th Infantry Division to finally cross the San river, five days after the launch of Operation Barbarossa.

On 28 June the Rapid Group was ordered to advance eastwards along the Załuż-Kuzmina-Krościenko-Chyrów-Dobromil-Nowe Miasto Przemyskie-Bylice route towards the Sadkowice-Koniuszki area. Its mission was to block the southern and southeastern passes and to dispatch an advance unit to Komarno to seize river crossings over the Vereshytsia river. The Group's progress was delayed due to a

The Slovak RS included a specialised armoured car component that consisted of three OA vz. 30 vehicles, primarily employed for reconnaissance and scouting missions, operating ahead of the main tank formations. Their role was to gather intelligence on enemy positions, terrain and potential obstacles, providing critical information to the advancing units. (*AC*)

When on the move, in non-combat conditions, the LT vz. 35 crews often chose to sit in the open hatches rather than remain fully enclosed inside the tank. This practice gave them the best possible view of their surroundings, which was particularly helpful when driving such heavy machinery. Since tanks like the LT vz. 35 could be challenging to manoeuvre, having a clear, unobstructed view helped the crew navigate obstacles, avoid hazards and maintain better spatial awareness. (*AC*)

damaged bridge south of Wojtkowa, which collapsed under the weight of an LT vz. 35, dropping it 5 metres into a ravine. Fortunately, no crew members were injured. After effecting repairs, the Group reached Chyrów, where local Polish and Ukrainian residents welcomed the Slovaks as liberators from communist rule.

On 1 July 1941 the Group received new orders to advance south through Sambor, towards Drohobycz and Stryi. Slovak reconnaissance units entered Stryi the next day without resistance, as Soviet forces had already withdrawn.

This LT vz. 35 (tactical no. 121, serial no. 13.855) of the 1st Company RS is seen here at the rear of a long marching column, awaiting the order to advance. The open engine access hatch is noteworthy—it was often left ajar during movement breaks to help cool down the engine, which had a tendency to overheat during the hot summer of 1941. (AC)

'Škodas' of the 1st Company RS parked for an overnight halt. Note the use of foliage to camouflage the tanks. Although the Luftwaffe maintained air superiority, it could not completely prevent individual Soviet bombers from conducting suicidal attacks against armoured formations. (AC)

An OA vz. 30 armoured car passing a long column of heavy trucks used to transport motorised infantry. The Slovak RS/RB employed a variety of four- and six-wheel-drive vehicles, with the Praga RV being the most prominent model in service. (*AC*)

Upon entering the Sambor area on 2 July, ten LT vz. 35 tanks were left behind due to mechanical failures—one had burned out entirely. At least two tanks were intentionally disabled by members of the Assault Vehicle Battalion. The disabled tanks were grouped and later returned to Slovakia. Including an LT vz. 38 lost near Zaluż, the battalion had lost eleven tanks. To compensate, a platoon of seven LT vz. 35 tanks was transferred from the Eleventh Army's Armoured Company to the Rapid Group. Between 5 and 7 July the Rapid Group was reorganised into the Rapid Brigade (*Rýchla brigade*, or RB), reinforced with elements from the 1st and 2nd Divisions, Artillery Regiment 11 and other support units. The Assault Vehicle Battalion was reorganised into two tank companies equipped with thirty-six light tanks: twenty LT vz. 35s, nine LT vz. 38s and seven LT vz. 40s.

On 9 July the Rapid Brigade moved along the Sambor-Rudki-Lviv-Winniki route towards the Szopki-Winniki-Kurowice sector. The roads were in poor condition due to heavy rains, and many vehicles broke down en route. Some were repaired at PÚV workshops in Sambor (Sambir), while others were sent to German repair facilities in Lviv. The following day, 10 July, the brigade arrived in the area between Szopki and Kurowice, and by 13 July it had reached Gródek, crossing into prewar Soviet territory for the first time.

On 14 July the 17th German Army Command ordered the Slovak Brigade to redeploy to the right flank near Buchach (Buczacz). The movement was carried out without incident, and the unit reached its destination on 15 July. It returned to Gródek the next day, reaching the pre-1939 Soviet border. The following two days were spent repairing vehicles, cleaning weapons and resupplying.

On 21 July the Rapid Brigade resumed its advance eastwards and arrived late that night in Vinnytsia, on the Southern Bug river. The city was still smouldering from earlier fighting between the German 4th Mountain Division and retreating Soviet forces. The Slovak units passed through the city without halting, crossing the river via a makeshift wooden bridge constructed by German engineers. Moving without headlights, the convoy navigated treacherous roads until 1 am on 22 July, when it reached Shchaslyve, halting en route to Lipovets.

THE BATTLE OF LIPOVETS

The town of Lipovets, with a population of around 15,000, was a crucial road junction where the Kalynivka–Haisyn road intersected with a secondary route to Vinnytsia. For a successful withdrawal to their new defensive line, the Soviets had to hold Lipovets. Defending the town was the responsibility of the 44th Mountain Rifle Division, composed of four rifle regiments and two artillery regiments—about eight thousand, five hundred troops in total. Lipovets mainly consisted of single-storey houses with gardens, but it also featured a tractor station, post office, collective farm (*kolkhoz*) and a small sunflower oil processing plant. The streets were unpaved and poorly maintained, typical of many agricultural towns in Ukraine. The town straddled both banks of the upper Sob river, a left tributary of the Southern Bug. The Sob, surrounded by marshes, was generally impassable; however, in summer the water level was low. In Lipovets the river had been regulated, with a key bridge crossing it.

Before the Slovak brigade arrived, the 44th Mountain Rifle Division was preparing a counterattack against the German XXXXIX Mountain Corps. The Slovak advance disrupted these Soviet plans.

River crossings posed a significant challenge for Slovak 'Škoda' tanks during the eastern advance. Fragile wooden bridges were often unable to support the 10-ton weight of the tanks, placing great pressure on the drivers. Fortunately, stranded vehicles could usually be recovered with the help of other tanks. Here, note the removed machine guns and the broken-off cupola hatch on the tank that fell through. (*AC*)

Above: An LT vz. 35 (tactical no. 224) stuck in the Sun river, being prepared for recovery by an LT vz. 40. The photo was taken in early June 1941. (*AC*)

Left: While the LT vz. 35s were deployed for the Soviet campaign, the older LT vz. 34s remained at home, relegated to training duties. (*AC*)

An LT vz. 35 (tactical no. 323, serial no. 13.835), assigned to the 3rd Company RS. The Slovak crew draped a German flag (red with a white circle and black swastika) over the tank turret to serve as an aerial recognition marker. This improvised identification method was intended to prevent attacks by the Luftwaffe, especially given that Slovak camouflage patterns more closely resembled Soviet styles than the standard German dark grey. (*AC*)

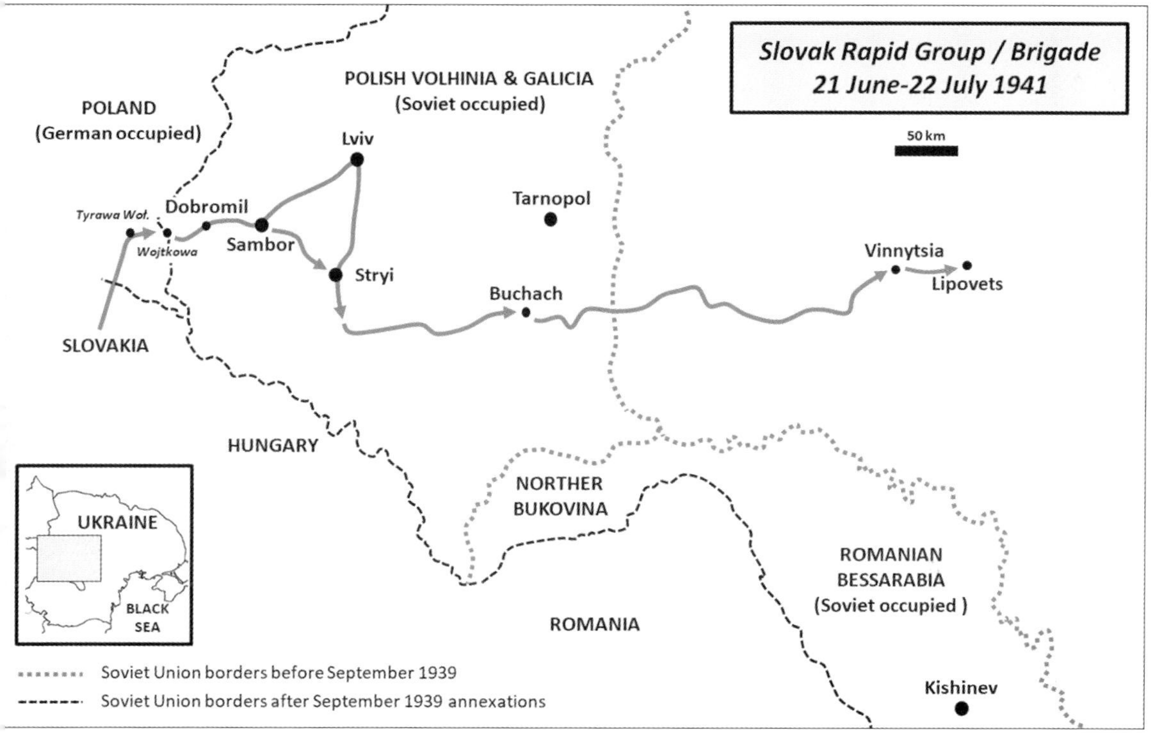

Above: Battle Trail Map of the Slovak RS/RB.

Right: An LT vz. 35 (serial no. 13.848 or 13.840) advancing into the Soviet Union and passing a column of German infantry. Notably, the rear of the turret features a hand-painted skull and crossbones—the only known instance of an individual marking used within the Slovak RB. (*AC*)

At approximately 4 am on 22 July 1941, as dawn broke, the approaching Rapid Brigade—numbering 4,902 men, supported by an artillery contingent and a tank unit—began its assault on Lipovets. Leading the column were three OA vz. 30 armoured cars, followed by two platoons of LT vz. 35 tanks from the 3rd Tank Company, with cyclists and artillery in support. The advancing column stretched over a kilometre in length. As the leading vehicles descended into Lipovets, Soviet artillery and mortar fire began raining down on them. Despite the initial shock, the Slovak troops managed to regroup and continue the attack.

Around 7 am, another two tank platoons from the 3rd Tank Company moved out from Shchaslyve. Due to heavy artillery fire and the mined, muddy terrain, they were unable to support the main infantry thrust along the road. Instead, they advanced along a creek through rolling ground towards the village of Kamionka. Once behind the next ridge, they took up firing positions and began shelling the village with their tank guns.

The Slovak cyclists, unable to dislodge the well-entrenched defenders, called for armoured support. Eight LT vz. 35 tanks responded and moved to assist. Despite neutralising several machine-gun nests, the second Soviet defensive line held firm. Two tanks from the 2nd Platoon then moved forwards to support the infantry directly. They left their positions near Kamionka, crossed the hill and broke through the Soviet lines on the right side of the road under small-arms fire. This manoeuvre allowed the Slovak infantry to occupy parts of the enemy's forward defences by 10 am. Two more LT vz. 35 tanks flanked Soviet positions near Lipovets, advancing from Kamionka. Although they continued pushing forwards, they did not reach the town itself.

By 10 am the forward Slovak units had captured the first Soviet defensive line near the ceremonial bridge, though the strategically important hills in front of Lipovets remained in Soviet hands.

The attack resumed at 12.30 pm, preceded by an artillery barrage. Slovak infantry and tanks advanced to secure the high ground flanking the road to Lipovets. A column of trucks carrying infantry formed along the road, with anti-tank batteries deployed in support. The tanks were tasked with protecting this column. However, Soviet artillery struck first, landing accurate and devastating fire along the route, destroying Slovak vehicles one by one. The Slovak artillery responded, and a prolonged exchange ensued for over an hour.

This LT vz. 35 (tactical no. 125) of the 1st Company RB is displaying a small Slovak national flag mounted on its radio antenna, which served as a quick identification marker. (*AC*)

Above: This LT vz. 35 (tactical no. 222, serial no. 13.838) was supplied by Skoda initially to PÚV-3. During the campaign in the Soviet Union it was assigned to the 2nd Company RB. (*AC*)

Below: Slovak LT vz. 35 tanks undergoing field repairs, which typically involved replacing road wheels, fixing track links, and addressing engine or gearbox problems. Due to limited spare parts and logistical support, many repairs had to be improvised using salvaged components or field-made tools. (*AC*)

By 4.30 pm the forward units had reached the outskirts of Lipovets. Reconnaissance patrols reported heavily fortified Soviet positions. During the fighting a mortar shell struck the turret of an LT vz. 35, killing its commander and severely damaging the vehicle. Another tank, an LT vz. 40, was hit by an anti-tank round, though the crew survived. Around the same time the 3rd Tank Company, which had been fighting near

Feliksówka and Kamionka, began withdrawing. Two LT vz. 35s became stuck in a muddy riverbed and were abandoned—one was destroyed by Soviet forces that night.

That evening Colonel Polifousek ordered a general regrouping. At around 10 pm Slovak units began their retreat. During the withdrawal, another LT vz. 35 was hit and abandoned, and one LT vz. 38 was destroyed. The following morning it was discovered that the Soviet forces had withdrawn from Lipovets during the night, and the town was taken without a fight. However, Slovak losses were considerable, including three LT vz. 35s and one LT vz. 40.

The Battle of Lipovets exposed numerous weaknesses within the Slovak Rapid Brigade. Its soldiers were poorly trained and inadequately led. German reports noted that Slovak troops panicked easily and that officers were often unable to restore order.

Shortly afterwards, the brigade's tank repair workshop command reported that it was incapable of repairing damaged vehicles in the field and recommended sending the tanks back to Slovakia. In reality, this was a deliberate effort—an internal conspiracy— to withdraw armoured assets from the front and preserve them for national defence. The plan succeeded. The armoured battalion was sent first to Tarnopol (Ternopil), then by train to Sambor (Sambir) and eventually back to Turčiansky Svätý Martin. On 1 January 1942 official records stated that none of the twenty-seven LT vz. 34 tanks was operational, and only seven of the forty-nine LT vz. 35s were combat-ready.

This LT vz. 35 (tactical no. 315, serial no. 13.835) was produced by Skoda in April 1937 and supplied to the Slovak-based PÚV-3. During the campaign in the Soviet Union it was assigned to the 3rd Company RB. (*AC*)

Above: One of the three LT vz. 35s destroyed near Lipovets on 22 July 1941. Standing atop the wreck is Major Dobrotka, commander of the Slovak Armoured Regiment within the RB. (*AC*)

Right: LT vz. 35 (tactical no. 325, serial no. 13.849) of the 3rd Company RB. Tanks of the 3rd Company were not marked with the Slovak national double cross. (*AC*)

However, the actual situation was far better—most of the supposedly 'written off' tanks could be easily repaired when spare parts became available. The workshop staff deliberately prolonged the process, inventing faults to avoid sending the tanks back into combat. While the LT vz. 35s were kept in reserve, the Ministry of National Defence decided to strengthen its front-line divisions with other tanks purchased from German stocks, including several LT vz. 40s and LT vz. 38s.

As of 23 May 1944 the Slovak-based PÚV still had forty-six LT vz. 35s, though its primary combat vehicles were now sixty-three LT vz. 38s. These were supplemented by sixteen PzKpfw IIs, five PzKpfw IIIs and eighteen Marder III tank destroyers.

The Slovak National Uprising (August–October 1944)

Romania's defection to the Soviet side in August 1944 caused alarm in Berlin and raised fears that other German satellite states in East and Central Europe might follow suit. To prevent a similar development, and to secure Slovakia against the advancing Red Army, German forces crossed Slovakia's northeastern border on the evening of 29 August 1944. In response, the Slovak National Uprising (SNP) broke out the same day. Among the German units tasked with suppressing the uprising was the improvised SS Division Tatra, which was primarily equipped with standard German tanks. However, some sources suggest it may have also operated a few LT vz. 35 tanks.

At the time, the Slovaks still had forty-six LT vz. 35 tanks in storage at the barracks in Turčiansky Svätý Martin. Of these, however, only about five were in combat-ready condition.

On 2 September 1944 four LT vz. 35s that had been restored to working condition by the local workshop in Turčiansky Svätý Martin were moved to Dubná Skala. The following day they formed a tank platoon that was caught off guard by two German medium tanks. Three of the 'Škoda' tanks were destroyed, and the fourth was knocked out by an anti-tank gun.

On 8 September another LT vz. 35 was repaired and assigned to a tank platoon tasked with defending Turčiansky Svätý Martin. After a general retreat, the platoon withdrew to Zvolen. On 22 September it was integrated into the IV Tactical Group.

Non-operational LT vz. 35s were evacuated from the Turčiansky Sv. Martin barracks using half-track tractors and transferred to the nearby railway station, from where they were transported by rail to Môťová near Zvolen. At least thirty-two tanks arrived there. Twelve of these were stripped of turrets or otherwise modified to assist in the construction and repair of improvised armoured trains (IPV-I, IPV-II and IPV-III).

Following orders from General Ján Golian, commander of the insurgent forces, non-operational LT vz. 35s were to be entrenched in fixed turret-down positions and used as stationary firing points. This task fell to the Engineering Battalion. Between 19 and 23 September 1944 twelve LT vz. 34 and LT vz. 35 tanks were entrenched near Svätý Kríž nad Hronom, as well as around Trnavá Hora and Jalná. Additional tanks were positioned along the Svätý Kríž–Zvolen road and near the Stará Kremnička–Hronská Breznica railway line, under the command of Lieutenant Jozef Ľ. Gandel. Another tank was dug in near Čremošné, at the confluence of the Biela Voda and Žarnovica streams.

Between 23 September and 10 October 1944 six more LT vz. 35s were entrenched in the area around Banská Bystrica (notably near Kremnička). These tanks had little tactical effect, however, and were often abandoned by their crews during combat. Some were later destroyed by German forces, while others were captured. After German forces captured the barracks of the Slovak PÚV, several LT vz. 35s likely fell into the hands of SS Division Tatra, although their exact fate remains unclear.

Above: LT vz. 35s, recently returned from the Russian campaign, being washed at the barracks in Turčiansky Svätý Martin. The vehicles still retain their original three-tone disruptive camouflage. However, those that underwent a general overhaul were likely repainted in overall green. (*AC*)

Below: On 27 October 1944, during the general retreat of the Slovak resistance units during the Slovak National Uprising, LT vz. 35s (serial no. 13.802 and serial no. 13.855) were part of the column retreating through Staré Hory. Tank serial no. 13.802 was abandoned at Donovaly near an improvised airport, and tank 13.855 retreated through Donovaly and was parked near Kečka, where its wreck remained until 1949. (*AC/PD*)

Several Slovak LT vz. 35s captured by the Germans during the Uprising were disarmed and repurposed to build a barricade protecting the Radiotechna/Telefunken factory in Přelouč in early May 1945. Before the arrival of the Red Army, the German garrison in the city was disarmed by local insurgents. (*Collection of the Přelouč Regional Museum*)

By the end of September the defenders of Turčiansky Svätý Martin had only one operational LT vz. 35; this was transferred to Kremnica, where it joined remnants of another platoon equipped with two LT vz. 38 tanks. On 30 September this detachment supported the 2nd Company of the 32nd Infantry Battalion in combat against SS Division Tatra. After the fall of Kremnica on 6 October, the last LT vz. 35 became bogged down at a crossroads near Skalka. The following day it was attacked by German tanks and aircraft but somehow managed to escape to the Görgely Tunnel, where it was repurposed as a recovery vehicle for the retreating forces. On 8 October it was moved to Tajov and later to Banská Bystrica and Môťová. Slovak sources also mention the use of one LT vz. 35 in October 1944 by the 'Vojtech' Battalion, with another possibly assigned to a reserve unit.

On 25 October two LT vz. 35s were deployed near the Tri Duby airfield, supporting a reconnaissance unit of the 2nd Czechoslovak Parachute Brigade. During the general retreat on 27 October both tanks withdrew through Staré Hory. One was abandoned near a makeshift airfield at Donovaly. The second tank continued past Donovaly but was abandoned beneath Kečka Hill, where it remained a wreck until 1949.

While the use of LT vz. 35s during the Slovak National Uprising was extensive, the tank's tactical success was extremely limited. By late 1944 the vehicle's outdated armour and weak armament were no match for modern German armoured fighting vehicles.

7

In Romanian Army Service

During the 1930s Romania was a member of France's 'Little Entente' alliance in Central Europe, and its military procurement reflected this orientation. Most of its equipment came from France (tanks) or from France-allied nations in Central Europe such as Czechoslovakia (tanks) and Poland (aircraft).

In the mid-1920s Romania operated only Renault FT-17 tanks, which formed the backbone of its early armoured forces, concentrated within the Tank Battalion based in Bucharest. It was only in the mid-1930s that Romania decided to expand its armoured forces to full regimental strength—specifically through the formation of the 1st Tank Regiment (*Regimentul 1 Care de Luptă*, or Rg.1.Cl.)—and turned to Czechoslovak manufacturers, particularly Škoda, to acquire modern tankettes and light tanks. After lengthy negotiations with both ČKD and Škoda, the Romanian Ministry of Defence decided in 1936 to purchase 126 Škoda S-II-aR light tanks (a slightly modified LT vz. 35 model). In Romanian service these vehicles were known as the R-2 (short for *tanc uşor* R-2).

Romanian officials requested a prototype within three months, and in the summer of 1937 demanded the immediate delivery of fifteen tanks. To meet this demand, Škoda was forced to redirect vehicles from batches originally intended for the Czechoslovak army. However, these tanks were still plagued by technical issues, which led the Romanians to begin questioning the quality and reliability of the design. The final prototype was not approved until August 1938. Production of the R-2 then commenced and continued from 1 September 1938 to 22 February 1939. The first fifteen vehicles were upgraded to match the approved prototype's specifications.

Škoda also attempted to sell to the Romanians a manufacturing licence for the R-2. The offer included a plan for local production of 280 R-2 tanks at the Malaxa Works in Bucharest, but this project never materialised. Although an improved version of the S-II-aR was demonstrated in Romania in the autumn of 1939, the Romanians declined the licence proposal.

During production and delivery of the tanks, the Romanian army insisted on several technical modifications. As a result, the latter half of the order—designated R-2c (*cimentate*)—featured a modified turret design. These tanks had a rear turret plate composed of two flat armour plates joined in a shallow 'V' shape, replacing the original single curved plate used in the first sixty-three units.

To supplement the Czechoslovak tanks, in May 1938 Romania placed an additional order for fifty French Renault R-35 infantry tanks. But the tank supply to Romania was abruptly cut off by the Munich Crisis and the outbreak of Second World War in September 1939. A minor boost to its armoured inventory came later that month, however, when elements of the Polish 21st Armoured Battalion crossed into Romania following Poland's collapse. This added twenty-three Renault R-35s to the Romanian army, increasing its total to seventy-three of that type.

In early 1940 the new R-2s were assigned to Rg.1.Cl. Alongside the 2nd Tank Regiment (Rg.2.Cl.), equipped with R-35s, they formed part of the Motorised Mechanised Brigade (*Brigada Moto-Mecanizată*).

R-2s of the Romanian Rg.1.Cl. parade before enthusiastic crowds of civilians. Events like this were both a demonstration of national pride and an opportunity to familiarise the public with the country's modern military capabilities. (*AC*)

An R-2 in central Bucharest, near the historic Fire Tower built in 1890. The tower once served as an observation post for firemen and now overlooks this display of modern military strength. (*AC*)

Above: A close-up view of the R-2c variant, featuring the distinctive 'V'-shaped turret rear. This design, unique to Romanian-built Škodas, used angled armour plates to deflect incoming rounds and improve ballistic protection. (*AC*)

Below: An R-2 likely photographed on its return from winter manoeuvres at the turn of 1940/1941. Interestingly, the tank commander standing in the cupola is wearing a garrison cap instead of the standard black beret, suggesting the photo may have been staged as a commemorative image. (*AC*)

Left and below: R-2 tanks were used to suppress the uprising by members of the so-called Iron Guard (*Garda de Fier*) in Bucharest in January 1941. With political support from Adolf Hitler, the Romanian army successfully crushed the rebellion. (*Photos by Willy Pragher*)

Rg.1.Cl. consisted of two tank battalions. Each battalion included a headquarters platoon (with two R-2s and four anti-aircraft guns) and three tank companies, each with sixteen R-2s. Additionally, each battalion had a workshop company (with three R-2s), and the regiment itself was supported by a regimental HQ platoon (with two R-2s) and an anti-tank/anti-aircraft platoon equipped with four 47mm anti-tank guns and two anti-aircraft guns.

Romania's efforts to strengthen its armoured forces met with only limited success, as in May 1940 France surrendered to Germany, leaving Romania without any strategic allies. This vulnerability was quickly exploited by its traditional adversaries—the Soviet Union and Hungary. On 28 June 1940 the Soviet Union issued an ultimatum demanding that Romania cede to it Bessarabia and Northern Bukovina. With no prospect of Western assistance, and under threat of force, the Romanian government acquiesced. Germany did not object to the Soviet demands, having already agreed to Soviet claims on the region under the secret terms of the Molotov-Ribbentrop Pact.

Soon afterwards, Romania lost Northern Transylvania to Hungary in the Second Vienna Award, a deal mediated by Nazi Germany and Fascist Italy. Isolated and diplomatically weakened, Romania experienced significant internal unrest. In the wake of these territorial losses, former Chief of the General Staff Ion Antonescu seized power in September 1940 and sought closer alignment with Nazi Germany. He hoped that by supporting Germany, Romania might regain Bessarabia and perhaps recover other lost territories—particularly Northern Transylvania, long contested with Hungary. In October 1940 German troops began arriving in Romania under the pretext of protecting it from British sabotage and influence.

In the spring of 1941, with the help of instructors from Germany's 13th and 16th Panzer divisions, Romania established its 1st Armoured Division (*Divizia 1 Blindată*, or D.1.Bl.) on 17 April. The unit was hastily built around a motorised brigade that had been originally formed in 1935. Training cooperation between Romanian and German personnel varied in effectiveness. Romanian artillery units, in particular, were reluctant to adopt German doctrine. Command of the new division was given to Brigadier General Ioan Sion, who, despite his lack of experience with armoured warfare, carried out his duties competently.

While still undergoing training, the division deployed to the Soviet border in April 1941 in preparation for Operation Barbarossa, Germany's invasion of the USSR. Romania's initial role was to reclaim Bessarabia and Northern Bukovina. Although some in the Romanian command believed the campaign would be limited to retaking those territories, it is likely that both military and political leaders understood that further engagement against the Soviet Union would be necessary to secure and retain their strategic gains.

The Liberation of Bessarabia (June–August 1941)

On 22 June 1941 Romania declared war on the USSR. To meet its obligations, it formed the Romanian Antonescu Army Group, composed of the Romanian Third and Fourth armies and the German Eleventh Army, which could field a combined force of twenty divisions (including six German) and six brigades. This force was tasked with launching an offensive against the Soviet Twelfth Army of the Kiev Military District. The Soviets already had six rifle divisions deployed in Bukovina; later reinforcements from the Odessa Military District brought in seven additional rifle divisions, two cavalry divisions and five fortified sectors along the border manned by NKVD border guards.

Crucially, the Soviet defences included the II and XVIII mechanised corps, with four tank divisions and two mechanised divisions—totalling over 760 tanks, including approximately sixty newly introduced KV-1 and T-34 models. The remainder consisted of large numbers of older T-26 and BT series tanks. While these older models were roughly comparable to the Romanian R-2 light tanks, the newer Soviet medium and heavy tanks outclassed them completely.

D.1.Bl., commanded by Brigadier General Ioan Sion—a career artillery officer with no prior experience in manoeuvre warfare—was deployed to Moldavia. The division

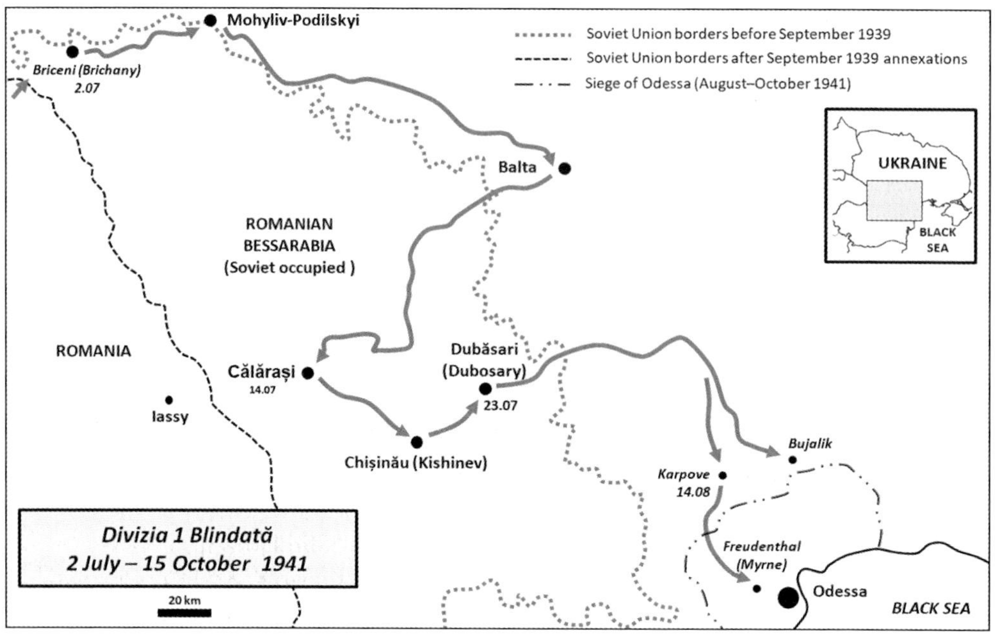

Above: Battle Trail Map of Rg.1.Cl.

Below: An R-2 crew, in black berets, taking a rest in a village in Bessarabia, 1941. Note the Romanian and German infantrymen standing on the left, each wearing their distinctive helmet types. The German M1935 helmet features a flared rim with extended neck protection, metal grommeted ventilation holes, and a complex multi-pad leather liner, making it heavier and more protective. In contrast, the Romanian Model 1938 helmet has a more rounded, shallower dome with simple punched ventilation holes and a simpler leather liner, reflecting a lighter, less angular design influenced by French Adrian helmets. (*AC*)

During breaks in combat the barrels of guns and machine guns were covered with special protective sleeves designed to shield the weapons from dust and dirt. (*AC*)

Above left and above right: Romanian and German troops entered Chişinău (Kishinev) on 16 July 1941; by 6 am R-2s had reached the northern outskirts of the city and by 8 am, under the command of Major Spirescu, they had captured the Old Post Office. From there, they advanced towards the city centre, followed by mechanised infantry. The quickest route was via Pavlov Street (today's Petru Rareş and Eugen Doga streets). Overcoming relatively weak resistance, the tanks captured the city centre, around the Cathedral. Another clash occurred at the Cathedral with Soviet cavalry hiding in the park. Some Romanian tanks moved to the southern part of the city to block the Soviet retreat but were destroyed by Soviet artillery on the Hînceşti highway near today's Telecentru area. Another group headed from the centre towards the railway station; several tanks remained there on guard while the others returned to the Old Post Office. (*AC*)

An R-2 on fire in front of the Cathedral of the Nativity of Christ in Chişinău (Kishinev). (*AC*)

spearheaded the Romanian Cavalry Corps, advancing alongside the 6th Infantry Division and 5 and 6 Cavalry Brigades through Bukovina towards Mogilev, in coordination with the German XI Army Corps. The German corps had no tanks but was supported by two assault gun batteries from *Sturmgeschütz-Abteilung* 190.

Although Operation Barbarossa began on 22 June 1941, the Romanian front remained relatively quiet for the next ten days, with only minor skirmishes and limited Soviet air raids, including ineffective attacks on the Ploieşti oil fields. The Soviets also launched small amphibious operations in the Danube Delta. Eventually, Romanian forces secured a bridgehead across the Prut river, and the broader offensive—codenamed 'München' (Munich)—began in earnest against a well prepared Soviet defence.

On 3 July D.1.Bl. crossed the Prut following the successful German XI Corps bridgehead and pushed towards the Dniester river. However, due to logistical and mechanical constraints, the division was already not operating at full strength. Rg.2.Cl., equipped with slow and lightly armoured Renault R-35s, could not keep up with the mobile operations and was reassigned to the Romanian III Corps of Fourth Army, where its tanks were more suited for infantry support roles.

Meanwhile, Rg.1.Cl., equipped with R-2 tanks, remained with D.1.Bl.—by this point effectively reorganised as a reinforced brigade—and entered combat on 4 July with the objective of capturing Brînzeni (Brynzeny). There, Romanian tanks encountered Soviet armour for the first time. In one engagement a Romanian tank platoon reportedly faced about a dozen Soviet tanks and, according to Romanian accounts, lost one R-2 while destroying two enemy tanks (likely T-26s, misidentified as T-28s).

After securing Brînzeni, the division advanced towards the Dniester, losing most of its vehicles to mechanical failures rather than enemy fire. However, it also captured several abandoned Soviet tanks. By 8 July it had reached the river. General Sion continued the push southwards, encountering scattered Soviet resistance before the Red Army retreated across the eastern bank to the fortified Stalin Line.

The Romanian armoured division then played a key role in the capture of Balta, approaching from the north and putting pressure on the hills of the Cornesti Massif (*Kornestiyskyi masyv*), which was stalling the 4th Army's advance.

R-2 tanks of the 5th Company Rg.1.Cl., photographed near the front line in a loose formation to minimise the risk of multiple vehicles being damaged by a single heavy shell burst. Such a formation also provided greater flexibility for evasive manoeuvres and rapid dispersal in case of emergency. (*AC*)

A Romanian tank driver inspects the Škoda engine, known for its tendency to overheat—an issue compounded by the fact that it was not originally designed for long, continuous marches over several weeks. As a temporary solution, crews cooled the engine manually by opening the hatches during halts. In more desperate situations, they even drove with the engine hatches open, despite the risk of dust intake, which could severely damage the engine. (*AC*)

R-2 tanks advancing across the open steppe, with Romanian infantry moving ahead while the tanks are temporarily halted. Foot soldiers were often sent forwards to scout villages or check for possible ambushes before the tanks proceeded. (*AC*)

On 14 July the division led the LIV Army Corps (composed of three infantry divisions, including one Romanian) in an attack on Soviet positions at Călăraşi (Kalarash). Romanian R-2 tanks successfully outflanked the Soviet defences, reportedly surprising and overrunning elements of the Soviet XXXV Rifle Corps' artillery, at the cost of only two R-2 tanks.

The following day, 15 July, the Soviet 47th Tank Division launched a counterattack west of Chişinău (Kishinev), deploying T-26 tanks against Romanian R-2s. On 16 July D.1.Bl. entered Chişinău from the north, destroying Soviet rear guards and losing just one R-2, with five others damaged. The Romanian tanks bypassed the retreating Soviet artillery, which managed to destroy three R-2s but was forced to abandon several of its guns.

On 19 July Soviet forces fully withdrew across the Dniester, while D.1.Bl. turned north to assist advancing German infantry. On 23 July LIV Corps crossed the Dniester at Dubăsari (Dubosary).

Although the Romanian forces had avoided major combat losses by this point, the poor condition of the roads had caused severe mechanical wear to much of their equipment, especially the fragile Czech-designed R-2 tanks.

By the end of July the Romanian strategic objective—the recapture of Bessarabia and Northern Bukovina—had been achieved. However, at Adolf Hitler's direct request, Romania chose to continue its advance beyond its pre-1940 borders, committing to the broader German campaign into Soviet territory.

The Siege of Odessa (August–October 1941)

In early August 1941 the Romanian Third Army and German Eleventh Army continued their advance eastwards, while the Romanian Fourth Army, including D.1.Bl., pivoted to the southeast to encircle the Ukrainian port city of Odessa. The aim was to seize the city in a rapid assault before its defences could be fully reinforced.

After a necessary maintenance pause, General Ioan Sion's understrength armoured 'division' resumed operations. During the night of 5/6 August it crossed the Dniester river and advanced southeastwards towards the town of Bujalik, then turned south towards the coast. On 8 August, as heavy rains turned the terrain to mud and slowed even tracked vehicles, the division encountered Odessa's outer defensive lines.

To the right, along the Voznesensk–Odessa railway, the 1st Cavalry Brigade, supported by R-2 tanks from Rg.1.Cl., pushed back a regiment from the Soviet 95th Rifle Division and encircled parts of its artillery, capturing around two hundred prisoners. However, reinforcements from the Soviet 2nd Cavalry Division, supported by naval infantry and NKVD units, stabilised the front and slowed the Romanian advance.

Soon after, the Romanian high command dispersed D.1.Bl., detaching its artillery, infantry and tanks to support various corps. The R-2 tanks were relegated to supporting infantry units in III Corps, alongside the older Renault R-35s. Starting from 11 August, as the tanks began supporting the 15th Infantry Division—an untrained formation for combined-arms operations—they encountered increasingly organised Soviet resistance.

That day, the R-2s suffered their first significant losses, with five tanks either destroyed or disabled. The following day Soviet naval infantry of the 1st Regiment, supported by a gunboat and 180mm coastal artillery, repelled a number of Romanian attacks. The R-2 tanks, unwilling to advance without infantry cover, remained static.

An R-2 tank pauses briefly in a newly captured Ukrainian town, its armament carefully shielded against dust during the advance. Romanian tanks typically faced only light resistance in most urban areas, and engagements rarely escalated into intense street fighting. (*AC*)

Ukraine is known for its vast, flat steppe terrain—sparsely wooded but ideal for wheat cultivation. While moving through such open areas, R-2 tanks had little to no cover, leaving them vulnerable to long-range fire from well-camouflaged, dug-in anti-tank guns. (*AC*)

An R-2 tank (tactical no. 1101) assigned to the 2nd Battalion HQ Platoon, with one of the commanding officers posing in front of the vehicle. Romanian tank crews of all ranks wore khaki-green denim overalls and black berets. (*AC*)

Above: R-2s (tactical nos 333 and 332) belonging to the 3rd Company Rg.1.Cl. advancing in a tightly packed column formation during a movement to the front. (*AC*)

Below: Maintaining an armoured column on the move required meticulous planning, including in-motion refuelling, often supported by fuel-carrying track-tanks that accompanied the main force. Tank crews were trained to carry out minor repairs on their own, while field engineers intervened only for more serious issues that could render a vehicle immobile. The movement of tanks from rear support areas to forward assembly zones was typically conducted in tight formations to minimise the length of the column—though this increased their vulnerability to air attack. (*AC*)

A Ukrainian peasant woman passes an R-2 light tank (tactical no. 313). The attitude of the Ukrainian population towards the Romanian soldiers varied, ranging from cautious neutrality to moments of guarded cooperation. However, this sentiment was often short-lived, shaped by harsh occupation policies, requisitions and the brutal realities of the Eastern Front. (*AC*)

On 13 August the 72nd Infantry Division arrived from the east with a company of tanks, probably additional R-2s, according to Soviet reports. Yet the attack faltered again and nine more R-2s were destroyed. Continued attacks by the Romanian V Corps failed to achieve a breakthrough. By the evening of 14 August four more tanks had been knocked out. R-2s were vulnerable to artillery and infantry anti-tank tactics, including Molotov cocktails, and suffered heavily when isolated from supporting infantry. As a result of its mounting losses, Rg.1.Cl. was reassigned entirely to III Corps.

Despite these setbacks, the Romanian high command still hoped to capture Odessa quickly. Now that the city was surrounded, they aimed for a decisive breakthrough. The regiment was given a brief rest, during which some R-2s were repaired. However, its combat strength had diminished to about seventy vehicles—more akin to a reinforced battalion than a division.

Sion's division, which had effectively become a brigade, was assigned to exploit a breach near the Karpovo railway station, made by Romanian infantry advancing along the railway from Tiraspol. The assault was to begin before dawn, but the R-2 tanks, having been reassigned, were delayed. On 18 August the attack commenced in darkness, with tanks only arriving at daybreak. Soviet troops from the Fortified Region opened fire at close range, pinning down the infantry. Still the R-2s advanced. To the east, one battalion of the 90th Rifle Regiment was pushed back, but counterfire from artillery and armoured cars forced the tanks to retreat. West of the 161st Regiment several R-2s were destroyed by Molotov cocktails.

In the centre the initial Romanian gains were lost when three R-2s were destroyed near a village defended by remnants of the 95th Rifle Division. After this, the rest of the tanks withdrew. Although Romanian engineers and a few tanks captured the Karpovo station, the offensive failed. Total losses were heavy: eleven R-2s destroyed, twenty-four damaged. This marked the end of major combat operations for Rg.1.Cl., which was henceforth relegated to secondary duties.

By 20 August only twenty R-2s remained operational in what became known as the 'Eftimiu Detachment', led by Lieutenant Colonel Eftimiu. Meanwhile, forty-six damaged tanks were sent back to Târgovişte for overhaul. The Eftimiu Detachment joined I Corps, assigned to attack the town of Freudenthal (a German settlement, today part of Myrne). The mission was not to be a breakthrough but slow, deliberate progress.

On 24 August, during a Soviet counterattack on a nearby village, Eftimiu sent six R-2s to cut off the Soviet 31st Rifle Regiment. Despite NKVD resistance, the Romanians reclaimed the village and held Freudenthal. Around this time, the dwindling R-2 numbers were supplemented by the few remaining R-35s from Rg.2.Cl. On 28 August, after a brief artillery barrage, Eftimiu launched an attack east of Freudenthal but it failed. Fighting continued, and by mid-September the detachment— now renamed the 1st Assault Detachment (*Detaşamentul 1 Asalt*)—was reduced to just twelve R-2s and ten R-35s.

In the face of determined defence by the Soviets, who were preparing to evacuate Odessa by sea to Crimea, the Axis forces failed to effectively disrupt the operation. On 15 October Romanian and German forces discovered that the last Soviet troops

An R-2 travels along a dusty road during the summer of 1941. The crew members are taking advantage of the slow movement to observe their surroundings and ventilate the cramped interior. (*AC/Postcard*)

R-2s of the 2nd Company Rg.1.Cl. march through a Bessarabian city. Urban operations posed significant risks for lightly armoured 'Škodas', as they were especially vulnerable to ambushes, improvised explosives and infantry armed with anti-tank weapons in the close confines of city streets. (*AC*)

R-2 assisted by German soldiers while crossing a town centre paved with cobblestones. After rainfall, the surface became extremely slippery and treacherous, creating hazardous driving conditions and increasing the risk of skidding or loss of control. (*AC*)

had evacuated Odessa the night before. The next day, *Detaşamentul 1 Asalt* entered the abandoned city and captured around seven thousand stragglers. A week later the unit was disbanded. Thus ended the 73-day Siege of Odessa, which cost the Romanian army ninety-three thousand casualties (some sources say ninety-eight thousand) out of three hundred and forty thousand troops committed. Rg.1.Cl. lost twenty-six R-2 tanks destroyed and sixty seriously damaged but repairable. Almost all the rest had suffered mechanical breakdowns or light damage. Following the Soviet evacuation of Odessa, all the R-2s—including damaged and destroyed ones—were returned to Romania for repairs.

In early 1942 forty R-2s were sent back to the Škoda factory in Plzeň for complete overhaul, and another fifty went to the Škoda repair facility in Ploieşti for partial repairs—essentially stripping the regiment of armoured strength. To compensate, at least in part, Germany agreed in October 1941 to sell Romania twenty-six refurbished PzKpfw 35(t) tanks, which were delivered in June–July 1942. Still, the R-2 was hopelessly obsolete against newer Soviet tanks and Romanian pleas for more modern German armour went unanswered.

The Stalingrad Disaster (August 1942–January 1943)

The fully refurbished and retrained D.1.Bl., equipped with 109 R-2 tanks, arrived on the Eastern Front in mid-1942. The division detrained at Stalino on 29 August under the command of General Gheorghe, serving as a mobile reserve for the Romanian Third Army, which was guarding the left flank of the German Sixth Army at Stalingrad. Initially, D.1.Bl. remained away from the combat zone, continuing its training and familiarisation with local conditions but by early October it had moved to the vicinity of the Third Army's headquarters at Chernyshevskaya. During the deployment, twelve R-2 tanks broke down and had to be sent to Dnepropetrovsk for major repairs. Ten replacements arrived later from Romania.

Before engaging in combat, the R-2 crews continued intensive training exercises to prepare for the challenges ahead. As part of these drills, they used several captured Soviet T-34 tanks as live targets to test the effectiveness of their main armament. The crews fired their 3.7cm guns at the T-34s, hoping to assess their ability to penetrate the enemy's armour. To their dismay, they quickly discovered that the 3.7cm guns were almost completely ineffective against the T-34's thick, sloped armour.

These tests also convinced the Germans that the division needed better equipment. Consequently, in October 1942 D.1.Bl. received a small number of PzKpfw III and IV tanks intended to reinforce Rg.1.Cl. These tanks formed a medium company integrated into each of the two R-2 battalions.

While D.1.Bl. was still rearming and retraining, the Soviet counteroffensive began on 19 November 1942. Despite stubborn Romanian resistance, their infantry lines were breached in several places by overwhelming Soviet tank and infantry forces. Army Group B ordered its armoured reserves—including D.1.Bl., now reduced to eighty-four R-2s, nineteen PzKpfw III and IV tanks, and two captured Soviet tanks—to counterattack. On 20 November, D.1.Bl., supported by the 5th Infantry Division's reserves, engaged in heavy fighting between Sredne-Zarinski and Zhirkovski with the Soviet 19 and 216 Tank Brigades, supported by infantry and a 76.2mm anti tank regiment. The division lost twenty-five tanks (five R-2s due to mechanical failure, four Panzers, and at least fourteen R-2s knocked out in combat), but claimed to have destroyed sixty-two Soviet tanks and sixty-one motor vehicles, and taken 332 prisoners.

The following day the division lost an additional twenty tanks amid intense fighting. The situation worsened as Soviet motorised units began dividing and bypassing the weakened Romanian forces. On 22 November D.1.Bl. attempted to break through to 22.Pz.Div., then engaged in fighting the Soviet 8 Tank Brigade. It lost ten more tanks while destroying sixty-five Soviet tanks. The division also suffered heavy losses among its anti-tank units and fuel trucks.

Following the collapse of the overstretched Romanian infantry divisions at Golovski, D.1.Bl. tried to retreat to its depots at Chernyshevskaya. By this time it was down to 50 per cent of its original strength and was running critically low on fuel. However, the Soviets blocked the way, forcing the division to abandon twenty-one R-2 tanks due to lack of fuel. The division eventually regrouped at Oserski with eleven PzKpfw III and IV tanks and nineteen R-2s, many of which had to be towed due to mechanical failures or fuel shortages.

Above: A military parade in Bucharest following the capture of Odessa, October 1941. (*AC/Postcard*)

Right and below: Close-up views of R-2 tanks bearing a large Michael's Cross painted on their engine hatches, facilitating aerial identification. Each tank had an individual registration number displayed on the rear hull, starting with the prefix 'U039' followed by a unique three-digit identifier (for example, U039139, U039247). When stationed on home soil, the tanks were also marked with the King's Crest on both sides of the turret. (*AC/PD*)

Nevertheless, the division participated in further heavy fighting and by 2 December had only three operational tanks and 944 men left. It had suffered over five thousand casualties, and lost 129 tanks and 457 trucks. Despite reinforcement with hastily repaired tanks, it took part in the final defensive battles that culminated in the total destruction of the Romanian Third Army by the end of the year.

From 19 November onwards, the division's irrecoverable vehicle losses totalled seventy-seven R-2s, five PzKpfw IIIs, seven IVs, the two captured Soviet tanks, 457 all-wheel-drive trucks and 335 motorcycles.

On 4 December the surviving combat elements on the Chir river were organised into a detachment under Colonel Nistor. Four repaired tanks returned that day, and in early December they were reinforced by one R-2 tank and 700 men from the division's depots in Romania. The Nistor Detachment (*Detașamentul Nistor*) retained some combat capability and continued fighting the Soviets until the last few days of December, when it was forced to abandon four tanks due to mechanical failures.

On 1 January 1943 the remnants of D.1.Bl. crossed the Donets river at Novoshakhtiorsk and left the operational zone. At that point, it still had forty tanks, mostly unserviceable R-2s held in rear workshops. Rg.1.Cl. lost a total of eighty-one R-2 tanks during the campaign: thirty due to fuel shortages, twenty-four from mechanical failure and twenty-seven destroyed in combat. The survivors of D.1.Bl. had returned to their base in Romania by 31 March 1943. During the subsequent rearmament phase, the Romanians received PzKpfw IV and fifty PzKpfw 38(t) tanks from Germany, relegating the obsolete R-2 tanks to reserve status.

From Iron Cross to Red Star

On 1 April 1943 the Romanian army still possessed fifty-nine R-2 tanks, including some hulks destroyed in 1941, but only sixteen were serviceable.

Table 6. R-2 tank distribution, as at 30 August 1943

Unit	In Service	Under Repair
Rg.1.Cl.	25	30
Rg.2.Cl	0	–
Cavalry and Training	4 (?)	–

For the next year R-2s were mostly used as training vehicles, but with the rapidly advancing Soviet spring offensive of 1944, which threatened to occupy eastern Romania, the Romanian High Command decided to engage all its available tank forces, including some obsolete R-2s, and on 24 February 1944 formed a tank group intended for front-line operations. Named the Cantemir Mixed Tank Group (*Grupul Mixt de Tancuri 'Cantemir'*), it was composed of equipment drawn from Rg.1.Cl. and Rg.2.Cl., and totalled seventy-six armoured fighting vehicles, including a single company of ten R-2 tanks. This group's subunits participated in battles around Rahnîi-Leskovie and Mîtki in Transnistria but it was disbanded shortly afterwards, on 18 April 1944.

Above left and above right: Two photographs taken in sequence during R-2 operations around Stalingrad, possibly in early November 1943, while D.1.Bl. served as a mobile reserve for the Romanian Third Army, tasked with guarding the left flank of the German Sixth Army near Stalingrad. While the division was still in the process of rearming and retraining, the Soviet counteroffensive started. By January 1943, after intense fighting against an enemy with overwhelming advantages in manpower and armour, the Romanians had lost approximately 75 per cent of their R-2 tanks. (*AC/PD*)

One of the few surviving R-2s had returned to its base in Romania by the end of March 1943. (*AC*)

On 20 August 1944 the Soviets launched a massive offensive against Romania, targeting the cities of Iași (Jassy) and Chișinău (Kishiniev), smashing through the Romanian defensive lines. Following his failure to defend Romanian territory, Marshal Antonescu was arrested and King Michai was asked to form a new government. To save Romania from total destruction, an agreement was soon reached with the Soviet Union for Romania to switch sides and join the Allies.

The Romanian armoured forces were then effectively subordinated to Soviet command. In early September they were ordered to halt the offensive of the Hungarian 2nd Army and, from 9 September onwards, to advance towards Târnăveni and Luduș. The Armoured Detachment, supporting the Romanian Fourth Army, was equipped with twelve PzKpfw IV tanks, twelve tank destroyers and twelve (later increased to sixteen) TACAM R-2 tank hunters. These TACAM R-2s were self-propelled anti-tank guns based on the R-2 chassis, built by the Romanian Leonida company between July 1943 and June 1944.

The TACAM R-2 prototype was created between July and September 1943 by removing the R-2 turret and mounting a Soviet ZIS-3 76.2mm M1936 anti-tank gun in an open, lightly armoured superstructure made from armour plates salvaged from captured Soviet BT-7 and T-26 tanks. The gun was modified to use Romanian ammunition (Costinescu-model high explosive and armour-piercing rounds), and the original sights were replaced by Romanian Scptilici anti-tank sights produced by the Romanian Optical Industry (IOR), as well as German panoramic sights. This tank hunter was designated TACAM R-2 (*Tun Anticar cu Afet Mobil*, meaning 'self-propelled anti-tank gun').

After performance and firing tests at the Suditi proving grounds in late 1943, the Mechanised Troops Command approved serial production of TACAM R-2s by the Leonida company. However, work was delayed until late February 1944 due to slow German deliveries of R-2 replacements. By then, the M1936 gun was replaced on the TACAM R-2 by the more modern M1941 L/46 gun.

Table 7. R-2s vs. TACAM R-2s inventory

Type	30 August 1943	25 March 1944	19 July 1944
R-2	59	63	44
TACAM R-2		1	20

Above and opposite above: Romanian sources do not mention any R-2 tanks converted into recovery tractors, but photographs taken during the campaign in the Soviet Union prove that at least one such vehicle existed. This turretless variant was used to tow damaged tanks, including captured Soviet T-26 Model 1939s, which had been incorporated into Romanian service. Interestingly, the Romanians also operated at least one R-2 command tank equipped with a frame antenna. The design of the antenna appeared to be a Romanian modification rather than a standard German PzBefWg 35 (t). (*AC*)

An R-2, identified by the Romanian flag hanging from its radio antenna, is passed by a German *Kübelwagen* on a dusty road—highlighting the coordination between Romanian and German forces on the Eastern Front. The flag served both as a symbol of national identity and as a visual recognition signal to prevent friendly fire in the fluid, multinational operational environment. (*AC*)

By June 1944 twenty R-2 tanks had been converted into TACAM R-2 tank destroyers. However, the conversion of the remaining R-2s was halted after it became clear that the 7.62mm gun was largely ineffective against the newer Soviet IS-series heavy tanks. There were plans to replace it with the more powerful German 8.8cm gun, but these plans were abandoned after Romania switched sides on 23 August 1944.

The TACAM R-2s, organised as the 63rd TACAM Company, appear to have entered service with the 1st Training Armoured Division in late July 1944. They participated in the liberation of Bucharest, Ploieşti and Northern Transylvania up to 26 October 1944, during which ten vehicles were lost.

In November 1944 the remaining vehicles (twelve TACAM R-2s and five R-2s) were issued to Rg.2.Cl., where they formed a mixed company alongside PzKpfw 38(t) tanks. This unit took part in the campaigns in Moravia and Austria in 1945. Only on 14 May 1945, after Germany's final surrender, were the remnants of Rg.2.Cl. formally returned to the Romanian 1st Army. The unit returned with only a single PzKpfw IV tank, as the Soviets had taken most of the damaged vehicles to their own depots for captured equipment. In exchange, they provided Romania with a limited number of captured PzKpfw IVs and StuG IIIs.

The TACAM R-2 combined the obsolete R-2 chassis with a captured Soviet 76mm ZiS-3 model 1942 divisional gun to create a makeshift tank destroyer. Although built in 1944, these vehicles did not see combat until after Romania switched sides in August of that year. By July 1944 a total of twenty units had been produced. In September sixteen of them were deployed to defend the Transylvanian frontier against an Axis counteroffensive launched from Hungary. Later, they were also used on the Czechoslovak front. (*AC/PD*)

Above left and above right: By the time Romanian forces returned to Bucharest on 14 May 1945, none of the TACAM R-2s were officially recorded as operational. However, at least one vehicle survived, and it is preserved today at the Romanian National Military Museum in Bucharest. (*AC*)

8

In Bulgarian Army Service

Bulgaria, as an ally of Germany in the First World War, faced restrictions during the interwar period due to treaty limitations—particularly concerning the possession of armoured forces. As a result, Czechoslovakia was reluctant to negotiate the sale of military equipment to Bulgaria during the 1930s. Ironically, it was only after the German annexation of Czechoslovakia that the Škoda company agreed to enter discussions with Sofia regarding the potential supply of LT vz. 35 tanks. However, the German authorities ultimately intervened and blocked the deal.

In June 1939 a Bulgarian delegation visiting Berlin presented the pressing needs of the Bulgarian Army to both the German Foreign Ministry and the Wehrmacht High Command, requesting the supply of twenty-six light tanks (without specifying the type). In early July the Bulgarian Prime Minister also visited Berlin and requested thirty to forty Czech-made tanks. On 22 July 1939 Hitler decided to prioritise the supply of military equipment to politically important countries, placing Bulgaria at the top of the list. This included fulfilling Bulgaria's request for thirty to forty Czechoslovak tanks.

Following this decision, a Bulgarian military delegation visited Pz.Rgt.11 in Paderborn, where they were introduced to the capabilities of the Czech-built Škoda LT vz. 35 tank. The Bulgarian representatives immediately expressed interest in acquiring twenty-six of these tanks, and the deal was approved by the German authorities. The sale was arranged through AGK (*Ausfuhrgemeinschaft für Kriegsgerät GmbH*), the German war industry's export agency based in Berlin. Each captured tank was priced at 65,000 Reichsmarks, bringing the total contract value to 1,965,000 Reichsmarks. The order also included ten thousand high-explosive shells, five thousand anti-tank rounds, spare parts and maintenance tools. As both parties agreed that refurbished tanks would be delivered, PzKpfw 35(t)s were shipped from Wehrmacht stocks to the Škoda factory in Plzeň for overhaul.

The refurbished tanks—referred to in Bulgaria as the light 'Škoda' tank—arrived in February 1940. They were assigned to the 3rd Armoured Company (*Бронирана рота/Bronirana rota*) of the 1st Armoured Battalion (*Брониран батальон/Bronen battalion*), under the command of Captain Alexander Ivanov Bosilkov. At that time the 1st Company operated fourteen Italian CV33 tankettes, while the 2nd Company was equipped with eight Vickers 6-ton tanks, purchased from Britain in 1938.

From July to November 1940 the Vickers and Škoda tanks were concentrated near the villages of Lozen and Lyubimets in the Svilengrad region, where they were deployed to guard the Turkish border and to participate in joint training exercises with infantry units aimed at improving cooperation in the use of armoured vehicles.

Expansion of Armoured Forces (1940–1944)

On 26 March 1940, during ongoing military negotiations in Berlin, the Bulgarian delegation inquired about the possibility of procuring an additional forty tanks of the same type previously delivered (PzKpfw 35(t)s). In response, on 31 May 1940 the Škoda Works informed Bulgarian representatives that it could supply ten light tanks of the T-11 type—a variant originally intended for Afghanistan but undelivered due to wartime disruptions.

The T-11, structurally based on the LT vz. 35, was fully equipped and cleared for export. It was armed with the Škoda A8 model 1939 37.2mm cannon, a modernised version of the earlier A3 (3.7cm vz. 34). This newer gun featured a short recoil, an internal recoil mechanism, enhanced shell ejection and a semi-automatic breech, but remained compatible with the existing ammunition stock. A formal contract for the purchase of the ten T-11 tanks was signed on 20 June 1940, stipulating delivery by 24 September 1940. The order also included: four thousand high-explosive rounds, a thousand armour-piercing rounds, ten spare track sets, a hundred spare road wheels with rubber rims, and forty spare drive and idler wheels. Deliveries were made in two

The Bulgarian Army's 1st Armoured Battalion paraded through central Sofia in May 1940, in front of the Tsar/King and members of the High Command Staff. (*AC*)

This commemorative photo shows crew members of the Bulgarian 'Škodas' wearing full dress uniform and garrison caps. While on duty, tank crews wore overalls consisting of a jacket and trousers, along with an Italian-style tanker helmet. By 1944 a black tanker uniform, similar in cut to the German version, had been adopted. (*AC*)

Tsar Boris III inspecting T-11 tanks during field manoeuvres in 1941. Field tests conducted in 1941 and 1942 confirmed that the 'Škodas' offered clear advantages over the R-35s in terms of mobility, firepower and tactical versatility. (*AC*)

'Škoda' tanks on parade along Tsar Osvoboditel Boulevard in the centre of Sofia, 6 May 1940. All the vehicles are painted in dark grey camouflage, with quick aerial recognition crosses on top of the hull hatch. (*AC*)

Bulgarian officers of the 1st Armoured Battalion pose in front of a T-11 tank during the royal manoeuvres near Nova Zagora, 1942. The officer wearing the side cap, standing next to the German officer, is likely *Podpolkovnik* (Lieutenant Colonel) Geno Genev. (*AC*)

The T-11 tank during summer field exercises. The dry and dusty summer environment tested the mechanical reliability of the vehicle, including engine performance and suspension durability. Exercises like these were essential for familiarising soldiers with the T-11's handling characteristics and preparing units for potential deployment. (*AC*)

batches, somewhat later than specified: seven tanks were delivered on 27 November 1940 and the remaining three on 14 February 1941. The total value of the transaction was 15,071,250 Protectorate Crowns.

Following Bulgaria's accession to the Tripartite Pact, in April 1941 Germany sold to Bulgaria forty French Renault R-35 light tanks, at a favourable rate, and dispatched Wehrmacht instructors to train Bulgarian personnel. These vehicles enabled the formation of the 4th Tank Company.

In the same month the 1st Armoured Battalion participated in joint training exercises with the Wehrmacht's 16.Pz.Div. in the vicinity of Pazardzhik, under the observation of Tsar Boris III. Impressed by the performance of the German armoured forces, the Tsar ordered the formation of a new armoured regiment. Following a partial mobilisation in the spring of 1941, and the arrival of the Renault R-35 tanks, the 2nd Armoured Battalion was duly created, composed of the newly established 4th, 5th and 6th Tank Companies. On 25 June 1941 the 1st and 2nd armoured battalions were consolidated to form the 1st Armoured Regiment (*1-ви Брониран полк/1-vi Broniran polk*). The unit was garrisoned in the former barracks of the 1st Cavalry

Above and below: A 'Škoda' tank taking part in the manoeuvres held from 7 to 21 September 1941. These large-scale military exercises, organised under royal command, served as a demonstration of the army's strength, coordination and readiness in the face of growing regional tensions. During the manoeuvres the tanks were put through a variety of tactical scenarios, including simulated breakthroughs, defensive operations and mobility tests across diverse terrain, allowing both commanders and observers to evaluate their performance in near-combat conditions. (*AC/PD*)

Tsar Boris III in a
Škoda LT vz. 35.
(AC/PD)

Regiment and placed under the direct command of the Army General Staff. Command of the regiment was assumed by Major Todor Ivanov Popov.

During the summer field exercises of 1941, the 'Škodas'—equipping the 1st Battalion's Headquarters Platoon (two tanks), 1st Company (seventeen tanks) and 2nd Company (seventeen tanks)—proved superior to the French R-35 in mobility, firepower and tactical versatility. This assessment was reaffirmed in March 1942 during live-fire drills: the 'Škodas', equipped with 3.7cm cannons, demonstrated clear firepower advantages over the R-35s.

Both German and Bulgarian commands recognised the need to further reinforce the regiment, ideally with more 'Škoda' tanks or newer medium tanks armed with 7.5cm guns. By the end of 1942 Bulgarian military planners had concluded that the formation of a fully structured armoured brigade, modelled on the German Panzer division, was essential. This plan received German approval, and delivery of PzKpfw 38(t) tanks (designated 'Praga' in Bulgarian service) commenced in May 1943, followed by shipments of PzKpfw IV medium tanks. In preparation for the royal manoeuvres scheduled for the summer of 1943, the Armoured Regiment undertook extensive training with the newly delivered German tanks in the Sofia region.

Due to a shortage of medium tanks, the 'Škodas' remained in front-line service, while outdated vehicles such as the Ansaldo-Fiat CV33, the Vickers 6-ton and the Renault R-35 were reassigned to form two training companies based in Sliven.

By 1 October 1943, with a total of 143 armoured vehicles in its inventory—including thirty-six 'Škodas' and ten T-11 'Praga's—the Armoured Regiment was formally expanded into the Armoured Brigade (*Бронирана бригада/Bronirana brigada*). The key component of the brigade was the armoured regiment, composed of three battalions, each consisting of three tank companies. The brigade comprised an armoured regiment, a motorised infantry regiment and a motorised artillery regiment, as well as reconnaissance, anti-tank and engineer battalions, along with anti-aircraft and signals detachments and workshop, supply and transport units. In total, the brigade numbered some 9,950 men. In January 1944, in response to intensified Allied

The assembly area of the Bulgarian 1st Armoured Regiment. It was composed of two battalions equipped with a diverse mix of foreign armoured vehicles, including Czech Škodas, French Renault R-35s, British Vickers tanks and Italian L3 tankettes. This eclectic composition reflected the challenges of pre-war and early-war procurement. The assortment of designs, each with differing armour, armament and mechanical systems, presented logistical and training difficulties for maintenance crews and tank operators. (*AC*)

'Škoda' tanks on the royal manoeuvres, 7–21 September 1941. (*AC/ PD*)

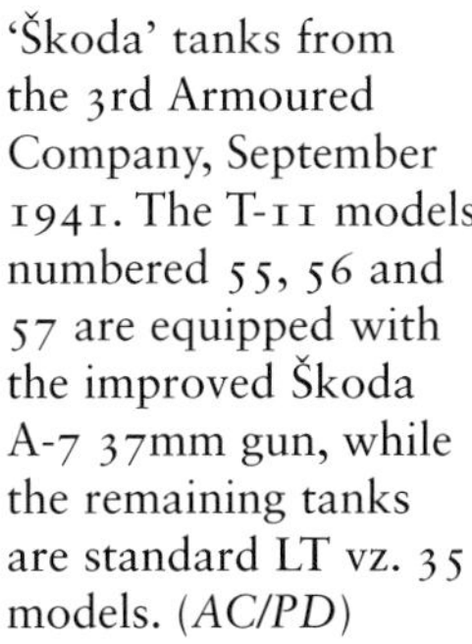

'Škoda' tanks from the 3rd Armoured Company, September 1941. The T-11 models numbered 55, 56 and 57 are equipped with the improved Škoda A-7 37mm gun, while the remaining tanks are standard LT vz. 35 models. (*AC/PD*)

bombing raids over Sofia, the brigade was relocated to the Vakarel-Ihtiman region, where it remained until the beginning of September 1944.

Bulgarian 'Škodas' in Combat (September–December 1944)

Romania's sudden capitulation at the end of August 1944, which brought Soviet forces to the Danube frontier weeks ahead of Bulgarian expectations, triggered political panic in Sofia. On 4 September 1944 the Bulgarian government publicly announced its intention to withdraw from the Axis alliance. Nevertheless, the very next day the Soviet Union declared war on Bulgaria and on the morning of 6 September elements of the 3rd Soviet Ukrainian Front began crossing unopposed into Bulgaria. Despite the absence of hostilities between Bulgarian and Soviet forces, Bulgaria's internal situation rapidly deteriorated into political upheaval.

On 7 September the Armoured Regiment, along with other elements of the Armoured Brigade, engaged and disarmed a retreating German motorised column near the village of Vakarel. The enemy force, consisting of several dozen vehicles, was defeated after brief but intense combat.

On 8 September Bulgaria formally declared war on Germany. The following day a military *coup d'état* was carried out in Sofia. A new government was established, proclaiming its intent to join the Allied cause and contribute to the expulsion of German forces from the Balkan Peninsula. The Soviet Union ceased hostilities against Bulgaria on the evening of 9 September.

On 15 September the Armoured Brigade was deployed to the Pirot region in Yugoslavia/Serbia under the operational control of I Army Corps. The unit was tasked with initiating offensive operations against German forces along the Pirot–Bela Palanka axis. On the same day a 'Škoda' platoon conducted a reconnaissance-in-force during which tank no. B60026 was struck by anti-tank fire and destroyed. Despite limitations in armour protection and firepower, the light Czechoslovak tanks performed effectively in the mountainous terrain, leveraging their agility and mechanical reliability.

At dawn on 17 September the 2nd and 3rd Armoured Battalions launched their main assault. During the advance the Bulgarian armoured vehicles were ambushed on a narrow mountain road and subjected to concentrated German artillery and anti-tank fire. Ten tanks were destroyed, and forty-one Bulgarian tank crewmen were killed. The surviving vehicles were ordered to withdraw to their original assembly area near the Bulgarian border, and the brigade was placed in reserve under I Corps command on 18 September.

The Armoured Brigade was next committed to combat on 10 October 1944, in cooperation with the 12th Infantry Division, tasked with breaching German defensive lines in the Vlasotince area, thereby enabling operations toward Niš. The Armoured Regiment, spearheading the advance, penetrated enemy positions and captured the village of Kočane, threatening to encircle German forces in Niš. In response, the enemy began a hasty withdrawal. On 14 October the Armoured Regiment intercepted and destroyed a retreating column of the 7th SS Volunteer Mountain Division 'Prinz Eugen' near the village of Merošina. In the subsequent two weeks Bulgarian

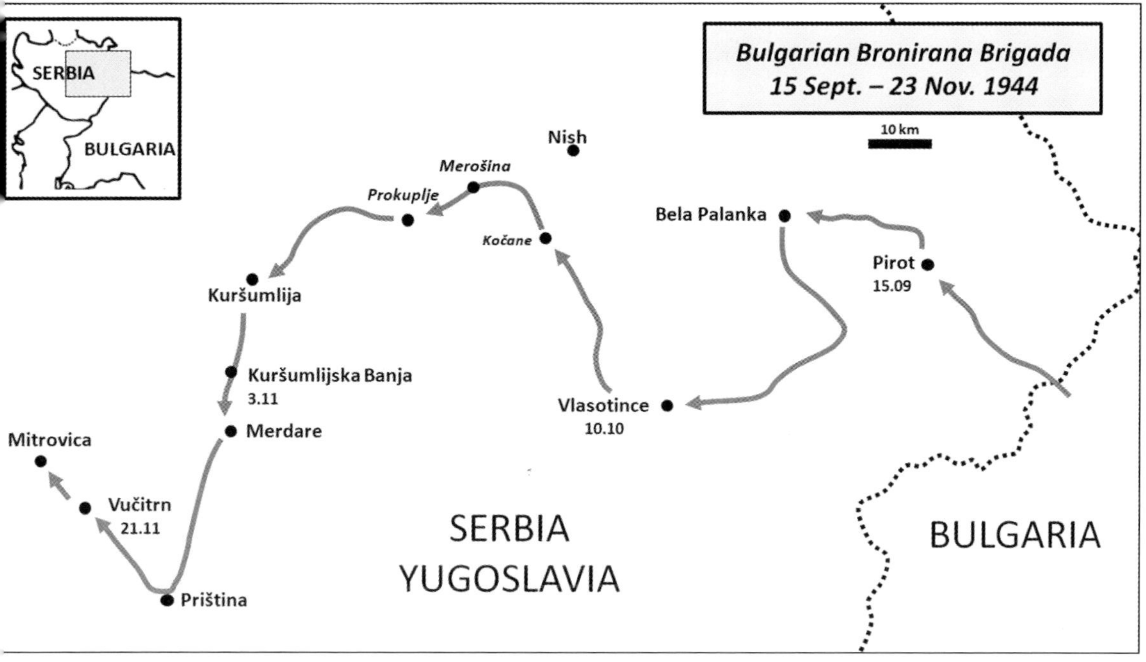

Battle Trail Map: the Bulgarian Armoured Brigade.

A group of parked T-11/LT vz. 35, PzKpfw 38(t) and PzKpfw IV tanks being prepared for the parade ceremony held in December 1944 in Sofia, in front of the St Aleksander Nevski Orthodox Cathedral. The T-11 in the foreground displays a prominent white St Andrew's Cross, along with a large tactical number '33' painted in white. (*AC/PD/Bulgarian National Library [BNL]*)

A column of 'Škoda' tanks from the 7th Tank Company advances through the streets of the capital during the December 1944 parade ceremony. (*AC/PD/BNL*)

armoured forces engaged German units in battles around Prokuplje, Kuršumlija and the Merdare Heights.

However, by 1 November 1944, due to attrition and mechanical losses, the Armoured Regiment reported only eighty-eight combat-ready tanks. This led to a structural reorganisation since the existing battalion structure—comprising mixed companies—was no longer sustainable. Under the revised order of battle a new battalion was formed, composed entirely of light tanks. Its 7th and 8th Companies were equipped with PzKpfw 35(t)/T-11 'Škoda' tanks, while the 9th Company operated PzKpfw 38(t) 'Praga' tanks.

On 3 November the restructured regiment liberated Podujevo, losing two tanks in the process. The unit then withdrew to Kuršumlijska Banja, where it remained until 16 November, undergoing maintenance. During this period eighty-two damaged vehicles were repaired by service and repair crews. On 15 November 1944 the Armoured Regiment was divided into three operational detachments, named after their commanding officers: Momchilov, Tzenov and Dikov.

The Momchilov Detachment, comprising the 3rd Light Armoured Battalion, an armoured reconnaissance battalion and an anti-tank platoon, advanced under heavy enemy fire and captured Shaikovska Čuka on 17 November. On 20 November the detachment reached Dolno Ljubče, where it was halted by a well fortified anti-tank ditch. Later that day the 9th Company successfully manoeuvred around the obstacle via the Kopunok Ridge, allowing the advance to continue. The Dikov Detachment, equipped with PzKpfw IV tanks, followed in support. On 21 November both detachments engaged in fierce combat to seize Vučitrn, paving the way for an assault on the critical objective: Mitrovica. After heavy fighting the town was secured by the evening of 22 November.

Following the liberation of Mitrovica, the Armoured Regiment was ordered to withdraw to Vučitrn on 23 November, as the 4th and 9th Infantry Divisions assumed the lead. The regiment was subsequently ordered to return to Bulgarian territory.

On 2 December 1944 the Armoured Regiment returned to Sofia, where it received a ceremonial welcome from the public. It was formally demobilised on 5 December. The campaign had been costly for the Bulgarian armoured forces, with twenty tanks lost in combat. A significant number of surviving vehicles required repairs, but this was hampered by a lack of German spare parts. By early 1945 only twenty-two PzKpfw IVs remained operational. The remaining 'Škoda' and 'Praga' tanks were retained in the 1st Armoured Brigade, garrisoned near Sofia, for training and auxiliary duties.

In March 1945, due to ongoing shortages, thirteen 'Škoda' tanks were scrapped and the remaining twenty-three units were integrated into the brigade. In October 1945 Bulgaria placed an order with Škoda Works in Plzeň for spare parts for its remaining 'Škoda' and 'Praga' tanks. A contract was signed, and in 1948 spare parts and components valued at 1,195,500 Czechoslovak crowns were delivered.

Although gradually superseded by Soviet armoured vehicles, the 'Škoda' tanks remained in service into the postwar period. After 1948 the LT vz. 35/T-11 tanks no longer appeared in the inventories of front-line units. Some were reassigned to anti-tank training schools, while others were converted by engineer units for specialised support roles. The majority were eventually scrapped, with their turrets repurposed as fixed defensive emplacements along Bulgaria's southern and southeastern frontiers.

A Bulgarian T-11 (35) tank during the December 1944 parade. The inscription 'Mitrovica' commemorates its involvement in the campaign against German forces in Yugoslavia/Serbia. (*AC/PD/BNL*)

Above: A T-11 (tactical no. 89, registration no. B60048) in Sofia on 2 December 1944. (*AC/PD/BNL*)

Below: 'Škoda' tanks from the 7th and 8th Companies, accompanied by 'Praga' light tanks (PzKpfw 38(t)s), make their way through the streets of Sofia en route to a military parade in December 1944. Crowds of civilians line the streets, watching the procession with a mix of curiosity and patriotic pride, marking a significant public display of Bulgaria's shifting military alignment in the final months of Second World War. (*AC/PD/BNL*)

9

Camouflage and Markings

Czechoslovakia

Camouflage

The Czechoslovak camouflage scheme was introduced in 1930 for all types of armoured vehicles, including the LT vz. 35. It consisted of matte dark green, yellow and dark brown paints. Green served as the base colour, while the yellow and brown were applied as irregular patches measuring approximately 25–100cm in length and 5–40cm in width. The edges between colours were sharply defined, and the pattern was intended to break up the vehicle's silhouette. The paints were manufactured by the Josef Palfy company in Smolnice and designated as Yellow no. 125 (~FS.30257), Green no. 169 (~34096 or RAL 7033) and Brown no. 141 (~30051).

The insides of engine hatches were camouflaged in the same manner as the exterior. In contrast, the interiors of crew hatches were upholstered in dark brown leather. The entire fighting compartment was painted in an ivory colour.

Tactical Markings

The first tactical markings—likely unofficial—appeared on LT vz. 35 tanks during the 1936 military manoeuvres and consisted of white stripes painted on the sides of the turret. The 1st Platoon had a single vertical stripe, the 2nd two vertical stripes, the 3rd a single horizontal stripe and the 4th two stacked horizontal stripes. The same markings were also painted on the front right armour plate.

Battalion affiliation was indicated by white Roman numerals, followed by a dash and the Arabic numeral of the company. These were typically painted on the sloped side covers of the engine compartment.

Following field tests in 1936 the Tank Brigade invited its subordinate regiments to propose a standardised system for tactical markings. By the submission deadline, numerous proposals had been received, including coloured numbers or turret stripes, French-style playing card symbols, animal silhouettes and various geometric shapes. The most unusual submission came from the 3rd Tank Regiment (PÚV-3) based in Turčiansky Svätý Martin, which featured elements of Slovak national symbolism—namely, a double cross on three hills. Ultimately, the proposal from PÚV-2 in Vyškov was selected, which used coloured geometric symbols for unit identification.

In mid-1937 the Ministry of Defence formally approved this system for use across all PÚV units. Defined by decree no. 15669 (MNO č.j. 15669 taj. 1/7 odd. 1937), the regulation required all tanks to display a symbol on both sides and the rear of the turret indicating the platoon number, while the colour of the symbol denoted the company. The symbols, 20cm in diameter, were made from aircraft fabric and glued directly onto the armour.

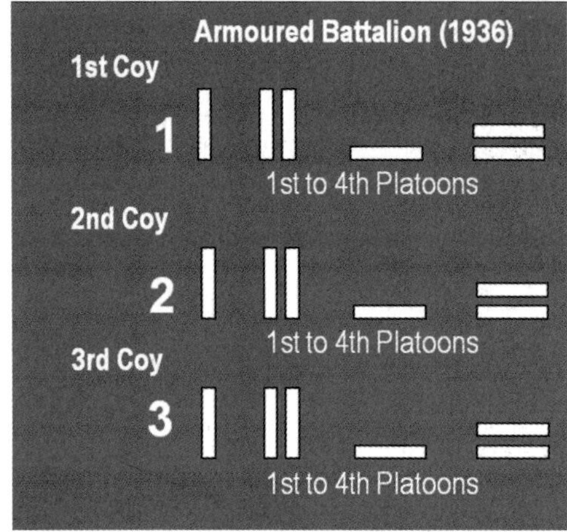

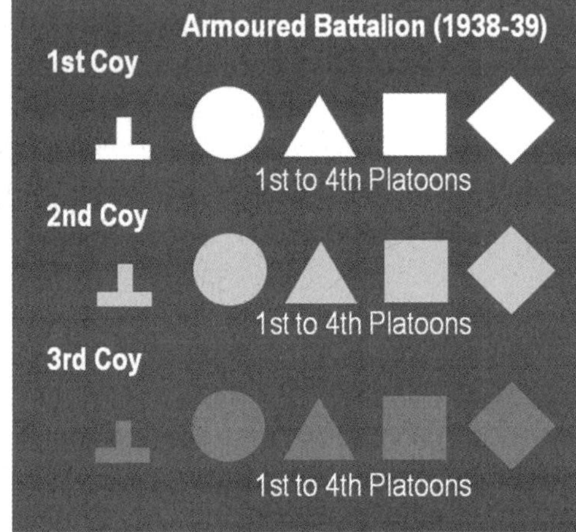

Above left and above right: In the mid-1930s a temporary tactical marking system was developed to identify tanks within an armoured battalion. Interestingly, while many countries adopted tactical markings inspired by the French 'playing card' symbols, in 1936 the Czechoslovaks experimented with a system based on combinations of white stripes. Eventually, in 1938–1939, they adopted coloured (white, yellow, and red) geometric shapes as the standard marking system.

The original Czechoslovak camouflage scheme, introduced in 1930, consisted of matte dark green (~FS.34096), yellow/sand (~ FS 30257), and dark brown (~ FS. 30051) paints, applied in irregular patches. Vehicle identification was based on individual registration numbers, which were painted on the front and rear hull armour. (*AC*)

LT vz. 35 (serial no. 13.696), Kp.1, 1st Platoon (1936). (*AC*)

LT vz. 35 (13.759) Kp 1, 3rd Platoon, marked with a white square (1939) (*AC*)

LT vz. 35, Kp 1, 2nd Platoon, marked with a red triangle (1939). (*AC*)

LT vz. 35, Kp.2, Commander's tank (1939). (*AC*)

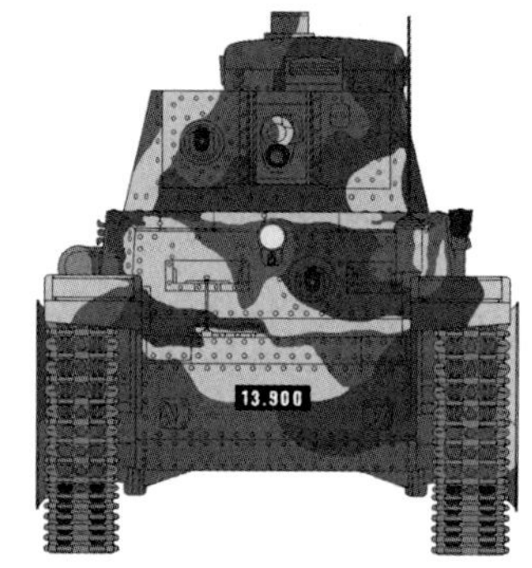

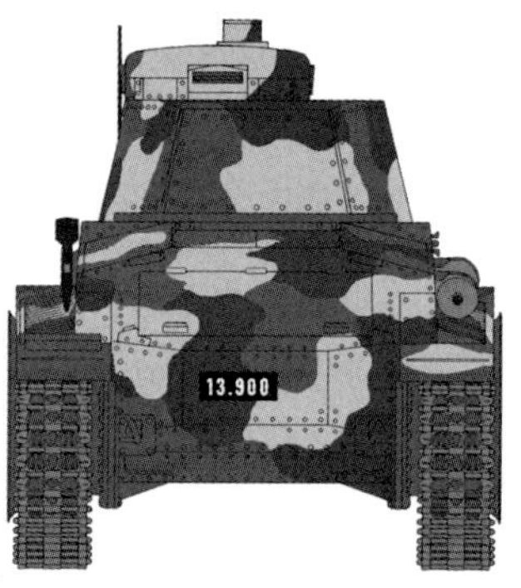

LT vz. 35 (serial no. 13.900), delivered by Škoda in 1937 to PUV-3. Dark gray patches represent brown (~FS 30051), medium gray represents green (~FS 34096 or RAL 7033), and the lightest areas indicate yellow (~FS 30257). (*AC*)

LT vz. 35 (serial no. 13.917), delivered by ČKD in 1937 to *PÚV-1*, was marked with red circle, as belonging to Kp.3, 1st Platoon. (*AC*)

LT vz. 35 (serial no. 13.691), delivered by Škoda in 1937 to the *PÚV-1*, was marked with a white triangle as belonging Kp.1, 2nd Platoon. (*AC*)

Table 8. Tactical markings, 1937 (MNO č.j. 15669 taj. 1/7 odd. 1937)

Armoured Regiment	Company colour	1st Platoon	2nd Platoon	3rd Platoon	4th Platoon
1st Company	White				
2nd Company	Yellow	●	▲	■	◆
3rd Company	Red				

The company commander's tank carried a tactical marking in the form of an inverted 'T' on the turret. This symbol featured a 20cm-wide base with arms 5cm in width, and was painted in the designated colour of the company. Reserve vehicles—three per company—as well as battalion command tanks did not carry any tactical symbols.

Vehicles within individual platoons were generally not marked with unique identifiers. However, in Herbert Cline's 1938 documentary 'Crisis', a dark number 3 is clearly visible within a white triangle on the turret of one Czechoslovak tank, suggesting that such markings may have been applied experimentally or unofficially in some units.

REGISTRATION NUMBERS (LICENCE PLATES)

All Czechoslovakian tankettes and tanks were assigned registration numbers, functioning similarly to police licence plates. They consisted of five Arabic numerals painted in white on black plates mounted on the front and rear of the vehicle. The plates measured 340 × 140mm and featured a 3mm-wide white border. Armoured fighting vehicles, including the LT vz. 34 and LT vz. 35, were issued registration numbers from a dedicated block starting with the prefix '13.XXX.'

Table 9. LT vz. 35 registration numbers allocation

Tank type and producer	Number manufactured	Registration (police) number/s	Introduced into Service (mth/year)
S-II-a prototype	1	13.620	03/1935
LT vz.35 (by Škoda)	149	13.666–13.720; 13.818–13.860; 13.864–13.914	12/1936–4/1938
LT vz.35 (by CKD)	149	13.721–13.817; 13.915–13.966	1937

Slovakia

CAMOUFLAGE

Throughout the war, LT vz. 35 tanks in Slovak army service retained the original Czechoslovak camouflage scheme of matte dark green, yellow and dark brown, along with their original registration numbers from the '13.XXX' series.

National Markings

For the June 1941 invasion of the Soviet Union, Slovak LT vz. 35s were marked with the white Slovak double cross, applied to the sides of the turret. These were sometimes used in combination with tactical numbers, though they also appeared alone.

A decree from the Slovak Ministry of Defence, issued on 21 May 1942, mandated a change to national markings. Tanks were now required to display a vertical white-blue-red tricolour on a shield measuring 15cm wide by 20cm high, positioned on the sides of the turret in place of the earlier white double cross.

LT vz. 35 with markings used in the summer of 1941, just before the start of Operation Barbarossa. (*AC*)

LT vz. 35 (tactical no. 224), marked as belonging to Kp.2, 2nd Platoon, RB. Summer 1941, Russian campaign. (*AC*)

LT vz. 35 (tactical no. 325, serial no. 13.849), marked as belonging to Kp.3, 2nd Platoon, RB. Summer 1941, Russian campaign. (*AC*)

LT vz. 35 following complete refurbishment and repainting in the summer of 1944. The overall colour is presumed to be green (~FS 34096 or RAL 7033). The turret is marked with a shield in Slovak national colours: white, blue, and red. (*AC*)

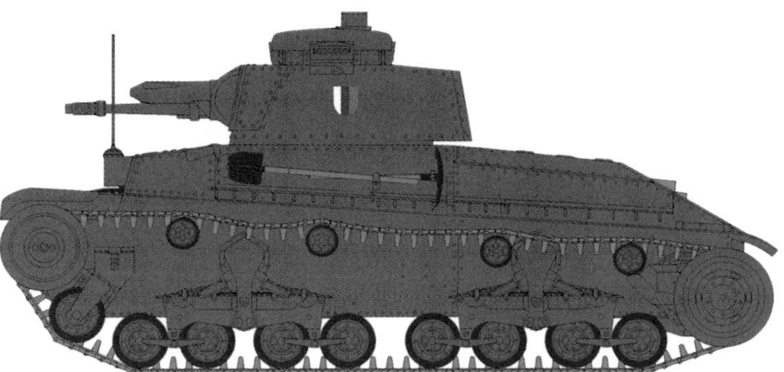

In Slovakian service

LT vz. 35 tanks retained by the Slovak armoured forces after the partition of Czechoslovakia maintained their original three-colour disruptive camouflage and registration markings. The need for improved visual identification only arose with the outbreak of the invasion of the Soviet Union, when a large white Slovak double

LT vz. 35 of the RS with early tactical markings, summer 1941. (*AC*)

LT vz. 35 from the Kp.2, 2nd Platoon, RB, 1941. Note the German flag draped over the front armour, used for aerial recognition. (*AC*)

LT vz. 35 from the Kp.1,
2nd Platoon, RB, 1941.
(*AC*)

LT vz. 35 from the Kp.2,
2nd Platoon, RB, 1941.
(*AC*)

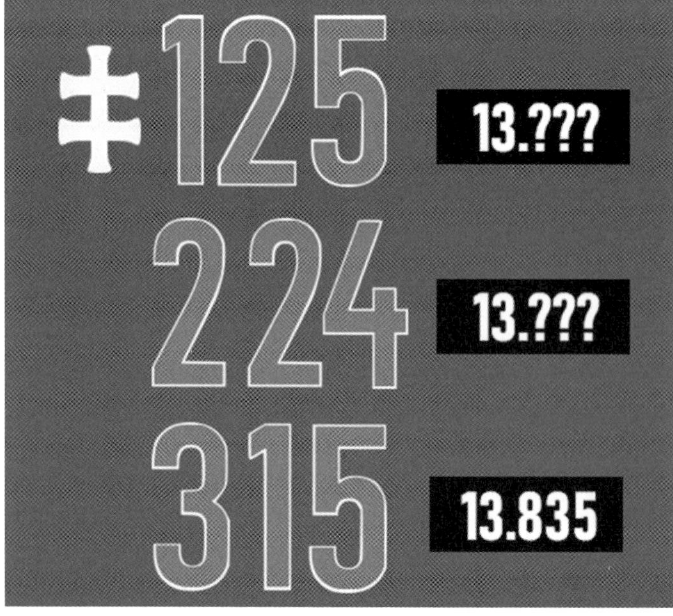

Slovak tactical numbers
were modelled on the
German three-digit system
but were adapted for
improved visibility. They
were significantly larger
in size than their German
counterparts, and were
painted in bright red,
making them more easily
distinguishable in the field.
(*AC*)

cross was painted on the sides of the turret, often accompanied by a three-digit tactical number in red, outlined in white. Interestingly, some LT vz. 35s displayed only the cross, while others carried only the number. To further enhance battlefield recognition, some tanks were fitted with a small Slovak national flag (white-blue-red) mounted on the radio antenna mast. In general, individual markings were not commonly applied to Slovak vehicles; however, photographic evidence exists of at least one tank marked with a white, hand-drawn skull and crossbones on the rear of the turret.

TACTICAL NUMBERS

During the Eastern Front campaign, Slovak LT vz. 35s were further marked with large red three-digit numbers outlined in white, painted on both the sides and the rear of the turret. These numbers identified the tank's company and platoon assignment. Slovak tanks followed the German system of tactical numbering, with three digits identifying the company, platoon and individual vehicle (for example, tank 321 was the first tank in the 2nd Platoon, 3rd Company). Battalion headquarters vehicles used numbers beginning with 0 (for example, 099). In later years these tactical numbers were gradually abandoned and eventually fell out of use.

Hungary

CAMOUFLAGE

Two LT vz. 35 tanks captured from Slovakia by Hungary were repainted in standard Hungarian olive green.

NATIONAL MARKINGS

Until 1944 Hungarian tanks bore the national insignia of a green beam cross with a white outline and a red triangle at the centre. From 1944 onwards, this marking was replaced by a white cross within a black rectangle, typically applied to the hull or turret sides. Additionally, tanks featured white tactical numbers on the turret, similar to German conventions.

Alongside the national symbols on the hull, the captured LT vz. 35s also displayed the small insignia of the Hungarian Armoured Forces on the turret sides.

Germany

CAMOUFLAGE

Following the German occupation of Czechoslovakia in the spring of 1939, most LT vz. 35s were repainted according to the standard *Panzerwaffe* two-tone camouflage scheme, introduced on 12 July 1937. This scheme combined *Dunkelgrau* nr. 46 (dark grey, roughly RAL 7021) and *Dunkelbraun* nr. 45 (dark brown, roughly RAL 7017) in a 3:1 ratio.

Vehicles undergoing repair or modification by Škoda were repainted using paint produced by the Tebas company in Prague, likely according to German RAL specifications. The camouflage consisted of large, soft-edged patches arranged in a random 'cloud' pattern to obscure the tank's outline. Smaller details were painted entirely in either *Dunkelgrau* or *Dunkelbraun*.

The choice of a dark grey-brown camouflage in the 1930s was based on the assumption that the main threat to tanks came from aerial observation. Dark grey was especially effective at concealing vehicles parked in shaded areas, such as under trees or alongside buildings. Pre-war exercises demonstrated that the combination of camouflage paint and natural dust or mud significantly enhanced concealment, often more effectively than the paintwork alone.

After the Polish campaign, the German military adopted a simplified camouflage scheme to conserve paint and streamline logistics, switching to overall dark grey (*Dunkelgrau*) as the new standard.

NATIONAL MARKINGS

In the summer of 1939 the OKH issued a directive requiring all tanks and armoured vehicles to carry a white *Balkenkreuz* (beam cross) for battlefield identification. This order, dated 13 July 1939 (OKH AHA/In 6 (I.Kav./IV) Nr. 3003/39 g.), specified dimensions tailored to each vehicle type—for example, 27cm arm length for the PzKpfw I and 55cm for the SdKfz 231/2. On the PzKpfw 35(t)s the cross was applied to the front right of the turret, both turret sides, and the rear.

In German service (Polish campaign)

The early German camouflage scheme, introduced in 1937, was applied to all types of armoured vehicles. It consisted of a matte dark grey base (~FS 37038) with irregular patches of dark brown (~FS 30045) covering about one-third of the vehicle's upper surfaces.

Prior to the Polish campaign, all PzKpfw 35(t) tanks were marked with large white *Balkenkreuze*, typically painted on the front left of the turret, the sides and the rear. However, these high-contrast markings quickly proved problematic on the battlefield, as they provided convenient aiming points for enemy anti-tank gunners. As a result tank crews attempted to obscure the crosses with mud or grey paint. (*AC*)

No divisional insignia or large tactical numbers were used in 1939. However, the tanks retained rhomboid plates displaying small three-digit tactical numbers, typically mounted on the hull sides and rear. The typeface and style of these numbers were likely designed by each unit individually, which to some extent made it possible to identify the battalion or regiment. (*AC*)

Tanks of Pz.Rgt.11 during a break, featuring prominent aerial recognition markings in the form of a white rectangle painted across the engine deck. (*AC*)

At least a few tanks of Pz.Rgt.11 were marked with a *Balkenkreuz* featuring additional symbols in the centre: a '/' represented Kp.1, while an 'X' indicated Kp.2. (*AC*)

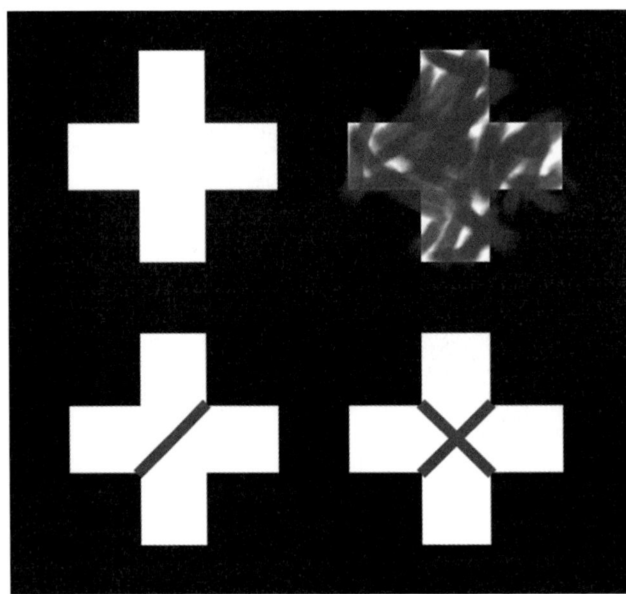

Left: Various types of German national markings used by Pz.Rgt.11 in September 1939. (*AC*)

Bottom: PzKpfw 35(t) marked as belonging to Kp.1, 3rd Platoon, Pz.Rgt.11, Poland, September 1939. Dark grey patches represent brown (RAL 7017) camouflage applied over a dark grey base (RAL 7021). (*AC*)

Below: During pre-war exercises in the summer of 1939 several Pz.Rgt.11 tanks were marked with a white triangle or circle, identifying Abt.I and Abt.II, respectively. (*AC*)

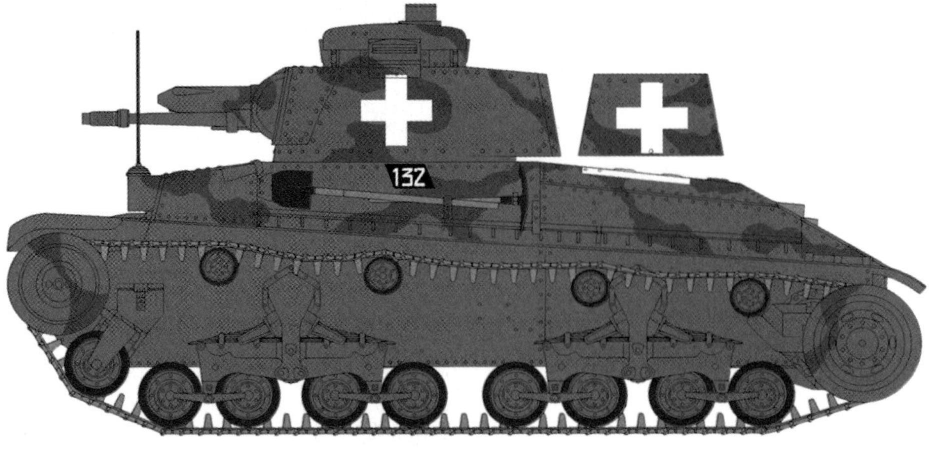

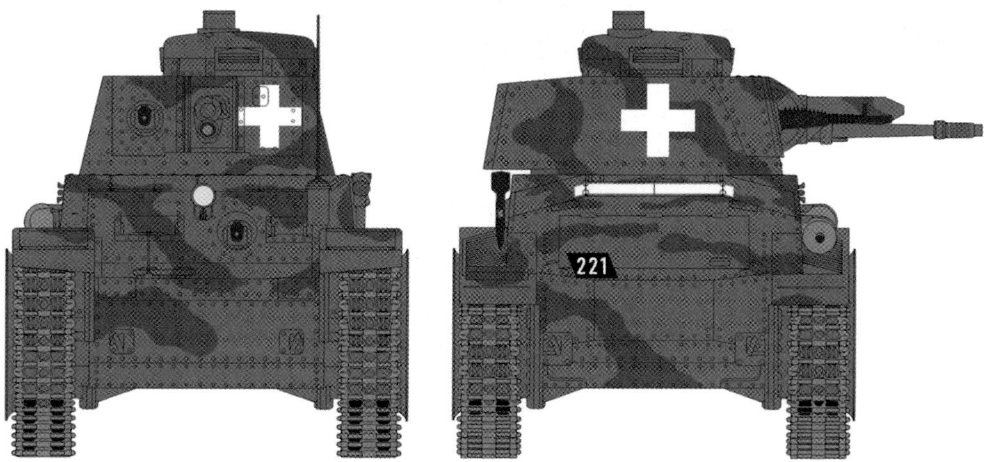

PzKpfw 35(t) marked as belonging to Kp.2, 2nd Platoon, Pz.Rgt.11, Poland, September 1939. Note the white rectangular panel painted across the engine deck, serving as an air recognition marking. (*AC*)

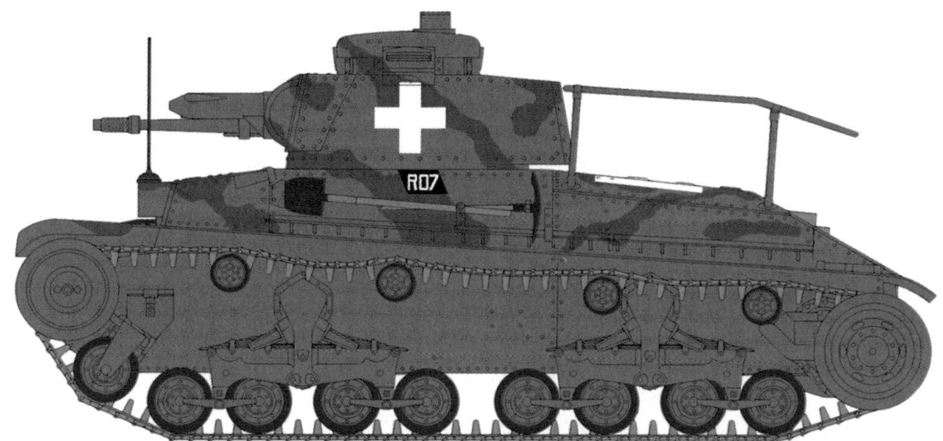

Above: PzBefWg 35(t) marked as belonging to HQ Company Pz.Rgt.11, identifiable by the tactical number R07. (*AC*)

Right: Divisional markings of 6.Pz.Div, May 1940–May 1941 (inverted Y**) and June 1941–January 1942 (XX). A skull emblem was applied to the Škoda-built tanks used by the Totenkopf Division's Heavy Reconnaissance Company. (*AC*)

In German service (French campaign)

However, the white cross quickly proved problematic, as it created a convenient aiming point for enemy anti-tank gunners. During the early stages of the Polish campaign many crews attempted to obscure the symbol with mud or grey paint. Improvised modifications emerged, including partial crosses, white outlines or hand-drawn lines. As a result, Inspectorate 6 issued a revised order on 26 October 1939 replacing the

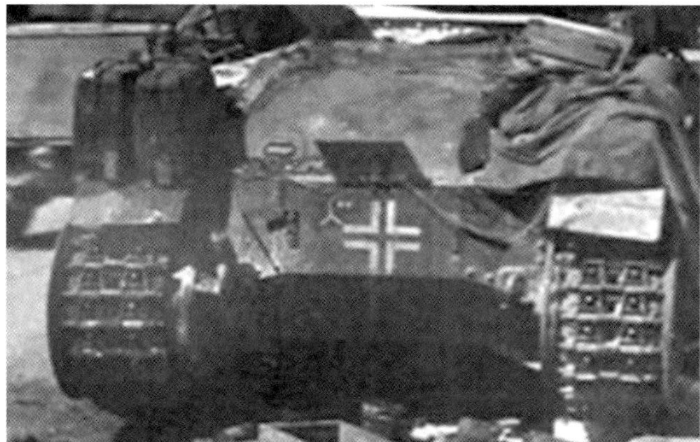

Closer views of 6.Pz.Div.'s symbol, used from November 1939 to early 1941, show a yellow emblem resembling an inverted 'Y' with two dots, painted on the front and rear of the hull. Due to their small size, these markings were intended for internal identification, while combat recognition was achieved by replacing the solid white *Balkenkreuz* with a black cross outlined by a 2.5cm white border, applied only on the sides and rear of the hull. (*AC*)

While some 35(t)s retained white rectangular markings painted on the upper surfaces of the engine cover during the French campaign, air recognition was mostly based on red flags draped over the rear engine covers, bearing black swastikas. (*AC*)

A 35(t) of Kp.3, Pz.Abt.65, displays a standing lion on its turret side, created by spraying white paint over a cut-out lion silhouette. Two other tanks from this unit's HQ platoon had individual markings painted on their turret sides, based on the letters N/Z and Z/O, possibly representing the respective commander's initials. (*AC*)

Above and below: PzKpfw 35(t), painted overall in dark grey and marked as belonging to Company 3, 2nd Platoon, Panzer Regiment 11, France, May–June 1940. Note the aerial recognition markings, which remained in use throughout the French campaign. However, as the engine deck was loaded with jerry cans, the markings became barely visible, so red flags were draped over the rear hull. (*AC*)

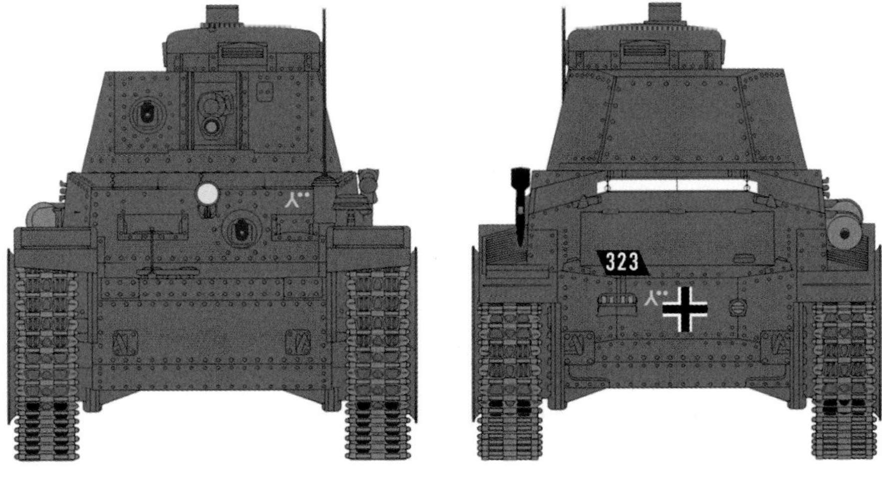

Above and below: PzKpfw 35(t) marked as belonging to SS Totenkopf Div.'s *Aufkl.Abt., Schw. Kp.*, France, May–June 1940. (*AC*)

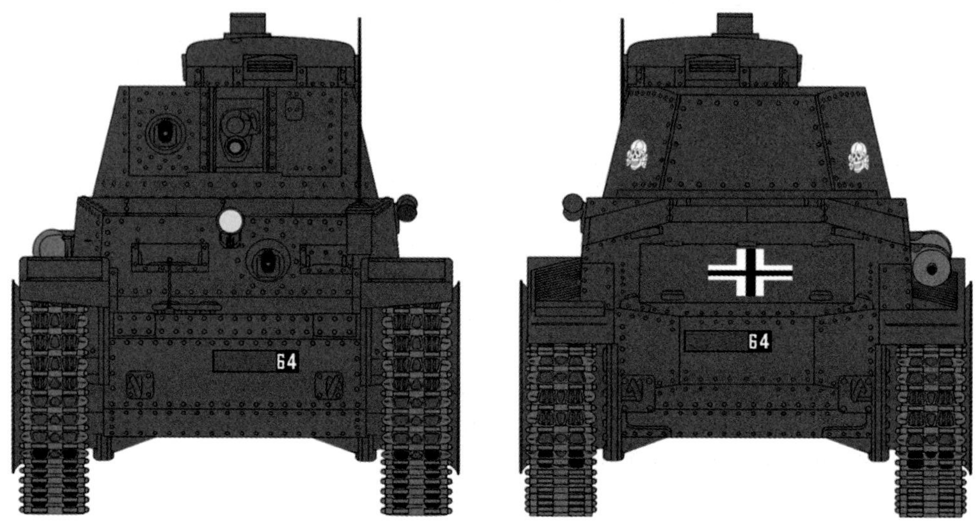

solid white *Balkenkreuz* with a black version outlined with a 2.5cm white border, to be applied only on the sides and rear of the hull. No national markings were to be visible from the front. This new marking standard remained in force, with minor adjustments, until August 1944.

TACTICAL NUMBERS

By 1938 the *Panzerwaffe* had adopted a standardised three-digit tactical numbering system: the first digit indicating the company, the second digit the platoon and the third digit the tank's position within the platoon (so, for example, Tank no. 124 was the 4th vehicle in the 2nd Platoon, 1st Company). Platoon commanders typically used numbers like 111, 121, 131, etc.

Battalion command vehicles used a variant of this system, incorporating Roman numerals (thus, I for the 1st Battalion and II for the 2nd Battalion). For example, I01 was the Commander of the 1st Battalion, and II01 was the Commander of the 2nd Battalion. Within the 1st Battalion, supporting roles were indicated as follows: I02—Radio Officer (RAO); I03—Signals Officer; and I04—Ordnance Officer. Tank I02 often served as a back-up vehicle for the battalion commander; if it happened that the CO had to take over I02, the RAO would switch to a different vehicle.

The same system was used to mark Pz.Rgt.11's HQ platoon, though instead of Roman numerals, the letter 'R' was used to designate the Regimental tanks (for the 'independent' Pz.Abt.65 the letter 'A' was used to mark HQ platoon).

Table 10. Allocation of tactical numbers within Pz.Rgt.11

Stab. Regiment/Regiment HQ Platoon			
Nos R00–R08 (R06, R07—Pz.Bef.Wg.)			
Stab./Abt. I 1st Bn HQ	Tactical number	Stab./Abt. II 2nd Bn HQ	Tactical numbers
Nos. I01–I08	Nos.	Nos. II01–II08	Nos.
Kp. 1	101–145	Kp.5	501–545
Kp. 2	201–245	Kp.6	601–645
Kp. 3	301–345	Kp. 7	701–745
Kp. 4	401–445	Kp.8	801–845

Three-digit tactical numbers—typically white or yellow—were painted on small, removable rhomboid plates affixed to the hull sides and the rear of the tank. Due to their limited dimensions (approximately 20cm long by 15cm high), these numbers were visible only at short distances and were therefore primarily used for vehicle identification while in bivouac or during the organisation of march columns, rather than as combat identification markings.

Prior to the campaign in Russia, 6.Pz.Div. changed its divisional emblem to a double 'XX', which was painted on the front (left upper corner) rear armour and sometimes also on the hull sides. (*AC*)

Above left and above right: By June 1941 all German tanks were marked with permanent tactical numbers painted on the sides and rear of the turret. These three-digit numbers were painted in white or yellow, using a standardised font across all companies, except for Kp.3, which used a wider typeface. No changes were made to the national marking's shape or positioning, which remained on the hull rear and sides, just in front of the turret. Before the invasion of the Soviet Union the 'Škodas' were modified to carry additional equipment mounted on the fenders and engine deck, giving them the appearance of small trucks. A ditching beam was mounted on the right fender, while a rack for three jerry cans was retained on the left side of the engine deck. Two additional jerry cans were secured on their long sides on the rear left fender, held in place by metal clamping bands. The jacking block was positioned directly below them. A pair of spare road wheels was mounted on the front left fender, and a rack for six jerry cans was installed on the sloped rear section of the engine deck. Crews often attached additional personal and utility items to the rear of the vehicle, including helmets, buckets and even bundles of fascines for overcoming terrain obstacles. This externally mounted equipment was typically covered with heavy tarpaulins on the sides and rear of the vehicle for protection and concealment. A large stowage box was commonly mounted on the left fender. In some vehicles a wooden plank was mounted upright on two metal brackets along the left side of the superstructure, serving as a makeshift rack where the crew stored personal gear between the plank and the hull. In some cases, an armoured box, similar to those seen on PzKpfw IIs, was fitted to the rear armour plate for storing smoke-grenade launchers.

On this PzBefWg (command/radio tank) the 'XX' is in a non-standard position, appearing on both turret sides, replacing the absent tactical numbers. (*AC*)

This system of removable plate-mounted tactical numbers was employed during both the Polish campaign (1939) and the French campaign (1940). During the Soviet campaign in 1941, however, the tactical numbers were painted directly onto the tank—white numbers of the same size (20 × 15cm) were applied to both sides and the rear of the turret.

Some tanks also bore their chassis number (a six-digit serial) painted in white below the driver's visor and on the inner side of the right track guard.

AERIAL RECOGNITION MARKINGS

Ahead of the war with Poland, on 15 July 1939 the German High Command issued an order requiring aerial recognition markings for armoured vehicles. The directive called for the application of white rectangular markings measuring 100cm by 50cm on the upper surfaces of tanks, using washable white paint or lime. These were intended to enable friendly aircraft to easily distinguish German tanks from the air.

On PzKpfw 35(t) tanks these recognition panels were typically applied across the engine deck. These markings remained in use throughout the Polish and French campaigns. Additionally, in May 1940 many German tanks—including PzKpfw 35(t) s—were seen displaying large red flags bearing black swastikas in white circles, draped over the rear engine covers to further aid in air recognition.

DIVISION SIGNS

At the outbreak of war in 1939 not all Wehrmacht units had adopted divisional insignia. Notably, 1.le.Div., which operated the PzKpfw 35(t), initially lacked such markings. However, as the utility of unit symbols became evident during early operations, the practice of using division signs expanded significantly. On 1 November 1939 the OKH introduced a standardised system of simple geometric signs for all Panzer divisions, including upgraded light divisions. These signs were to be stencilled in yellow on the vehicle's dark grey base paint for visibility and ease of application. The symbols were to be applied to the front, rear and left side of the tank's superstructure. For wheeled vehicles, they were to be painted on the left front mudguard, the rear and the left side near the tactical number.

6.Pz.Div., which absorbed the former 1.le.Div., was initially assigned a symbol resembling an inverted 'Y' with two dots. This insignia was used during the French campaign (1940) but was replaced by a double 'X' symbol for the 1941 Soviet campaign.

INDIVIDUAL MARKINGS

A few PzKpfw 35(t) tanks featured unique individual symbols, most notably during the French campaign. Command tank 'A03', for example, belonging to *Oberleutnant* Marquardt, executive officer of Pz.Abt.65, carried the letters 'N' and 'Z' painted in white on the sides of the turret. Another tank from the same unit bore a monogram combining the letters 'Z' and 'O'. A vehicle from 3rd Company, Pz.Abt.65, displayed a standing lion on its turret side. The symbol was created by spraying white paint over a cut-out lion silhouette; after removing the stencil, a sharply outlined Panzer grey lion remained, surrounded by a white border.

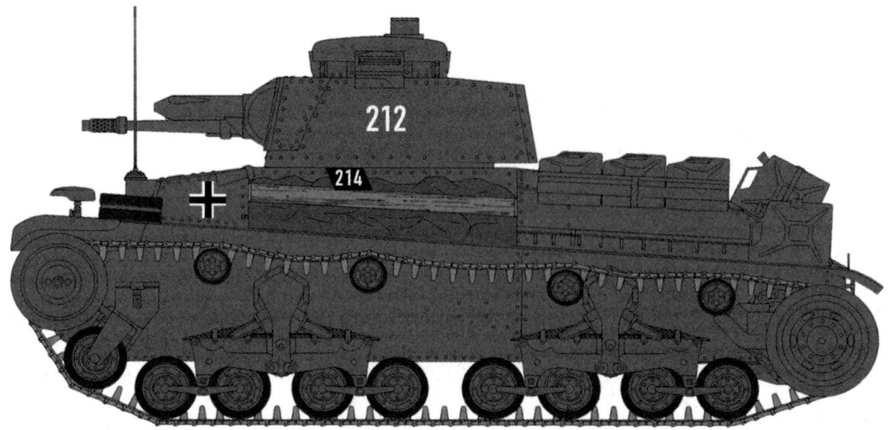

PzKpfw 35(t) marked as belonging to Kp.2, 1st Platoon, Pz.Rgt.11, Baltic/Soviet Union, June 1941. (*AC*)

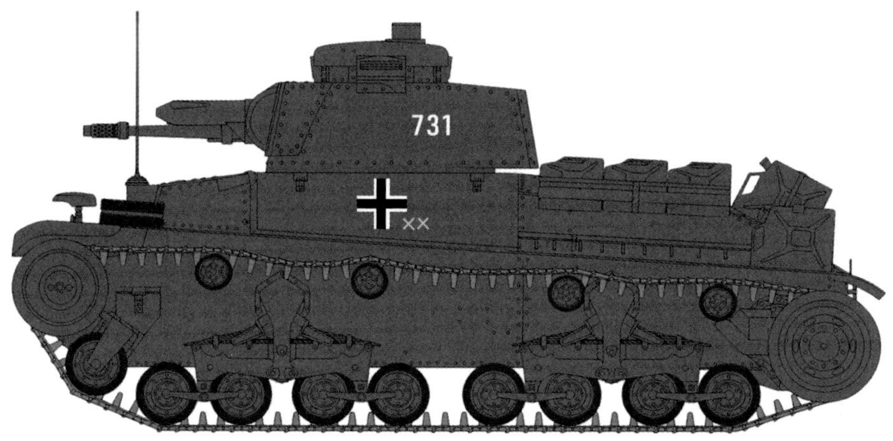

Above and below: PzKpfw 35(t) marked as belonging to Kp.7, 3rd Platoon, Pz.Rgt.11, Baltic/Soviet Union, June 1941. (*AC*)

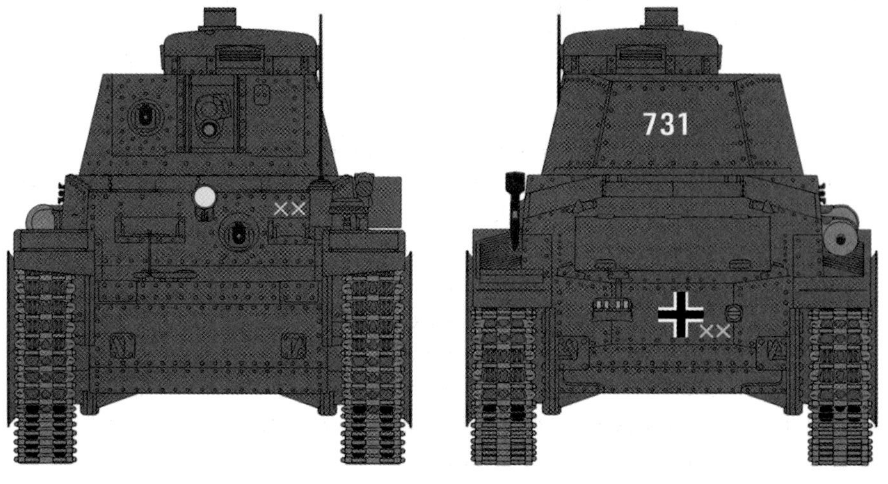

Radio tank of the HQ Platoon Pz.Rgt.11, Baltic/Soviet Union, summer 1941. (*AC*)

SS-Totenkopf Division

Several PzKpfw 35(t) tanks assigned to the SS-Totenkopf Division in the spring of 1940 were marked with the division's distinctive emblem—a white skull ('Totenkopf')—painted on both the turret and the hull. These tanks also bore registration numbers prefixed with 'SS', although partially overpainted to avoid vehicle identification.

Romania

Camouflage

Romanian LT vz. 35 tanks—designated R-2s—were initially delivered in an overall green-grey paint scheme applied by Škoda. During the harsh winter campaign of 1942 on the Eastern Front this was temporarily overpainted with white, washable paint or lime for improved camouflage in snowy conditions.

National Markings

From 1937 the royal crest of King Carol II was painted on the turret of each R-2 in black or dark grey, surrounded by a laurel wreath and topped with a royal crown. Below the turret, on the hull sides, tanks displayed a white-outlined St Michael's Cross and a black registration number, ranging from 'Sr.1' to 'Sr.126'.

In 1940 and 1941 R-2s were marked with white geometric symbols (a square, circle or triangle) on the turret sides and rear, crossed by red diagonal lines. Although exact assignments are not confirmed, these symbols likely mirrored the German system, using a square for the first subunit (for example, the 1st Company), a circle for the second subunit and a triangle for the third subunit. The red diagonal lines may have distinguished between 1st and 2nd battalions.

Table 11. Speculative allocation of Romanian R-2 tanks

Rg.1.Cl.			
1st Battalion		**2nd Battalion**	
1st Company	■	4th Company	■ with red line
2nd Company	●	5th Company	● with red line
3rd Company	▲	6th Company	▲ with red line

During preparations for the invasion of the Soviet Union in the summer of 1941 the royal crest and geometric tactical markings were overpainted and replaced by three-digit tactical numbers modelled on the German system.

National identity was indicated by the St Michael's Cross, composed of four letter 'M's joined to form a cross, painted in white with a central roundel in the blue-yellow-red Romanian tricolour. These symbols were painted on the hull sides and across the full width of the engine hatch. In 1943 and 1944 German-origin tanks also bore the 'Michael Cross' painted in white. It is possible that command tanks had a blue stripe running along the turret to distinguish them. After 1 September 1944 the 'Michael Cross' was removed from all armoured vehicles to avoid confusion with German tanks by Romania's new Soviet allies. It was replaced by the tricolour roundel.

During fighting in Slovakia, Austria and the Czechoslovak lands in early 1945, the 2nd Tank Regiment displayed either a khaki star within a white circle or a white star on the turret.

In Romanian service

A close-up view of an R-2 turret marked according to Romanian specifications, which required the Romanian royal crest to be painted on both sides of the turret. In addition, every tank was assigned an individual tactical number painted on the hull side, here Sr.82, below the crest. (*AC*)

An R-2 photographed in January 1941. Its geometric markings likely identify it as belonging to the 1st Company of the 2nd Battalion. (*AC*)

R-2 tanks featuring a marking composed of the royal crest alongside a national marking modelled after the German *Balkenkreuz*. (*AC*)

Various types of markings used by the Romanian armoured forces. Note: tactical numbers starting with (II) were reserved for Battalion HQ units, while those beginning with (R) indicated Regiment HQ units. Line tanks were marked with three-digit numbers in the German style. (*AC*)

Battalion and company markings used in early 1941. (*AC*)

Sr.82.

An R-2 marked with the royal crest of King Carol II and serial no. Sr.82, Romania, 1940. The overall colour is presumed to be green (~FS 34096 or RAL 7033). (*AC*)

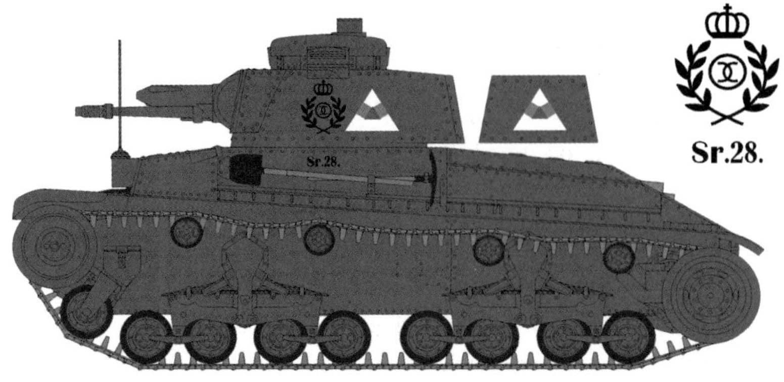

Sr.28.

At the end of 1940 or early 1941 R-2 tanks were marked with geometric symbols for identification. This particular R-2 was likely assigned to the 6th Company Rg.1.Cl. (*AC*)

An R-2 marked as belonging to the 1st Platoon, 3rd Company Rg.1.Cl., Soviet Union, summer 1941. (*AC*)

An R-2 marked as belonging to the 2nd Platoon, 6th Company Rg.1.Cl., Soviet Union, winter 1942/1943. (*AC*)

TACTICAL NUMBERS

As noted, at the outbreak of war with the Soviet Union Romanian R-2 tanks received large, white, three-digit tactical numbers on the turret, similar to those used by German and Slovak armoured forces. These numbers were painted in broken white lines over an olive background and were used for identification. For example, '634' signified the fourth tank of the 3rd Platoon, 6th Company. The 1st Battalion included companies numbered 1 to 3, while the 2nd Battalion included companies numbered 4 to 6. This marking system became standard on Romanian tanks and tank destroyers until November 1944.

REGISTRATION NUMBERS

From September 1939 R-2 tanks were marked with registration numbers (licence plates) painted on the front and rear of the vehicles on a white rectangular background. These numbers were preceded by the numbers 010 (for example, 010015, 010180, 010206), indicating army ownership. In early 1941 the registration system was updated so that the number was preceded by the letter U (for example, U039247, U039139) for 'Unitate' ('Military Unit'). On front-line vehicles the numbers were changed over time to painted black on an olive background.

Bulgaria

CAMOUFLAGE

Bulgarian LT vz. 35s were delivered in an overall dark grey colour, either German RAL 7021 *Schwarzgrau* or the slightly lighter Czechoslovak variant RAL 7027. A few

Škodas used in the Socialist Labour Day parade on 1 May 1945 were repainted in olive green; however, most ex-Czechoslovak tanks retained their original dark grey colour even after the war.

REGISTRATION AND TACTICAL NUMBERS

All Škoda tanks bore individual registration numbers painted directly on the hull's front and rear left side. These numbers consisted of the letter B (an abbreviation of the Cyrillic word for Voiska, meaning Troops), identifying the vehicle as a military vehicle, followed by a five-digit code. The first three digits (600) indicated the vehicle class. The subsequent digits identified the vehicle's serial number in the army (23–49 for LT vz. 35s and 48–57 for T-11s). The registration number was painted on a white rectangle (48cm by 17cm). The B and digits measured 14cm by 7cm, and were painted in black or possibly red, using a standardised font.

The last two digits of the registration number were also painted as a large white tactical number on both turret sides. Some Škodas had these tactical numbers outlined with a thin black line, probably applied by crews when refreshing the paint.

QUICK RECOGNITION MARKINGS

In May 1940 'Škodas' were marked with the Andreev's Cross for aerial recognition. This emblem, consisting of two beams crossed at a 45-degree angle, was painted prominently across the full width of the engine hatch on the rear deck. After Bulgaria switched sides and joined the Allies on 9 September 1944, the Andreev's Cross was applied more extensively. It was added to both sides of the turret, positioned behind the tactical number, as well as on the rear of the turret, to clearly identify the vehicles as friendly to Allied forces.

In Bulgarian service

A rear view of T-11 (48) shows a clearly visible registration number (B.60048) painted on a white rectangular background. Note that on the rear of the vehicle the registration number is positioned towards the left side, while on the front lower armour it was painted centrally. (*AC*)

This close-up view shows T-11 turrets marked with large, two-digit tactical numbers (nearest is no. 56, chassis no. 283, registration number B.60056) and armed with Škoda A7 guns. All Bulgarian armoured fighting vehicles imported from Czechoslovakia—including tankettes and tanks—were marked using double-digit numbers. The LT vz. 35/T-11s were delivered in German dark grey overall, but it is likely that by 1944 some tanks had been repainted during refurbishment. If German paints were used, the original colour was maintained; if local paints were applied, a change in shade is probable. (*AC*)

From September 1944, when Bulgaria joined the Allies, all Bulgarian tanks began to be marked with a quick recognition symbol composed of two beams crossed at a 45-degree angle—the Andreev's Cross—to aid both ground and air identification. (*AC*)

A Škoda from the 8th Company during the victory parade in December 1944. This vehicle was marked with several non-standard identifiers, including multiple '8/8p' markings, indicating its assignment to the 8th Company. (*AC*)

LT vz. 35 (Czech
serial no. 13.776,
Bulgarian registration
no. B.60035) of the 1st
Armoured Battalion,
1940. The overall
colour is presumed to
be dark gray. (*AC*)

LT vz. 35 (Czech
serial no. 13.757,
Bulgarian registration
no. B.60033) of the 1st
Armoured Battalion,
1941. (*AC*)

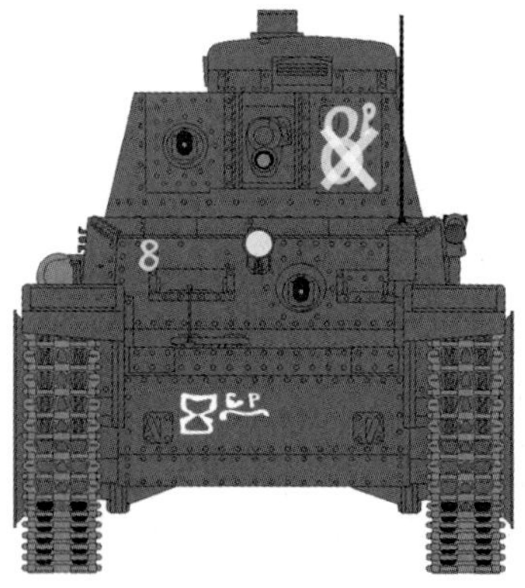
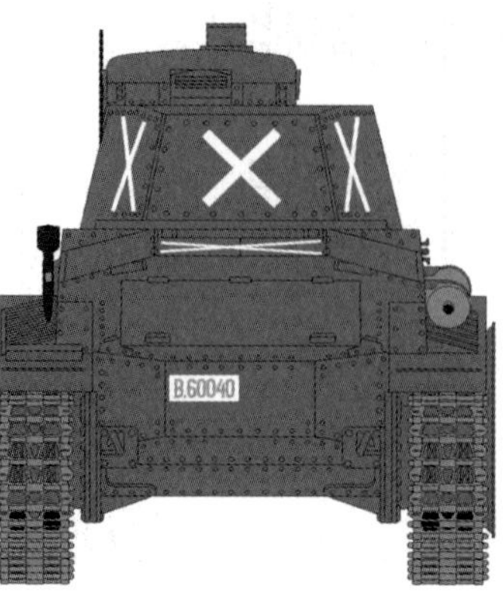

A Škoda from
the 8th Company
(Bulgarian registration
no. B.60040 painted in
red or black) of the 1st
Armoured Battalion
during the victory
parade in December
1944. (*AC*)

Non-standard tactical markings

Individual Markings

Škodas returning from the 1944 Yugoslav campaign, especially those that participated in the victory parade in Sofia on 2 December 1944, were often marked by their crews with the names of battle sites, towns and villages (notably Mitrovica) where they had fought, or with the company number to which the vehicle belonged.

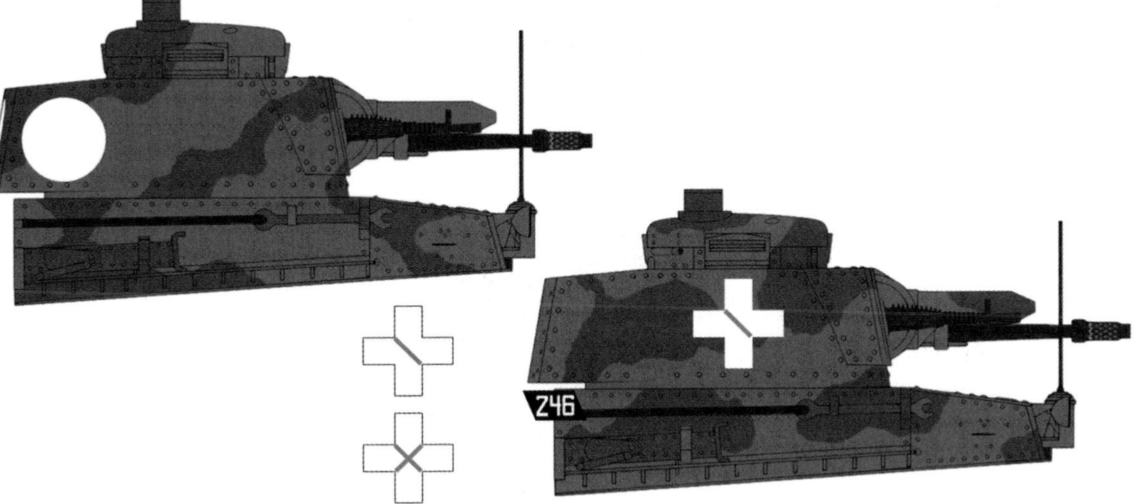

Above: During pre-war exercises in the summer of 1939 several Pz.Rgt.11 tanks were marked with a white triangle or/and circle, identifying Abt.I and Abt.II respectively. During the Polish campaign the symbol '/' was used on some tanks of Abt.I, while 'X' marked some tanks of Abt.II. (*AC*)

Below: During the French campaign a tank from Kp.3, Pz.Abt.65, was marked with a standing lion emblem on the turret side, created by spraying white paint over a cut-out lion silhouette. During both the French and Russian campaigns several tanks were marked with their commanders' initials on their turret sides, as shown. (*AC*)

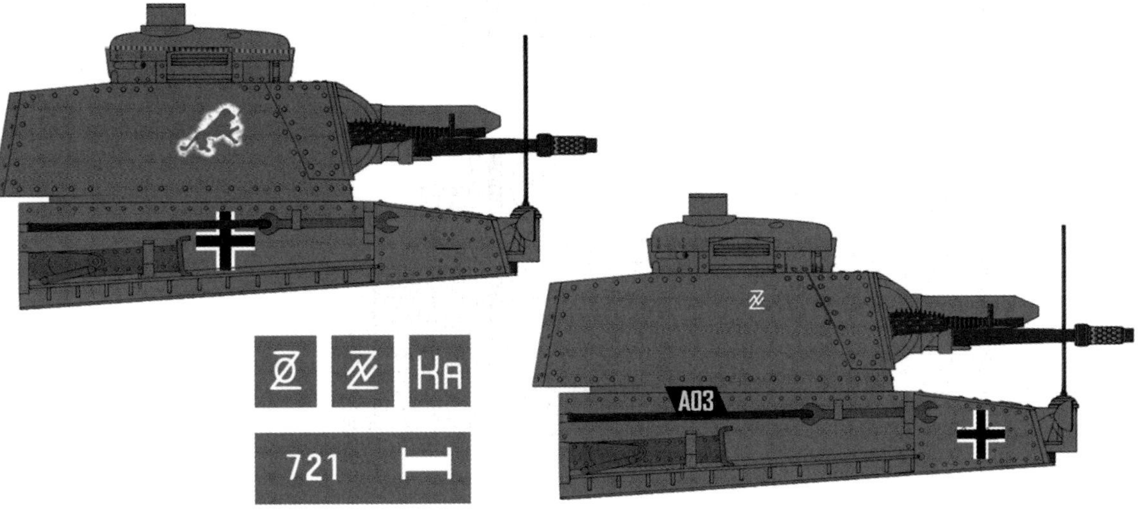

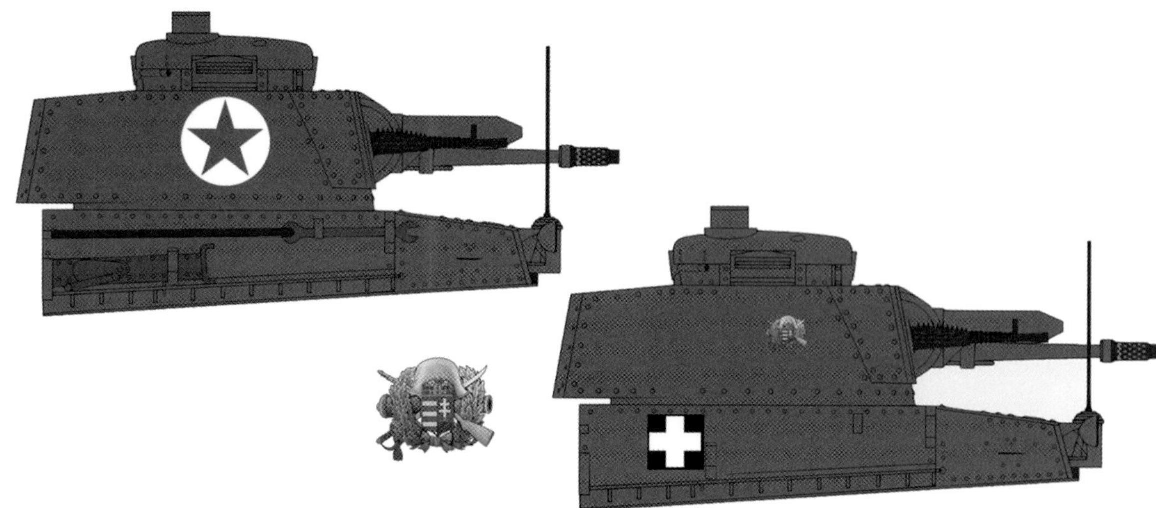

Late war (spring 1945) markings on Romanian 'Škodas' during the fighting in Czechoslovakia alongside the Red Army, as well as on Hungarian LT vz. 35 tanks used by the tank training center. The overall colour is presumed to be green (~FS 34096 or RAL 7033) for both machines. (*AC*)

Epilogue

When the LT vz. 35 rolled off the production lines of Škoda and ČKD in the mid-1930s, it stood as a symbol of Czechoslovak ingenuity and modern military engineering. Built to meet the rigorous standards of the Czechoslovak army, it represented a fine balance of firepower, mobility and tactical flexibility. By 1935 the LT vz. 35 was among the most advanced light tanks in the world—its performance reflecting the cutting-edge doctrine and industrial prowess of its creators.

The tank's mobility—peaking at a respectable 35km/h—gave it operational flexibility on the move, a crucial trait in the fluid battles of the early war. Its main armament, the 3.7cm gun, proved more than adequate against the lightly armoured vehicles that dominated Europe's pre-1941 battlefield. This combination made the LT vz. 35 a capable cavalry tank in the truest sense: fast, responsive and sufficient for rapid mechanised advances.

However, no design is without compromise. The LT vz. 35's relatively thin armour, barely effective against contemporary anti-tank weapons, soon revealed its vulnerability. Additionally, it suffered from mechanical unreliability—particularly in extreme cold—a flaw that would become painfully apparent during the brutal Russian winters.

In a twist steeped in the cruel irony of geopolitics, the tank that was engineered to defend Czechoslovakia from German aggression ended up serving in the ranks of the Wehrmacht, and became an essential component of the German Panzer divisions, bolstering a mechanised force that was still in the midst of rapid rearmament.

In the invasions of Poland and France the PzKpfw 35(t) performed admirably, outclassing many of its adversaries in mobility and firepower. These campaigns represented the tank's zenith—its moment of greatest utility. But by 1941, on the vast and unforgiving plains of the Eastern Front, the tide had turned. The rise of the T-34 and KV-1, with their superior armour and firepower, quickly rendered the 35(t) obsolete. Most tellingly, it wasn't enemy fire but mechanical failures and logistical shortages that sealed its fate. Harsh winter conditions, lack of spare parts and dwindling fuel supplies led to widespread abandonment of the type during Operation Barbarossa.

Even as the Wehrmacht phased it out, the LT vz. 35 found new life among Germany's allies. In the armies of Slovakia, Romania and Bulgaria these tanks continued to serve as the backbone of armoured forces well into the war. Though eventually supplanted by more modern German medium tanks, the operational experience gained from the use of the LT vz. 35 proved invaluable. Its deployment provided critical lessons in crew coordination, maintenance under combat conditions and the evolving role of armoured units within combined arms tactics.

Remarkably, the LT vz. 35 stands out as one of the few armoured vehicles to serve in front-line roles from the earliest campaigns of 1939 through to the final clashes of 1945. A few surviving examples in service by 1945 served as enduring, silent witnesses to the full arc of the global conflict—armoured relics from the war's opening salvoes to its closing moments.

Most LT vz. 35s were scrapped in the postwar years, their metal hulls melted down, yet a handful of these machines somehow survived, becoming rare relics of a turbulent era. Perhaps the best known survivor was a PzKpfw 35(t) captured by American forces at the Hillersleben Proving Grounds in 1945. This specimen was shipped to the Aberdeen Proving Grounds in Maryland by Colonel Jarrett for testing and evaluation. After decades on display in the United States, it was repatriated to the Czech Republic in 2008. Lovingly restored by the Technical Museum in Lešany, it remains the only fully operational LT vz. 35 in the world—a living monument to both Czechoslovak engineering and the tank's remarkable journey through history. Other examples include a Romanian R-2 and a TACAM R-2 self-propelled gun displayed at the National Military Museum in Bucharest. A single T-11 survives in Sofia, Bulgaria. And one last captured PzKpfw 35(t) sits stoically in the moat of the Military Museum in Belgrade, Serbia—a weathered ghost of the Blitzkrieg era.

The story of the LT vz. 35/PzKpfw 35(t) is not simply one of military hardware—it is a narrative of national ambition, tragic irony, battlefield innovation and enduring legacy. Though overshadowed by the more famous tank types of the war, the 35(t) played a crucial role in shaping early armoured warfare. It marched in victory and retreat, across fields and steppes, through smoke and snow. And in its steel bones lie the echoes of an era now passed—one worth studying, preserving and remembering. A machine not just of war, but of history.

Appendix

LT vz. 35 Production, Numbers and Final Destination

Table 12. Czechoslovak tanks and secondary users

Date	Manufacturer	Chassis no.	Serial/ registration no.	Czechoslovak user	Secondary users	Third users
1935	Škoda	prototype	13620	Škoda	Waffen SS	
21.12.1936	Škoda	50130	13666	PÚV-1	1.le.Div./6.Pz.Div.	Romania
21.12.1936	Škoda	50131	13667	PÚV-1	1.le.Div./6.Pz.Div.	
21.12.1936	Škoda	50132	13668	PÚV-1	1.le.Div./6.Pz.Div.	
21.12.1936	Škoda	50133	13669	PÚV-1	1.le.Div./6.Pz.Div.	
21.12.1936	Škoda	50134	13670	PÚV-1	1.le.Div./6.Pz.Div.	Romania
21.12.1936	Škoda	50135	13671	PÚV-1	1.le.Div./6.Pz.Div.	scrapped 1940
21.12.1936	Škoda	50136	13672	PÚV-1	1.le.Div./6.Pz.Div.	
21.12.1936	Škoda	50147	13673	PÚV-1	Hungary	1H-406
21.12.1936	Škoda	50139	13674	PÚV-1	1.le.Div./6.Pz.Div.	
21.12.1936	Škoda	50140	13675	PÚV-1	1.le.Div./6.Pz.Div.	scrapped 43
21.12.1936	Škoda	50144	13676	PÚV-1	1.le.Div./6.Pz.Div.	
21.12.1936	Škoda	50148	13677	PÚV-1	1.le.Div./6.Pz.Div.	
21.12.1936	Škoda	50142	13678	PÚV-1	1.le.Div./6.Pz.Div.	
21.12.1936	Škoda	50143	13679	PÚV-1	1.le.Div./6.Pz.Div.	MZM[1] 1942
21.12.1936	Škoda	50137	13680	PÚV-1	1.le.Div./6.Pz.Div.	Romania
25.01.1937	Škoda	50138	13681	PÚV-1	1.le.Div./6.Pz.Div.	
25.01.1937	Škoda	50141	13682	PÚV-1	1.le.Div./6.Pz.Div.	
25.01.1937	Škoda	50149	13683	PÚV-1	1.le.Div./6.Pz.Div.	
25.01.1937	Škoda	50151	13684	PÚV-1	1.le.Div./6.Pz.Div.	MZM 1943
25.01.1937	Škoda	50152	13685	PÚV-1	1.le.Div./6.Pz.Div.	MZM 1943
25.01.1937	Škoda	50153	13686	PÚV-1	1.le.Div./6.Pz.Div.	

1 MZM (*Materialzeugmagazin*): strategic reserve.

Date	Manufacturer	Chassis no.	Serial/ registration no.	Czechoslovak user	Secondary users	Third users
25.01.1937	Škoda	50154	13687	PÚV-1	1.le.Div./6.Pz.Div.	damaged 1939
25.01.1937	Škoda	50157	13688	PÚV-1	1.le.Div./6.Pz.Div.	
25.01.1937	Škoda	50158	13689	PÚV-1	1.le.Div./6.Pz.Div.	MZM 1943
25.01.1937	Škoda	50161	13690	PÚV-1	1.le.Div./6.Pz.Div.	
25.01.1937	Škoda	50167	13691	PÚV-1	1.le.Div./6.Pz.Div.	damaged 1940
25.01.1937	Škoda	50150	13692	PÚV-1	1.le.Div./6.Pz.Div.	Bulgaria
25.01.1937	Škoda	50162	13693	PÚV-1	1.le.Div./6.Pz.Div.	
25.01.1937	Škoda	50163	13694	PÚV-1	1.le.Div./6.Pz.Div.	MZM 1943
25.01.1937	Škoda	50160	13695	PÚV-1	1.le.Div./6.Pz.Div.	MZM 1942
03.04.1937	Škoda	50195	13696	PÚV-1	1.le.Div./6.Pz.Div.	MZM 1942
03.04.1937	Škoda	50204	13697	PÚV-1	1.le.Div./6.Pz.Div.	Romania
03.04.1937	Škoda	50205	13698	PÚV-1	1.le.Div./6.Pz.Div.	
03.04.1937	Škoda	50206	13699	PÚV-1	1.le.Div./6.Pz.Div.	burned 1939
03.04.1937	Skoda	50207	13700	PÚV-1	1.le.Div./6.Pz.Div.	Romania
03.04.1937	Škoda	50194	13701	PÚV-1	1.le.Div./6.Pz.Div.	
03.04.1937	Škoda	50209	13702	PÚV-1	1.le.Div./6.Pz.Div.	
19.07.1937	Škoda	50186	13703	PÚV-1	1.le.Div./6.Pz.Div.	
19.07.1937	Škoda	50280	13704	PÚV-1	1.le.Div./6.Pz.Div.	
19.07.1937	Škoda	50279	13705	PÚV-1	1.le.Div./6.Pz.Div.	
19.07.1937	Škoda	50283	13706	PÚV-1	1.le.Div./6.Pz.Div.	Romania
19.07.1937	Škoda	50278	13707	PÚV-1	1.le.Div./6.Pz.Div.	MZM 1942
19.07.1937	Škoda	50282	13708	PÚV-1	1.le.Div./6.Pz.Div.	
19.07.1937	Škoda	50272	13709	PÚV-1	1.le.Div./6.Pz.Div.	
19.07.1937	Škoda	50281	13710	PÚV-1	1.le.Div./6.Pz.Div.	
19.07.1937	Škoda	50285	13711	PÚV-1	1.le.Div./6.Pz.Div.	Romania
31.07.1937	Škoda	50284	13712	PÚV-1	1.le.Div./6.Pz.Div.	MZM 1942
31.07.1937	Škoda	50289	13713	PÚV-1	1.le.Div./6.Pz.Div.	
31.07.1937	Škoda	50290	13714	PÚV-1	1.le.Div./6.Pz.Div.	Romania
31.07.1937	Škoda	50288	13715	PÚV-1	1.le.Div./6.Pz.Div.	
31.07.1937	Škoda	50277	13716	PÚV-1	1.le.Div./6.Pz.Div.	
31.07.1937	Škoda	50287	13717	PÚV-1	1.le.Div./6.Pz.Div.	PzBef35(t)
31.07.1937	Škoda	50286	13718	PÚV-1	1.le.Div./6.Pz.Div.	MZM 1943
31.07.1937	Skoda	50292	13719	PÚV-1	1.le.Div./6.Pz.Div.	MZM 1943
31.07.1937	Škoda	50291	13720	PÚV-1	1.le.Div./6.Pz.Div.	
1937	ČKD	1048	13721	PÚV-1	1.le.Div./6.Pz.Div.	

Date	Manufacturer	Chassis no.	Serial/ registration no.	Czechoslovak user	Secondary users	Third users
1937	ČKD	1027	13722	PÚV-1	1.le.Div./6.Pz.Div.	Bulgaria
1937	ČKD	1028	13723	PÚV-1	1.le.Div./6.Pz.Div.	Bulgaria
1937	ČKD	1029	13724	PÚV-1	1.le.Div./6.Pz.Div.	Bulgaria
1937	ČKD	1030	13725	PÚV-1	1.le.Div./6.Pz.Div.	
1937	ČKD	1031	13726	PÚV-1	1.le.Div./6.Pz.Div.	MZM 1942
1937	ČKD	1032	13727	PÚV-1	1.le.Div./6.Pz.Div.	
1937	ČKD	1033	13728	PÚV-1	1.le.Div./6.Pz.Div.	Bulgaria
1937	ČKD	1034	13729	PÚV-1	1.le.Div./6.Pz.Div.	
1937	ČKD	1035	13730	PÚV-1	1.le.Div./6.Pz.Div.	
1937	ČKD	1036	13731	PÚV-1	1.le.Div./6.Pz.Div.	Bulgaria
1937	ČKD	1037	13732	PÚV-1	1.le.Div./6.Pz.Div.	
1937	ČKD	1046	13733	PÚV-1	1.le.Div./6.Pz.Div.	
1937	ČKD	1047	13734	PÚV-1	1.le.Div./6.Pz.Div.	MZM 1942
1937	ČKD	1045	13735	PÚV-1	1.le.Div./6.Pz.Div.	
1937	ČKD	1049	13736	PÚV-1	1.le.Div./6.Pz.Div.	
1937	ČKD	1050	13737	PÚV-1	1.le.Div./6.Pz.Div.	
1937	ČKD	1051	13738	PÚV-1	1.le.Div./6.Pz.Div.	
1937	ČKD	1052	13739	PÚV-1	1.le.Div./6.Pz.Div.	
1937	ČKD	1053	13740	PÚV-1	1.le.Div./6.Pz.Div.	
1937	ČKD	1054	13741	PÚV-1	1.le.Div./6.Pz.Div.	Bulgaria
1937	ČKD	1055	13742	PÚV-1	1.le.Div./6.Pz.Div.	
1937	ČKD	1056	13743	PÚV-1	1.le.Div./6.Pz.Div.	
1937	ČKD	1057	13744	PÚV-1	1.le.Div./6.Pz.Div.	burned 1939
1937	ČKD	1058	13745	PÚV-1	1.le.Div./6.Pz.Div.	
1937	ČKD	1059	13746	PÚV-1	1.le.Div./6.Pz.Div.	
1937	ČKD	1060	13747	PÚV-1	1.le.Div./6.Pz.Div.	Bulgaria
1937	ČKD	1061	13748	PÚV-1	1.le.Div./6.Pz.Div.	Romania
1937	ČKD	1062	13749	PÚV-1	1.le.Div./6.Pz.Div.	scrapped 1942
1937	ČKD	1063	13750	PÚV-1	1.le.Div./6.Pz.Div.	PzBefWg 35(t)
1937	ČKD	1064	13751	PÚV-1	1.le.Div./6.Pz.Div.	PzBefWg 35(t)
1937	ČKD	1065	13752	PÚV-1	1.le.Div./6.Pz.Div.	MZM 1942
1937	ČKD	1066	13753	PÚV-1	1.le.Div./6.Pz.Div.	
1937	ČKD	1067	13754	PÚV-1	1.le.Div./6.Pz.Div.	MZM 1942
1937	ČKD	1068	13755	PÚV-1	1.le.Div./6.Pz.Div.	Romania

Date	Manufacturer	Chassis no.	Serial/ registration no.	Czechoslovak user	Secondary users	Third users
1937	ČKD	1069	13756	PÚV-1	1.le.Div./6.Pz.Div.	
1937	ČKD	1070	13757	PÚV-1	1.le.Div./6.Pz.Div.	Bulgaria
1937	ČKD	1071	13758	PÚV-1	1.le.Div./6.Pz.Div.	
1937	ČKD	1072	13759	PÚV-1	1.le.Div./6.Pz.Div.	scrapped 1942
1937	CKD	1073	13760	PÚV-1	1.le.Div./6.Pz.Div.	
1937	ČKD	1074	13761	PÚV-1	1.le.Div./6.Pz.Div.	MZM 1942
1937	ČKD	1075	13762	PÚV-1	1.le.Div./6.Pz.Div.	
1937	ČKD	1076	13763	PÚV-1	1.le.Div./6.Pz.Div.	Romania
1937	ČKD	1077	13764	PÚV-1	1.le.Div./6.Pz.Div.	scrapped 1942
1937	ČKD	1078	13765	PÚV-1	1.le.Div./6.Pz.Div.	
1937	ČKD	1079	13766	PÚV-1	1.le.Div./6.Pz.Div.	
1937	ČKD	1080	13767	PÚV-1	1.le.Div./6.Pz.Div.	
1937	ČKD	1081	13768	PÚV-1	1.le.Div./6.Pz.Div.	Bulgaria
1937	ČKD	1082	13769	PÚV-1	1.le.Div./6.Pz.Div.	
1937	ČKD	1083	13770	PÚV-1	1.le.Div./6.Pz.Div.	Bulgaria
1937	ČKD	1084	13771	PÚV-1	1.le.Div./6.Pz.Div.	
1937	ČKD	1085	13772	PÚV-1	1.le.Div./6.Pz.Div.	Romania
1937	ČKD	1086	13773	PÚV-1	1.le.Div./6.Pz.Div.	
1937	ČKD	1087	13774	PÚV-1	1.le.Div./6.Pz.Div.	
1937	ČKD	1088	13775	PÚV-1	1.le.Div./6.Pz.Div.	
1937	ČKD	1089	13776	PÚV-1	1.le.Div./6.Pz.Div.	Bulgaria
1937	ČKD	1090	13777	PÚV-1	1.le.Div./6.Pz.Div.	scrapped 1941
1937	ČKD	1091	13778	PÚV-1	1.le.Div./6.Pz.Div.	scrapped 1942
1937	ČKD	1092	13779	PÚV-1	1.le.Div./6.Pz.Div.	Bulgaria
1937	ČKD	1093	13780	PÚV-1	1.le.Div./6.Pz.Div.	Romania
1937	ČKD	1094	13781	PÚV-1	1.le.Div./6.Pz.Div.	
1937	ČKD	1095	13782	PÚV-1	1.le.Div./6.Pz.Div.	scrapped 1942
1937	ČKD	1096	13783	PÚV-1	1.le.Div./6.Pz.Div.	Romania
1937	ČKD	1097	13784	PÚV-1	1.le.Div./6.Pz.Div.	
13.02.1937	ČKD	1001	13785	PÚV-2	1.le.Div./6.Pz.Div.	MZM 1942
13.02.1937	ČKD	1002	13786	PÚV-2	1.le.Div./6.Pz.Div.	MZM 1943
13.02.1937	ČKD	1003	13787	PÚV-2	1.le.Div./6.Pz.Div.	Bulgaria

Date	Manufacturer	Chassis no.	Serial/ registration no.	Czechoslovak user	Secondary users	Third users
13.02.1937	ČKD	1004	13788	PÚV-2	1.le.Div./6.Pz.Div.	
13.02.1937	ČKD	1005	13789	PÚV-2	1.le.Div./6.Pz.Div.	Bulgaria
12.02.1937	ČKD	1006	13790	PÚV-2	1.le.Div./6.Pz.Div.	
13.02.1937	ČKD	1007	13791	PÚV-2	1.le.Div./6.Pz.Div.	scrapped 1940
13.02.1937	ČKD	1008	13792	PÚV-2	Slovakia	
13.02.1937	ČKD	1009	13793	PÚV-2	1.le.Div./6.Pz.Div.	Waffen SS
13.02.1937	ČKD	1010	13794	PÚV-2	1.le.Div./6.Pz.Div.	Romania
05.03.1937	ČKD	1011	13795	PÚV-2	1.le.Div./6.Pz.Div.	
05.03.1937	ČKD	1012	13796	PÚV-2	1.le.Div./6.Pz.Div.	
05.03.1937	ČKD	1013	13797	PÚV-2	1.le.Div./6.Pz.Div.	
05.03.1937	ČKD	1014	13798	PÚV-2	1.le.Div./6.Pz.Div.	
05.03.1937	ČKD	1015	13799	PÚV-2	1.le.Div./6.Pz.Div.	Bulgaria
05.03.1937	ČKD	1016	13800	PÚV-2	1.le.Div./6.Pz.Div.	Bulgaria
05.03.1937	ČKD	1017	13801	PÚV-2	1.le.Div./6.Pz.Div.	
05.03.1937	ČKD	1018	13802	PÚV-2	Slovakia	
05.03.1937	ČKD	1019	13803	PÚV-2	1.le.Div./6.Pz.Div.	Bulgaria
05.03.1937	ČKD	1020	13804	PÚV-2	1.le.Div./6.Pz.Div.	
05.03.1937	ČKD	1021	13805	PÚV-2	1.le.Div./6.Pz.Div.	
05.03.1937	ČKD	1022	13806	PÚV-2	Slovakia	
05.03.1937	ČKD	1023	13807	PÚV-2	1.le.Div./6.Pz.Div.	Bulgaria
05.03.1937	ČKD	1024	13808	PÚV-2	1.le.Div./6.Pz.Div.	Romania
05.03.1937	ČKD	1025	13809	PÚV-2	1.le.Div./6.Pz.Div.	Bulgaria
1937	ČKD	1038	13810	PÚV-2	Slovakia	
1937	ČKD	1039	13811	PÚV-2	1.le.Div./6.Pz.Div.	
1937	ČKD	1040	13812	PÚV-2	1.le.Div./6.Pz.Div.	
1937	ČKD	1041	13813	PÚV-2	1.le.Div./6.Pz.Div.	Bulgaria
1937	ČKD	1042	13814	PÚV-2	1.le.Div./6.Pz.Div.	Bulgaria
1937	ČKD	1043	13815	PÚV-2	1.le.Div./6.Pz.Div.	
1937	ČKD	1044	13816	PÚV-2	1.le.Div./6.Pz.Div.	MZM 1942
1937	ČKD	1026	13817	PÚV-2	1.le.Div./6.Pz.Div.	
10.04.1937	Škoda	50155	13818	PÚV-3	Slovakia	
10.04.1937	Škoda	50156	13819	PÚV-3	Slovakia	
10.04.1937	Škoda	50168	13820	PÚV-3	Slovakia	
22.02.1937	Škoda	50164	13821	PÚV-3	Slovakia	
22.02.1937	Škoda	50165	13822	PÚV-3	Slovakia	
22.02.1937	Škoda	50166	13823	PÚV-3	Slovakia	

Date	Manufacturer	Chassis no.	Serial/ registration no.	Czechoslovak user	Secondary users	Third users
10.04.1937	Škoda	50169	13824	PÚV-3	Slovakia	
10.04.1937	Škoda	50170	13825	PÚV-3	Slovakia	
10.04.1937	Škoda	50172	13826	PÚV-3	Slovakia	
10.04.1937	Škoda	50173	13827	PÚV-3	Slovakia	
10.04.1937	Škoda	50174	13828	PÚV-3	Slovakia	
10.04.1937	Škoda	50176	13829	PÚV-3	Slovakia	
10.04.1937	Škoda	50184	13830	PÚV-3	Slovakia	
22.02.1937	Škoda	50188	13831	PÚV-3	Slovakia	
10.04.1937	Škoda	50159	13832	PÚV-3	Slovakia	
10.04.1937	Škoda	50171	13833	PÚV-3	Slovakia	
10.04.1937	Škoda	50175	13834	PÚV-3	1.le.Div./6.Pz.Div.	
10.04.1937	Škoda	50177	13835	PÚV-3	Slovakia	
10.04.1937	Škoda	50179	13836	PÚV-3	Slovakia	
10.04.1937	Škoda	50181	13837	PÚV-3	1.le.Div./6.Pz.Div.	
10.04.1937	Škoda	50145	13838	PÚV-3	Slovakia	
10.04.1937	Škoda	50178	13839	PÚV-3	Slovakia	
10.04.1937	Škoda	50180	13840	PÚV-3	Slovakia	
10.04.1937	Škoda	50182	13841	PÚV-3	1.le.Div./6.Pz.Div.	Romania
10.04.1937	Škoda	50183	13842	PÚV-3	Slovakia	
10.04.1937	Škoda	50185	13843	PÚV-3	Slovakia	
15.03.1937	Škoda	50187	13844	PÚV-3	Slovakia	
15.03.1937	Škoda	50190	13845	PÚV-3	1.le.Div./6.Pz.Div.	
15.03.1937	Škoda	50192	13846	PÚV-3	Slovakia	
15.03.1937	Škoda	50200	13847	PÚV-3	Slovakia	
15.03.1937	Škoda	50189	13848	PÚV-3	Slovakia	
15.03.1937	Škoda	50191	13849	PÚV-3	Slovakia	
15.03.1937	Škoda	50193	13850	PÚV-3	Slovakia	
15.03.1937	Škoda	50196	13851	PÚV-3	Slovakia	
15.03.1937	Škoda	50198	13852	PÚV-3	Slovakia	
15.03.1937	Škoda	50199	13853	PÚV-3	1.le.Div./6.Pz.Div.	
15.03.1937	Škoda	50201	13854	PÚV-3	1.le.Div./6.Pz.Div.	
15.03.1937	Škoda	50203	13855	PÚV-3	Slovakia	
15.03.1937	Škoda	50208	13856	PÚV-3	Slovakia	
15.03.1937	Škoda	50202	13857	PÚV-3	Slovakia	
03.04.1937	Škoda	50210	13858/	PÚV-3	Slovakia	
03.04.1937	Škoda	50270	13859	PÚV-3	Slovakia	
03.04.1937	Škoda	50271	13860	PÚV-3	Slovakia	

Date	Manufacturer	Chassis no.	Serial/ registration no.	Czechoslovak user	Secondary users	Third users
02.10.1937	Škoda	50300	13864	PÚV-1	1.le.Div./6.Pz.Div.	
02.10.1937	Škoda	50299	13865	PÚV-1	1.le.Div./6.Pz.Div.	
02.10.1937	Škoda	50301	13866	PÚV-1	1.le.Div./6.Pz.Div.	
02.10.1937	Škoda	50298	13867	PÚV-1	1.le.Div./6.Pz.Div.	
02.10.1937	Škoda	50297	13868	PÚV-1	1.le.Div./6.Pz.Div.	
02.10.1937	Škoda	50296	13869	PÚV-1	1.le.Div./6.Pz.Div.	
02.10.1937	Škoda	50294	13870	PÚV-1	1.le.Div./6.Pz.Div.	
02.10.1937	Škoda	50293	13871	PÚV-1	1.le.Div./6.Pz.Div.	Romania
02.10.1937	Škoda	50295	13872	PÚV-1	1.le.Div./6.Pz.Div.	MZM 1942
02.10.1937	Škoda	50304	13873	PÚV-1	1.le.Div./6.Pz.Div.	
02.10.1937	Škoda	50302	13874	PÚV-1	1.le.Div./6.Pz.Div.	
02.10.1937	Škoda	50303	13875	PÚV-1	1.le.Div./6.Pz.Div.	scrapped 1940
12.11.1937	Škoda	50306	13876	PÚV-1	1.le.Div./6.Pz.Div.	MZM 1942
12.11.1937	Škoda	50313	13877	PÚV-1	1.le.Div./6.Pz.Div.	scrapped 1940
12.11.1937	Škoda	50314	13878	PÚV-1	1.le.Div./6.Pz.Div.	
12.11.1937	Škoda	50308	13879	PÚV-1	1.le.Div./6.Pz.Div.	MZM 1943
12.11.1937	Škoda	50309	13880	PÚV-1	1.le.Div./6.Pz.Div.	MZM 1942
12.11.1937	Škoda	50310	13881	PÚV-1	1.le.Div./6.Pz.Div.	scrapped 1942
12.11.1937	Škoda	50311	13882	PÚV-1	1.le.Div./6.Pz.Div.	damaged 1939
12.11.1937	Škoda	50307	13883	PÚV-1	1.le.Div./6.Pz.Div.	MZM 1942
23.11.1937	Škoda	50312	13884	PÚV-1	1.le.Div./6.Pz.Div.	
23.11.1937	Škoda	50315	13885	PÚV-1	1.le.Div./6.Pz.Div.	
18.12.1937	Škoda	50316	13886	PÚV-1	1.le.Div./6.Pz.Div.	MZM 1942
18.12.1937	Škoda	50317	13887	PÚV-1	1.le.Div./6.Pz.Div.	
18.12.1937	Škoda	50320	13888	PÚV-1	1.le.Div./6.Pz.Div.	MZM 1943
18.12.1937	Škoda	50323	13889	PÚV-1	1.le.Div./6.Pz.Div.	scrapped 1939
18.12.1937	Škoda	50319	13890	PÚV-1	1.le.Div./6.Pz.Div.	PzBefWg 35(t)
18.12.1937	Škoda	50322	13891	PÚV-1	1.le.Div./6.Pz.Div.	
18.12.1937	Škoda	50318	13892	PÚV-1	1.le.Div./6.Pz.Div.	MZM 1942
18.12.1937	Škoda	50321	13893	PÚV-1	1.le.Div./6.Pz.Div.	MZM 1942
08.01.1938	Škoda	50305	13894	PÚV-3	Slovakia	
28.01.1938	Škoda	50324	13895	PÚV-3	1.le.Div./6.Pz.Div.	

Date	Manufacturer	Chassis no.	Serial/ registration no.	Czechoslovak user	Secondary users	Third users
28.01.1938	Škoda	50325	13896	PÚV-3	Slovakia	
28.01.1938	Škoda	50326	13897	PÚV-3	Slovakia	
28.01.1938	Škoda	50316	13898	PÚV-3	Slovakia	
28.01.1938	Škoda	50327	13899	PÚV-3	Slovakia	
28.01.1938	Škoda	53914	13900	PÚV-3	1.le.Div./6.Pz.Div.	
28.01.1938	Škoda	53901	13901	PÚV-3	Slovakia	
28.01.1938	Škoda	53919	13902	PÚV-3	1.le.Div./6.Pz.Div.	MZM 1942
11.03.1938	Škoda	53918	13903	PÚV-1	Hungary	1H-407
11.03.1938	Škoda	53921	13904	PÚV-1	1.le.Div./6.Pz.Div.	MZM 1942
11.03.1938	Škoda	53917	13905	PÚV-1	1.le.Div./6.Pz.Div.	
11.03.1938	Škoda	53922	13906	PÚV-1	1.le.Div./6.Pz.Div.	Romania
11.03.1938	Škoda	53923	13907	PÚV-1	1.le.Div./6.Pz.Div.	
11.03.1938	Škoda	53924	13908	PÚV-1	1.le.Div./6.Pz.Div.	
11.03.1938	Škoda	53925	13909	PÚV-1	1.le.Div./6.Pz.Div.	scrapped 1942
11.03.1938	Škoda	53926	13910	PÚV-1	1.le.Div./6.Pz.Div.	Romania
11.03.1938	Škoda	53920	13911	PÚV-1	1.le.Div./6.Pz.Div.	burned 1942
08.04.1938	Škoda	50146	13912	PÚV-1	1.le.Div./6.Pz.Div.	
08.04.1938	Škoda	53928	13913	PÚV-1	1.le.Div./6.Pz.Div.	
08.04.1938	Škoda	53927	13914	PÚV-1	1.le.Div./6.Pz.Div.	Romania
1937	ČKD	1098	13915	PÚV-1	1.le.Div./6.Pz.Div.	Belgrade museum
1937	ČKD	1099	13916	PÚV-1	1.le.Div./6.Pz.Div.	MZM 1943
1937	ČKD	10100	13917	PÚV-1	1.le.Div./6.Pz.Div.	MZM 1942
1937	ČKD	10117	13918	PÚV-1	1.le.Div./6.Pz.Div.	Romania
1937	ČKD	10118	13919	PÚV-1	1.le.Div./6.Pz.Div.	scrapped 1942
1937	ČKD	10119	13920	PÚV-1	1.le.Div./6.Pz.Div.	Bulgaria
1937	ČKD	10120	13921	PÚV-1	1.le.Div./6.Pz.Div.	
1937	ČKD	10121	13922	PÚV-1	1.le.Div./6.Pz.Div.	scrapped 1940
1937	ČKD	10122	13923	PÚV-1	1.le.Div./6.Pz.Div.	
1937	ČKD	10123	13924	PÚV-1	1.le.Div./6.Pz.Div.	Bulgaria
1937	ČKD	10124	13925	PÚV-1	1.le.Div./6.Pz.Div.	
1937	ČKD	10125	13926	PÚV-1	1.le.Div./6.Pz.Div.	
1937	ČKD	10126	13927	PÚV-1	1.le.Div./6.Pz.Div.	Bulgaria
1937	ČKD	10127	13928	PÚV-1	1.le.Div./6.Pz.Div.	scrapped 1942

Date	Manufacturer	Chassis no.	Serial/ registration no.	Czechoslovak user	Secondary users	Third users
1937	ČKD	10128	13929	PÚV-1	1.le.Div./6.Pz.Div.	
1937	ČKD	10129	13930	PÚV-1	1.le.Div./6.Pz.Div.	damaged 1939
1937	ČKD	10130	13931	PÚV-1	1.le.Div./6.Pz.Div.	Romania
1937	ČKD	10131	13932	PÚV-1	1.le.Div./6.Pz.Div.	
1937	ČKD	10132	13933	PÚV-1	1.le.Div./6.Pz.Div.	
1937	ČKD	10133	13934	PÚV-1	1.le.Div./6.Pz.Div.	
1937	ČKD	10134	13935	PÚV-1	1.le.Div./6.Pz.Div.	Romania
1937	ČKD	10135	13936	PÚV-1	1.le.Div./6.Pz.Div.	MZM 1943
1937	ČKD	10136	13937	PÚV-1	1.le.Div./6.Pz.Div.	
1937	ČKD	10137	13938	PÚV-1	1.le.Div./6.Pz.Div.	Bulgaria
1937	ČKD	10138	13939	PÚV-1	1.le.Div./6.Pz.Div.	
1937	ČKD	10139	13940	PÚV-1	1.le.Div./6.Pz.Div.	Romania
1937	ČKD	10140	13941	PÚV-1	1.le.Div./6.Pz.Div.	
1937	ČKD	10141	13942	PÚV-1	1.le.Div./6.Pz.Div.	
1937	ČKD	10142	13943	PÚV-1	1.le.Div./6.Pz.Div.	
1937	ČKD	10143	13944	PÚV-1	1.le.Div./6.Pz.Div.	MZM 1942
1937	ČKD	10144	13945	PÚV-1	1.le.Div./6.Pz.Div.	scrapped 1940
1937	ČKD	10145	13946	PÚV-1	1.le.Div./6.Pz.Div.	MZM 1942
1937	ČKD	10146	13947	PÚV-1	1.le.Div./6.Pz.Div.	
1937	ČKD	10147	13948	PÚV-1	1.le.Div./6.Pz.Div.	scrapped 1940
1937	ČKD	10148	13949	PÚV-1	1.le.Div./6.Pz.Div.	
1937	ČKD	10149	13950	PÚV-1	1.le.Div./6.Pz.Div.	MZM 1942
1937	ČKD	10101	13951	PÚV-2	1.le.Div./6.Pz.Div.	MZM 1943
1937	ČKD	10102	13952	PÚV-2	1.le.Div./6.Pz.Div.	
1937	ČKD	10103	13953	PÚV-2	1.le.Div./6.Pz.Div.	
1937	ČKD	10104	13954	PÚV-2	Slovakia	
1937	ČKD	10105	13955	PÚV-2	Slovakia	
1937	ČKD	10106	13956	PÚV-2	Slovakia	
1937	ČKD	10107	13957	PÚV-2	1.le.Div./6.Pz.Div.	
1937	ČKD	10108	13958	PÚV-2	1.le.Div./6.Pz.Div.	
1937	ČKD	10109	13959	PÚV-2	Slovakia	
1937	ČKD	10110	13960	PÚV-2	1.le.Div./6.Pz.Div.	MZM 1942
1937	ČKD	10111	13961	PÚV-2	1.le.Div./6.Pz.Div.	MZM 1942
1937	ČKD	10112	13962	PÚV-2	1.le.Div./6.Pz.Div.	MZM 1942

Date	Manufacturer	Chassis no.	Serial/ registration no.	Czechoslovak user	Secondary users	Third users
1937	ČKD	10113	13963	PÚV-2	1.le.Div./6.Pz.Div.	
1937	ČKD	10114	13964	PÚV-2	Slovakia	
1937	ČKD	10115	13965	PÚV-2	1.le.Div./6.Pz.Div.	MZM 1942
1937	ČKD	10116	13966	PÚV-2	1.le.Div./6.Pz.Div.	
1937	Škoda	50197		prototype for Romania		in Pilsen until 1945
6/42	Škoda	50223		(*)		Romania
6/42	Škoda	50224		(*)		MZM
1937	Škoda	50255		(*)		Romania
1937	Škoda	50256		(*)		Romania
1937	Škoda	50257		(*)		Romania
1937	Škoda	50258		(*)		Romania
1937	Škoda	50259		(*)		Romania
1937	Škoda	50260		(*)		Romania
1937	Škoda	50261		(*)		Romania
1937	Škoda	50262		(*)		Romania
1937	Škoda	50263		(*)		Romania
1937	Škoda	50264		(*)		Romania
1937	Škoda	50265		(*)		Romania
1937	Škoda	50266		(*)		Romania
1937	Škoda	50267		(*)		Romania
1937	Škoda	50268		(*)		Romania
1937	Škoda	50269		(*)		Romania

Note: * = assembled from eleven scrapped tanks of the Czechoslovak army, which replaced those machines usin
chassis numbers 53901–53928.

Table 13. Bulgarian army tanks

Delivery date	Type	Chassis no.	Czechoslovak registration no.	Bulgarian registration no.	Bulgarian tactical no.
20.02.1940	LT vz. 35	50150	13.692	B.60036	36
04.03.1940	LT vz. 35	1027	13.722	B.60023	23
20.02.1940	LT vz. 35	1028	13.723	B.60042	42
07.03.1940	LT vz. 35	1029	13.724	B.60043	43
?	LT vz. 35	1033	13.728	B.60032	32
10.03.1940	LT vz. 35	1036	13.731	?	
04.03.1940	LT vz. 35	1054	13.741	?	

Delivery date	Type	Chassis no.	Czechoslovak registration no.	Bulgarian registration no.	Bulgarian tactical no.
04.03.1940	LT vz. 35	1060	13.747	B.60025	25
?	LT vz. 35	1070	13.757	B.60033	33
?	LT vz. 35	1081	13.768	?	
04.03.1940	LT vz. 35	1083	13.770	B.60046	46
?	LT vz. 35	1089	13.776	B.60035	35
20.02.1940	LT vz. 35	1092	13.779	B.60047	47
04.03.1940	LT vz. 35	1003	13.787	?	
10.03.1940	LT vz. 35	1005	13.789	?	
20.02.1940	LT vz. 35	1015	13.799	?	
08.03.1940	LT vz. 35	1016	13.800	B.60039	39
08.03.1940	LT vz. 35	1019	13.803	B.60029	29
08.03.1940	LT vz. 35	1023	13.807	?	
20.02.1940	LT vz. 35	1025	13.809	B.60041	41
04.03.1940	LT vz. 35	1041	13.813	B.60045	45
08.03.1940	LT vz. 35	1042	13.814	B.60024	24
04.03.1940	LT vz. 35	10119	13.920	?	
10.03.1940	LT vz. 35	10123	13.924	?	
	T-11	286	not applicable	B.60049	49
	T-11	287	not applicable	B.60050	50
	T-11	278	not applicable	B.60051	51
	T-11	279	not applicable	B.60052	52
	T-11	280	not applicable	B.60053	53
	T-11	281	not applicable	B.60054	54
	T-11	282	not applicable	B.60055	55
	T-11	283	not applicable	B.60056	56
	T-11	285	not applicable	B.60057	57
	T-11	284	not applicable	B.60058	58

Bibliography

Books

Axworthy, Mark, Cornel Scafeş and Cristian Crăciunoiu, *Third Axis, Fourth Ally: Romanian Armed Forces in the European War, 1941–1945* (London: Arms and Armour Press, 1995)

Bradford, George,. *German Early War Armoured Fighting Vehicles—World War II AFV Plans* (Mechanicsburg, PA: Stackpole Books, 2007)

De Sisto, Frank V., *German Leichte Panzer at War* (Concord Publications, 2009)

De Sisto, Frank V., *Early Panzer Victories* (Concord Publications, 2010)

Feist, Uwe, *Leichte Panzers in Action* (Squadron/Signal Publications, Armour No. 10, 1974)

Fleischer, Wolfgang, *Panzerkampfwagen 35(t): Entwicklung und Einsätze* (Waffen-Arsenal, Special Band 37, 2003)

Francev, Vladimir and Charles K. Kliment, *Škoda LT vz. 35* (Prague: MBI, 1995)

Francev, Vladimir, and Charles K. Kliment, *Czechoslovak Armoured Fighting Vehicles 1918–1948* (Atglen, PA: Schiffer Publishing, 1997)

Gil Martinez, Eduardo M., *Romanian Armoured Forces in World War II*. Library of Armed Conflict 05 (Lublin: Kagero Publishing, 2018)

Jentz, Thomas L. and Werner Regenberg, *Panzer Tracts No. 19-1: Beute-Panzerkampfwagen Czech, Polish and French Tanks Captured from 1939 to 1940* (Panzer Tracts, 2007)

Kliment, Charles K. and Hilary L. Doyle, *Czechoslovak Armoured Fighting Vehicles 1918–1945* (Bellona Publications, 1979)

Kliment, Charles K. and Bretislav Nakladal, *Slovenská armáda 1939–1945* (Prague: Naše Vojsko/Ares, 2003)

Matev, Kolyoan, *Equipment and Armour in the Bulgarian Army: Armoured Vehicles 1935–1945* (Sofia: Angela Publisher, 2000)

Micianik, Pavel, *Slovenská armáda v tažení proti Sovětskému svazu (1941–1944): V operaci Barbarossa* (Dali Print, 2007)

Raus, Erhard, *Panzer Operations: The Eastern Front Memoirs of General Raus, 1941–1945*. Edited by Steven H. Newton (Da Capo Press, 2005)

Rue, John L., *Panzerkampfwagen 35(t) (Škoda LT vz. 35)* (Nuts & Bolts, Vol. 11)

Sander, Friedrich, *Blood, Dust & Snow: Diaries of a Panzer Commander in Germany and on the Eastern Front* (Greenhill Books, 2022)

Scafeș, Cornel I., Horia Vl. Șerbănescu and Ioan I. Scafeș, *Trupele Blindate din Armata Română 1919–1947* (București: Editura Oscar Print, 2005)

Scheibert, Horst, *Panzerkampfwagen Škoda 35(t)* (Podzun-Pallas-Verlag, Band 21)

Spielberger, Walter J., *Die Panzer-Kampfwagen 35(t) und 38(t) und ihre Abarten* (Stuttgart: Motorbuch Verlag, Militärfahrzeuge Band 11)

Thomas, Paul, *Hitler's Light Panzers at War*. Images of War Series (Barnsley: Pen & Sword, 2020)

Articles

Francev, Vladimír, and Tomáš Jakl, 'Kamufláž a označení tanku LT vz. 35 československé armády', in Historie a Plastikové Modelářství, no. 2007/06.

Pilař, Pavel, 'Lehké tanky Škoda T-11, T-12 a T-13M', in Historie a Plastikové Modelářství, no. 2002/02.

Pilař, Pavel, 'Lehké tanky Praga P-IIa a Praga P-II-b', in Historie a Plastikové Modelářství, no. 2004/06.

Špitálský, Jaroslav, 'Zkoušky LT vz. 35 v SSSR', in Historie a Plastikové Modelářství, no. 2005/08.